Verge

STUDIES IN GLOBAL ASIAS

Volume 3, Issue 1
Spring 2017

Verge (ISSN 2373-5058) is published twice a year in the spring and fall by the University of Minnesota Press, 111 Third Avenue South, Suite 290, Minneapolis, MN 55401-2520. http://www.upress.umn.edu

Every effort was made to obtain permission to reproduce material in this issue. If any proper acknowledgment has not been included here, we encourage copyright holders to notify the publisher.

Postmaster: Send address changes to *Verge,* University of Minnesota Press, 111 Third Avenue South, Suite 290, Minneapolis, MN 55401-2520.

Essays (between 6,000 and 10,000 words) should be prepared using parenthetical documentation with a list of works cited. Authors' names should not appear on manuscripts; instead, please include a separate document with the author's name and address and the title of the article with your electronic submission. Authors should not refer to themselves in the first person in the submitted text or notes if such references would identify them; any necessary references to the author's previous work, for example, should be in the third person. Submissions and editorial queries should be sent to verge@psu.edu.

Books for review should be addressed to

Verge: Studies in Global Asias
c/o Department of Asian Studies
102 Old Botany
University Park, PA 16802

Address subscription orders, changes of address, and business correspondence (including requests for permission and advertising orders) to *Verge,* University of Minnesota Press, 111 Third Avenue South, Suite 290, Minneapolis, MN 55401-2520.

Subscriptions: Regular rates, U.S.: individual, 1 year, $35; libraries, 1 year, $100. Other countries add $5 for each year's subscription. Checks should be made payable to the University of Minnesota Press. Back issues are $17.50 for individuals, $50 for libraries (plus $6 shipping for the first copy, $1.25 for each additional copy inside the U.S.; $9.50 shipping for the first copy, $6 for each additional copy, outside the U.S.). *Verge* is available online through the JSTOR Current Scholarship Program at http://jstor .org/r/umnpress. A subscription to *Verge* is a benefit of attending Penn State's biennial Global Asias conference.

Essays

Editor's Introduction

TINA CHEN

Context, Coordinate, Circulation: The Postrepresentational Cartographies of Global Asias

PICTURE ANIDA YOEU ALI, the artist featured on the cover of this issue, standing with her back exposed, water and black ink dripping down to stain the ragged edges of her white dress. What has been inscribed on Ali's back are reminders of overlapping histories invoked by her Cambodian Muslim American past. Phrases like "Khmer Rouge Regime," "Family Trip: Niagara Falls," "From Somewhere Else," and "Site of Tourism and Atrocities" (among others) are juxtaposed, overwritten, and ultimately bleed into each other before being rendered illegible, impossible to fully trace, and only visible as stain once the artist leaves the installation space and all that remains is the disembodied dress.

This performance—inspired by Maxine Hong Kingston's retelling of the Fa Mulan story in *The Woman Warrior*—functions as a "textile testimonial," and I'm especially intrigued by the ways in which it suggests a more expansive way to conceptualize mapping history, identity, and place. As Cathy J. Schlund-Vials astutely notes in her analysis of Ali's work in this issue's *Portfolio* feature, the "cartographic coordinates" mapped onto Ali's back can only be understood in relation to the "absent presences" of the Killing Fields and their ongoing aftereffects. As such, any attempt to chart the various intersections between history, identity, and place must, of necessity, also acknowledge the dynamism of multiple migrations and returns as well as the embodied dimensions of cartography's cognitive and conceptual projects.

Although mapping as a kind of generic metaphor for constructing intellectual frameworks has thoroughly saturated humanistic fields of inquiry, especially in response to and as a reflection of the various geographically oriented turns signaled by "beyond nation," "transpacific," "regional/ regionness," and "Global North/South" approaches, perhaps some more targeted attention to recent developments in theories of mapping might help us usefully expand—in conjunction with alternative forms of mapping as enacted by Ali's performance—the ways in which we understand conceptual plotting to be both an epistemological endeavor and a series of ontological possibilities.

As Rob Kitchin, Chris Perkins, and Martin Dodge (2009) demonstrate in their introductory survey to *Rethinking Maps: New Frontiers in Cartographic Theory,* the philosophical terrain of contemporary cartography is itself quite dynamic, and there are ongoing assessments of how theories of mapping have shifted attention from the map itself as an object of knowledge to the manifold ways in which maps operate postrepresentationally. Specifically, they highlight how postrepresentational theories of mapping have directed critical attention to maps as *inscriptions* (John Pickles's [2004] conceptualization of maps as producers rather than mirrors of the world), *propositions* (Dennis Wood and John Fels's [2008] definition of maps as ideological constructions that produce the world through the spatial ontologies they advance), *immutable mobiles* (Bruno Latour's [1987] understanding of how formalized protocols of mapping create maps as "a stable, combinable, transferable form of knowledge that is portable across space and time"), *actants* (ANT-influenced social science paradigms of maps as historically contingent objects that are actualized through their interactions with other actants and actors), and *practices* (James Corner's [1999] emphasis on maps as forms of enablement; Vincent J. Del Casino and Stephen P. Hanna's [2005] poststructuralist conceptualization of "map spaces" that are co-constituted by both the makers and the users of maps).

Coupled with Ali's enactment of mapping as embodied relationality, these diverse ways of conceptualizing the possibilities and limits of cartography helpfully offer us a diversified way of thinking about the complicated mappings that the work in this issue—and indeed any issue—of *Verge* attempts. Even as these concepts make evident the challenges of mapping any geographical location like Asia, they also make manifest the impossibilities and potential of mapping Global Asias, that conceptually determined site that insists on its own indeterminacy and plurality as much as its global expanse.

This issue's **Convergence** section begins with an *A&Q* that attempts to map the fault lines between the academic discipline of political science and the interdisciplinary academic fields of area studies and ethnic studies. In response to questions about the potential incompatibilities between disciplinary methods and field methods, four political scientists working in disparate fields—comparative ethnic studies (Fred Lee), East Asian studies (Erin Aeran Chung), Asian American studies (Janelle S. Wong), and Southeast Asian studies (Erik Martinez Kuhonta)—meditate on both the constraints and prospects of working intersectionally or with a mixed-methods methodology. Although each respondent recognizes the ways that area and cultural knowledges often are subordinated to the epistemological and methodological priorities of political science as a disciplinary formation, a subordination that is aggravated by the methodological battles within political science itself between quantitative and qualitative methods, all of the contributors also suggest that it is possible to work synergistically between discipline and interdiscipline. As long as one understands what Donald K. Emmerson (2008) has identified as the "terms of enlistment"—the meanings and conditions that locate disparate institutional knowledge formations in relation to each other—that structure our research, these terms might be renegotiated such that a range of scholarly approaches can exist at points beyond the extremes of either mutual alienation or disciplinary hegemony.

In her meta-response essay to the *A&Q* essays, Leela Fernandes usefully reminds us that "if the relationship between disciplinarity and interdisciplinarity is to be fully addressed—both in relation to the study of Asia/ Asian diasporas and in relation to the broader question of knowledge production—it requires an exploration of the ways in which interdisciplinary fields of analysis (and their institutionalized sites) may also become disciplined by the cross-disciplinary formations that are dominant within them." Fernandes points out how the increasing marginalization of political science impacts the conditions of knowledge formation in South Asian studies in ways as overt as low levels of participation by political scientists at area studies conferences and as subtle as reinforcing certain styles, methods, and theories as exemplary of "cutting-edge interdisciplinarity." Collectively, the contributors to *A&Q* illuminate the possibilities of mapping as practice in their collaborative demonstration of how questions of method are always about the enablement of intellectual legitimacy.

Key to postrepresentational mapping theory is an acknowledgment of how changing modes of production and new technologies make possible heightened attention to the interaction between map and user. This issue's *Interface* profiles the Center for Art and Thought (CA+T), a web-based nonprofit that harnesses the potential of digital and new media technologies to facilitate dialogues between artists, scholars, and the broader public. CA+T understands global processes through the experiences of the Filipino diaspora. As Jan Bernabe, Clare Counihan, and Sarita Echavez See exemplify through their analysis of *Sea, Land, Air: Migration and Labor,* CA+T's inaugural virtual exhibit, mapping always entails perspective. While too often that perspective is a view from somewhere that gets universalized, CA+T's attentiveness to the Filipino diaspora "as a point of departure—rather than a point of arrival—for bringing into focus and understanding other histories, spaces, and communities" illuminates how the digital curation of such focalization serves as an invitation for users to participate in the mapping of CA+T's resources and engagements. Excitingly, the possibilities afforded by digital curation—archiving unconstrained by physical storage, a processual release of exhibit materials, the spatial unfixing of knowledge exchange—do more than enable CA+T to operate as an example of "cultural digital mobility that challenges the segregation between 'art' and 'scholarship.'" They also make possible a more interactive engagement between user and platform, the ability to create a "rhizomatic exhibition experience" that is participatory and continually evolving.

New technologies such as those employed by CA+T sometimes render invisible older technologies as technology. Our third **Convergence** feature, a *Field Trip* on "Book Histories, Material Culture, and East Asian Studies," begins with author Ann Sherif's engagement with the book as a physical object and opens up into a survey of how book studies (or history of the book) is a multidisciplinary field that "describes and analyzes the production, consumption, preservation, and destruction of the technologies [and] cultural modes" of not just individual books but entire "book worlds." In evoking a geographical image for her survey of the field, Sherif argues for the importance of challenging the universalist assumptions of Western book history scholarship, especially its persuasive identification of the printing press as signal technological change agent, and the emphasis on nation-state book cultures in East Asian book studies. By attending to the regionally interrelated yet locally distinctive book cultures of East Asia and their various points of intersection and divergence, scholars can more effectively map shared cultural contexts, different reading practices, and alternative patterns of circulation.

Circulation—of books and of people—is a dynamic movement that sometimes exceeds a map's representational capacity. So too is contestation and the frictive jockeying for territories already claimed and disputed. As the rise of ISIL attests, mapping new territory can be a violent act. We are witness to how ideologies are inscribed and proposed through cartographic claiming. In our final **Convergence** feature, Cathy J. Schlund-Vials introduces us to the multifaceted work of Anita Yoeu Ali, an activist/artist whose "agitative artistic politics" are designed to direct attention to the causes and consequences of Islamophobia. Such a project seems especially urgent at this moment when civil war rages in Syria, the Middle East is fractured by religious and sectarian violence, how to welcome and manage refugees is a globally contested issue, and the political climate of the West both fosters and reflects an unprecedented increase in anti-Muslim bigotry. As I have already suggested, while such conditions cannot be adequately captured in any single map, the work of artists like Ali might offer us different ways of coordinating and contextualizing the markers of past and present, here and there, home and away. Schlund-Vials traces Ali's development as an artist from her early involvement with the Asian American spoken word performance ensemble I Was Born with Two Tongues to her participation in Chicago-based feminist collective Mango Tribe to her more recent work as a multidisciplinary transnational performance artist. Through her detailed attention to Ali's transnationally conceptualized project *The Red Chador,* which highlights ongoing racial violence centered on religious identification and iconography, Schlund-Vials demonstrates how Ali's efforts to elicit unplanned and unscripted audience responses through her performance of the silent, inscrutable, and brilliantly sequined figure of "The Red Chador" generated multivalent engagements in diverse cities (Paris; Hartford, Connecticut; and Washington, D.C.) and diverse contexts (galleries, subway stations, cafés, the Smithsonian). Ali's commitment to embodiment—whether as The Red Chador or as the unnamed woman with ink and water running down her back—signals a mapping practice that is equally attentive to what is erased as it is to what is remembered.

The lead **Essay** for this issue is a wonderfully generative argument about transpacific circulation, global modernity, and ways of reading that exceed the discrete boundaries that separate Asian American literatures and Asian literary production. In "Oceanic Etymologies: Shanghai and the Transpacific Routes of Global Modernity," Steven Yao considers Shanghai not so much as a geopolitical locus but as a "polylingual verbal sign that appears in literary works from around the Pacific Rim as a figure or trope for the increasingly global scale of interactions that together make up economic and cultural modernity." Beginning with John Yau's poem "Shanghai Shenanigans" (1981), Yao illustrates the limits of reading Shanghai in biographical or referential terms, instead gesturing to the productive interpretive possibilities of reading Shanghai as "verbal token and historical impetus for experimentation with prevailing conventions of literary form and their associated protocols of legibility in various languages and locations around the Pacific Ocean." Yao argues that "charting this terrain" will clarify Asian American literature's complicated relation to modernist literary traditions and practices across Asia. Traveling through multiple ports of call—including New York, Hollywood, Shanghai, Tokyo, and Kobe—Yao carefully reads Mu Shi Ying (穆時英)'s "The Shanghai Foxtrot (a Fragment)" (上海的狐步舞-一個端片) (1932), Yokomitsu Riichi's *Shanghai* (serially published between 1928 and 1931), and Tani Joji's "The Shanghaied Man" (上海された男) (1925) to demonstrate how Shanghai as "figure, sign, and *topos*" indexes the crisscrossing circuits of the cultural flow that accompanies the global spread of modernity.

In "Semioscapes, Unbanality, and the Reinvention of Nationness: Global Korea as Nation-Space," Jerry Won Lee undertakes a semiotic analysis of how diaspora communities continually reinvent nationness through the use of symbolic resources in public space. Lee proposes that the "unbanality," which he defines as "singular conspicuousness," of Koreanness achieved through reconfigurations of space in Koreatowns across Asia and North America permits the reinvention of nation outside the nation-state. Building on Arjun Appadurai's (2001) notion of "process geographies" as geographies that map "significant areas of human organization as precipitates of various kinds of action, interaction, and motion—trade, travel, pilgrimage, warfare, proselytization, colonization, exile, and the like" (7), Lee advances a notion of the "semioscape" to highlight how "the ways in which everyday actors use language and semiotic resources to reconfigure space disrupt the very boundedness of communities to politically defined territories." Crucially, Lee's attention to the semiosis of space through his analysis of architectural choices and Koryo as chronotope develops criteria other than location and authenticity to understand distinctions between state and space.

The complicated interrelationship between location and authenticity is explored in Abigail De Kosnik's "Perfect Covers: Filipino Musical Mimicry and Transmedia Performance." Focusing on mimicry as a key characteristic of a certain "Filipino brand," De Kosnik argues that the international success of Filipino cover artists has helped to cement the reputation of Filipinos as excellent mimics suitable not only as performance labor but also as call center workers, nurses, and domestic help. De Kosnik adapts comparative media scholar Henry Jenkins's (2007) notion of transmedia, wherein corporations use multiple platforms to build different components of complex fictional worlds, to analyze the ways in which Filipinos have individually leveraged new media technologies and the Internet to transmediate their imitative skills to a global marketplace. As De Kosnik persuasively demonstrates, Filipinos' multiplatform performances of their mimetic talent are intimately tied to the United States's "twisted kinship with the Philippines" and can be analyzed as an effort to remap ongoing colonial legacies.

If mapping is always in some ways propositional, an effort to advance certain ideological positions and produce the world through the spatial ontologies they construct, then opportunities to highlight this constructive aspect of mapping are on special display at the World's Fair. In "The Biopolitics of Gratitude and Equivalence: Debt, Exchange, and Disaster Politics at the Shanghai World's Fair," Jennifer Hubbert draws on fieldwork undertaken at the 2010 Shanghai Expo to examine how "disaster politics" illuminate the politics of citizenship in the narrative constructed about the 2008 Sichuan earthquake. Engaged with recent scholarship in anthropology that links humanitarianism to biopolitical processes, Hubbert's examination of how Expo representations functioned as a technology of power does not assume the automatic triumph of biopolitical regulation. Instead, Hubbert focuses on the "structural prerequisites necessary for the state to accomplish its sovereignty project within the framework of humanitarian praxis" in an effort to focus "not on what a biopolitics of humanitarianism *does* but on what a biopolitics of humanitarianism theoretically *needs* to accomplish its goals." She draws attention to how victims of the earthquake were brought into the state's modernity project through a "biopolitics of gratitude" while volunteers were constructed as representatives of such state-sanctioned modernity through a "biopolitics of equivalence." Tellingly, the biopolitical dimensions of the disaster politics studied in this **Essay**, while overdetermined by the state, are also subject to alternative assessments. Such tensions bespeak the possibility of refusing the state's implied exchange of obligation for its help.

The tensions underlying China's rise within Asia and in the world are also the subject of Fan Yang's **Essay**, "Temporality and Shenzhen Urbanism in the Era of 'China Dreams.'" Yang argues that temporality, the complex and uneven relation to time, is central to understanding urbanism in Shenzhen, the first Special Economic Zone set up in 1979 by Deng Xiaoping. Yang's doubled perspective—deriving from her teenage years growing up in Shenzhen from 1986 to 1996 and her 2014 fieldwork in the city—creates a distinctive opportunity to map the incongruent, multiple temporalities that continue to structure the city despite its reputation for a kind of "Shenzhen Speed" that is always directed at the future.

In her productive attunement to Shenzhen as a "polyrhythmic space," Yang's work utilizes Henri LeFebvre's concept of "rhythmanalysis" to allow for a more critical engagement with the city and its inhabitants' heterogeneous relations to time and space. The result helps "to remap a geopolitical imagination of China/Asia that resituates these spaces and practices in the third world or Global South."

Josephine Nock-Hee Park shares this interest in the remapping of a geopolitical imagination in this issue's final **Essay**, "'A Strange Form of Love': The Global Asian American Subject in Richard E. Kim's *The Martyred*." Focused on Kim's 1964 existential account of the Korean War as narrated by a South Korean officer, the first part of the essay explores the novel's central mystery of Christian martyrdom in the context of a modern history of religious revivals in Korea, while the second half of the argument turns to the politics of the skeptical figure of the protagonist. Park reads the novel's "Cold War universalism as a significant and continuing mode of securing an American audience without the comforts of sentiment." According to Park, Christina Klein's reading of the middlebrow imagination elaborates a new mapping of Asia that aimed "'to replace a national imaginary based on separation from a global imaginary based on connection' (Klein 2003, 13), and in Richard E. Kim's curious fiction, we discover a highbrow aspiration derived from the modes of Cold War integration Klein significantly revealed as the other side of the coin of Manichean division." Through her careful analysis of how Kim enacts a Cold War alignment through his existential novel, Park shows how converting political interests into philosophical terms reveals on ongoing process by which Asians become Americans.

By reading the work collected in this issue of *Verge* through the insights of postrepresentational cartography, I direct our attention to processual modes of understanding, the debated ontological propositions created by acts of mapping, the interactive engagements that contribute to the actualization of mapping as a means of organizing our epistemologies— and the provisional nature of any effort to map something as vast, as complex, as imagined as Global Asias and its diasporas.

■ **WORKS CITED**

Appadurai, Arjun. 2001. "Grassroots Globalization and the Research Imagination." In *Globalization,* edited by Arjun Appadurai, 1–21. Durham, N.C.: Duke University Press.

Corner, J. 1999. "The Agency of Mapping: Speculation, Critique and Invention." In *Mappings,* edited by Denis Cosgrove, 213–52. London: Reaktion Books.

Del Casino, V. J., and S. P. Hanna. 2005. "'Beyond the "binaries"': A methodological intervention for interrogating maps as representational practices." *ACME: An International E-Journal for Critical Geographies* 4, no. 1: 34–56.

Emmerson, Donald K. 2008. "Southeast Asia in Political Science: Terms of Enlistment." In *Southeast Asia in Political Science: Theory, Region, and Qualitative Analysis,* edited by Erik Martinez Kuhonta, Dan Slater, and Tuong Vu, 302–24. Palo Alto, Calif.: Stanford University Press.

Jenkins, Henry. 2007. "Transmedia Storytelling 101." *Confessions of an Aca-Fan: The Official Weblog of Henry Jenkins* (blog), March 22. http://henryjenkins.org/2007/03/transmedia_storytelling_101.html.

Kitchin, Robert, Chris Perkins, and Martin Dodge. 2009. "Thinking about Maps." In *Rethinking Maps: New Frontiers in Cartographic Theory,* edited by Martin Dodge, Rob Kitchin, and Chris Perkins, 1–25. New York: Routledge.

Klein, Christina. 2003. *Cold War Orientalism: Asia in the Middlebrow Imagination, 1945–1961.* Berkeley: University of California Press.

Latour, Bruno. 1987. *Science in Action.* Cambridge, Mass.: Harvard University Press.

Pickles, J. 2004. *A History of Spaces: Cartographic Reason, Mapping, and the Geo-Coded World.* London: Routledge.

Wood, Dennis, and John Fels. 2008. *The Natures of Maps: Cartographic Constructions of the Natural World.* Chicago: University of Chicago Press.

Convergence

Political Science and the Study of Global Asias

It is certainly desirable for a social science to be rigorous, empirical and seek general rules of human behavior. But as Aristotle explained, it should not try to achieve a rigor that goes beyond what is possible given the limitations inherent in the subject matter. In fact, most of what is truly useful for policy is context-specific, culture-bound and non-generalizable. The typical article appearing today in a leading journal like the *American Political Science Review* contains a lot of complex-looking math, whose sole function is often to formalize a behavioral rule that everyone with common sense understands must be true. What is missing is any deep knowledge about the subtleties and nuances of how foreign societies work, knowledge that would help us better predict the behavior of political actors, friendly and hostile, in the broader world.

> —Francis Fukuyama, "How Academia Failed the Nation: The Decline of Regional Studies" (2004)

What does or should an "area studies political scientist" do? Within the past two decades, this question has at times led to heated debates. For some, area studies research is at best the source of footnotes that more analytically oriented political scientists may employ fruitfully and effectively. For others, "political science" embodies pompous pretense in its own name and, at its worst, profoundly misrepresents politics as real human beings ordinarily understand it, experience it, and believe it. These two caricatures could be readily dismissed if they were to have no impact on careers, appointments, funding decisions, or collegiality within universities.

> —Jorge I. Domínguez, "Don't Stay Home: The Utility of Area Studies for Political Science Scholarship" (2009)

Southeast Asian studies and political science are compatible. It will always be possible to define these two fields in exclusionary ways. At the extreme, they can be made to refute one another, methodologically and epistemologically. Yet there is no reason why one cannot study an area and do political science at

the same time—and satisfy criteria for quality research on both sides of that polemicized divide, *depending on what those criteria are.*
> —Donald K. Emmerson, "Southeast Asia in Political Science: Terms of Enlistment" (2008)

1. Do you perceive any conflicts or even incompatibilities between (1) the methods commonly used in political science and the study of specific Asian regions and/or (2) the methods commonly used in political science and the study of specific Asian diasporic populations? If so, what might this suggest about the relationship between (1) disciplinary and area knowledges and/or (2) disciplinary and cultural knowledges?
2. Conversely, in what ways can distinctive epistemological and methodological approaches work together to create new models for both political science and the study of Asia and various Asian diasporas?
3. Certain institutional presuppositions and conditions of knowledge formation can enable or block, facilitate or discourage, productive interchanges between political science and area studies and/ or ethnic studies. In what ways have you had to negotiate field and subfield, discipline and area study, in your own research on specific Asian regions or specific Asian populations?

Working on the Boundaries of Political Science and Ethnic Studies

FRED LEE

My claim is a rough parallel to a claim Donald Emmerson makes in the introduction to this *A&Q*: there is no reason why one cannot do both ethnic studies and political science well, depending on how one articulates the boundaries and relationships between them. Now, I do not want to overstate the case for differentiating them, but I do conceive of these fields as relatively distinctive, epistemologically and methodologically speaking. We might even find a polemicized divide between political science and ethnic studies, one analogous to the distinction Francis Fukuyama's epigraph draws between political science and area studies. But we would have to look harder to find it, especially if we turn to the (once again relative) distinction between Asian studies as an area studies and Asian American studies as an ethnic studies.

Political science engages more with Asian studies than Asian American studies due to the interdisciplinary orientations of its subfields.[1] Scholars of comparative politics and international relations who specialize in Asian countries or regions have at least a passing familiarity with area studies. By contrast, scholars of political theory and public law who focus on the United States or the Americas are not particularly conversant in Asian American studies. And these are the political scientists working in the subfields most engaged with cultural productions, *longue durée* histories, and other concerns of ethnic studies. Their understandings of ethnic studies, however, are more likely to be informed by black studies than Asian American studies—or Latino/a studies, or American Indian studies, for that matter. As a consequence, political theory and public law scholars will with some exceptions situate U.S. racial dynamics within conceptual frames more appropriate to Africana/transatlantic than Asian/transpacific politics. They might, for example, interpret U.S. racist formations exhaustively in light of claims of biological inferiority (most relevant to antiblack scientific racism) as opposed to claims of civilizational otherness (most relevant to Orientalist discourses).

There is little fundamental conflict between the intellectual practices of political theory and public law scholars in political science and those of, say, historians or literary scholars in Asian American studies. Many of us in political theory and public law already see ourselves as akin to philosophers, legal scholars, and others formally outside of our discipline. That is, we already see ourselves as "interpretive social scientists" or "humanistic social scientists." However, political scientists working in the American politics subfield often see themselves differently. Many of them are epistemically committed to the social scientific enterprise of nomothetic explanation, meaning their methodologies (e.g., formal modeling or process tracing) work on quantitative or qualitative "data." This is where potential conflicts between an American politics scholar who analyzes survey data and an Asian Americanist who historicizes racial formations could cut deepest.

I should stress that, despite its predominant tendencies, the American politics subfield has always included humanistic social scientists. A scholar of race in American political development (APD), for instance, would find the historicist sensibility of an Asian Americanist familiar; what the former would find unfamiliar is the subject matter of the latter, because APD is better informed about African American than Asian American politics (e.g., Lowndes, Novkov, and Warren 2008). Furthermore, students of U.S.

racial politics will combine interpretive, qualitative, and quantitative methods more often than other practitioners of the American politics subfield. Exemplary of this mixed-methods approach are Ange-Marie Hancock's (2004) *The Politics of Disgust* and Lisa García Bedolla's (2005) *Fluid Borders,* both of which enact what Lewis Gordon (2010) calls a "teleological suspension of disciplinarity." Gordon's idea is, roughly, that our disciplinary methods, despite their constitutive incompleteness, tend toward solipsism; hence he recommends that we "suspend" and reach beyond (rather than ignore or discard) disciplinarity in the pursuit of transdisciplinary inquiries (the "telos").

Political science as a nomothetic enterprise has its own disciplinary logics, whose suspension could facilitate closer connections of our discipline to Asian American and other transdisciplinary studies. The results of infusing American politics scholarship with contemporary currents in critical theory, ethnography, and historiography can be seen in Claire Kim's (2000) *Bitter Fruit.* Beyond pushing race scholarship in the American subfield beyond "black and white," Asian Americanists such as Kim are pressuring political science more broadly to loosen its grip on two widely held presuppositions: (1) the state and the market are the conceptual markers, if not the transhistorical locations, of politics and (2) analyses of cause and effect are necessary, if not sufficient, for the explanation of political phenomena. Such questions about the boundaries of the political realm and the modes of scientific investigation cut to the core of political science as a disciplinary formation. Might the concept of "politics" cover cultural production, psychic formation, family life, and other domains where Asian Americanists have explored it? Might the meaning of "explanation" also extend to psychoanalytic and deconstructive or, to shift the inflection, legal historical and critical philosophical modes of analysis—explanatory modalities more common to Asian Americanists than political scientists?

Political science as an interpretive enterprise is already methodologically akin to Asian American studies in the humanities, at least insofar as both sets of scholarly practices aim at the disclosure or creation of historically situated meanings rather than abstract causal models.[2] Humanistic political scientists and humanistic Asian Americanists also share an affinity for avowedly "value-laden" practices of knowledge production that, in their employ, yield liberal to left political positions. That said, I hold that political theory in particular ought to pluralize its relationships to ethnic studies, which largely consist in engagements with Africana studies. Recent studies of black political thinkers such as Frederick Douglas, W. E. B. Du Bois, or Frantz Fanon have somewhat decentered the European intellectual tradition in our understanding of what counts as "political theory." To move further in this direction, we might, for example, read Asian American thinkers (e.g., Fred Ho) alongside black or indigenous contemporaries (e.g., Angela Davis or Vine Deloria Jr.). Another potential path of investigation has been opened by Lisa Lowe's (2015) *The Intimacies of Four Continents*, which historicizes liberalism in relation to "canonical" thinkers, British colonial practices (i.e., another archive of liberalism), and transnational racial formations. This study exemplifies how political theorists could read European thought in less self-contained ways or more transdisciplinary terms.

These articulations of the actual and possible relations of political science and ethnic studies are informed by my self-understanding as a contemporary political theorist who works in comparative ethnic studies. I have not always identified myself as such, although I have long considered myself a student of both political thinking and racial politics. As a PhD student in political science, I almost exclusively framed my research in disciplinary terms, often treating ethnic studies literatures as "sources of footnotes," to redeploy Jorge Domínguez's phrase (e.g., Lee 2007). The reasons for this disciplinary orientation were only partly conscious and idiosyncratic. I perhaps wanted to quell any doubts fellow political theorists might entertain about my ability to handle German and French "high theory." I also likely had the sense that political science, on the whole, does not reward young scholars for working in the vein of ethnic studies.

Lately, I have started to more consciously negotiate the boundaries between political science and ethnic studies in my own research. For example, my current book project, *The Racial Politics of the Extraordinary*, began as an exploration of the political theoretical distinction between extraordinary and everyday politics at the sites of southeastern American Indian removals, Japanese internment, the civil rights movement, and selected racial power movements (Black Power, Red Power, and Asian American). I soon came to recognize that this relationship of instituting, episodic, and transformative politics to institutionalized, processual, and reproductive politics has also been theorized by ethnic studies scholars (e.g., Omi and Winant 2015). I also became more attuned to the potential promise and perils of thinking black, Amerindian, and Asian racial formations together from the standpoint of comparative ethnic studies. This process of negotiating boundaries has not entailed any radical epistemological breaks, but it has encouraged me to seek out new interlocutors and interdisciplinary resonances.

Fred Lee is an assistant professor of political science and Asian/Asian American studies at the University of Connecticut, Storrs. His current book project is *The Racial Politics of the Extraordinary: Four Events in the Informal Constitution of the United States.*

■ **NOTES**

1. Almost all government, politics, or political science departments are formally organized into comparative politics, international relations, and American politics. Most will also include a political theory subfield. Some will also include public law or race, ethnicity, and politics subfields.

2. Some political theorists, Sheldon Wolin (1969) among them, reject the notion that political theory can be construed as a methodological enterprise at all. I use "method" and its cognates loosely to refer to a rough bundle of scholarly practices rather than an explicit set of rules for knowledge production.

■ **WORKS CITED**

García Bedolla, Lisa. 2005. *Fluid Borders: Latino Power, Identity, and Politics in Los Angeles.* Berkeley: University of California Press.

Gordon, Lewis. 2010. "Theory in Black Teleological Suspensions in Philosophy of Culture." *Qui Parle* 18: 193–214.

Hancock, Ange-Marie. 2004. *The Politics of Disgust: The Public Identity of the Welfare Queen.* New York: New York University Press.

Kim, Claire. 2000. *Bitter Fruit: The Politics of Black–Korean Conflict in New York City.* New Haven, Conn.: Yale University Press.

Lee, Fred. 2007. "The Japanese Internment and the Racial State of Exception." *Theory and Event* 10. https://muse.jhu.edu/article/213866.

Lowe, Lisa. 2015. *The Intimacies of Four Continents.* Durham, N.C.: Duke University Press.

Lowndes, Joseph, Julie Novkov, and Dorian Warren, eds. 2008. *Race and American Political Development.* New York: Routledge.

Omi, Michael, and Howard Winant. 2015. *Racial Formation in the United States.* 3rd ed. New York: Routledge.

Wolin, Sheldon. 1969. "Political Theory as a Vocation." *American Political Science Review* 63: 1062–82.

The Relevance Question

ERIN AERAN CHUNG

Last fall, I facilitated a workshop aimed at mentoring junior scholars who study Korean politics. The quality of the papers presented and the discussions that ensued were indistinguishable from those in other political science workshops in which I had participated in the past. But one recurring grievance stood out: why, asked the participants, do we constantly have to justify studying Korean politics?

I have heard this complaint before from junior scholars in the United States working on East Asian politics. Some note that publication opportunities and jobs are few and far between for scholars of East Asian politics—unless one studies China. Students of Korean politics or Japanese politics cannot afford to be single-country specialists. In an effort to be "relevant" within political science, many add non-Asian cases to their research, cover all of Northeast Asia, or choose a topic that has strategic value for the United States. Others apply models derived from U.S. and European cases to East Asian democracies or adopt mainstream political science methodologies and frameworks to explain East Asian politics. These efforts have yielded rich comparative studies, valuable data sets, and diverse methodologies for investigating East Asian politics. Nonetheless, they have elided the question of whether East Asia is analytically and empirically relevant in its own right.

Is the study of East Asia relevant in political science only insofar as it applies ostensibly universal formal models? Are Korean and Japanese politics significant for political scientists only as comparative cases? Must political scientists who study East Asia forgo historically informed, single-country specialization to conduct research that is accepted as mainstream political science? Does East Asia matter only when it directly impacts U.S. interests?

The answer to these questions clearly seems to be no, and yet they persist—for historical reasons. The sui generis epistemology of area studies and the universalist ambitions of comparative politics have long been uneasy bedfellows despite their intertwined development.[1] Until the end of World War II, the study of East Asia—and most other regions outside the United States and Europe—was marginal because U.S. political scientists and policy makers assumed they had little to learn from other countries, especially non-Western countries. Japan's entrance into the Pacific War and, less than a decade later, the spread of communism in East Asia made the region relevant to the United States. Yet this relevance stemmed not from what East Asia could teach U.S. scholars but from its strategic import in curbing the spread of communism in the region. With the end of the Cold War, the relevance question reemerged: do we need deep knowledge of particular countries outside the United States when they are no longer critical to U.S. strategic interests? Instead of engaging in single-case studies, why not use the tools of comparative politics to test hypotheses on large numbers of countries and thus generate knowledge that can be applied to the rest of the world?

While these questions continue to saddle work that straddles area studies and political science, the last few decades have challenged the core concepts, methodologies, and even the traditional subfield divisions of political science. Political scientists are increasingly debating the relevance of established definitions of politics and the variables we use to explain what we call the political (Blyth 2006; Rudolph 2005; Schmitter 2009). And U.S. policy makers, political analysts, and prominent commentators have publicly questioned the relevance of political science—in particular, the study of American politics—to political practices in the United States (Hero 2016; Jaschik 2010; Smith 1997). The relevance question should therefore be reversed: we should be less concerned about whether the study of a particular country, such as Japan or Korea, is relevant to political science and more focused on whether existing concepts and methodologies in political science can sufficiently explain the events, institutions, ideas, and actors in Japan, Korea, and elsewhere.

Area studies and comparative politics have much to offer each other. The deep, interdisciplinary immersion required in area studies research—including language skills and layered cultural and historical knowledge—is critical to identifying new actors, institutions, and modes of political activity that do not conform to the boundaries of the national state, formal organizations, and established policies and practices. Comparative politics, likewise, gives us the tools to analyze patterns and practices that may reveal internal contradictions, subnational variations, and transnational iterations. Both sets of tools serve to reassess political science's core questions and concepts in the twenty-first century.

These tools have been central to my own work on migration, citizenship, and racial politics in Northeast Asia. Like my colleagues, I routinely contend with questions about the relevance of Japan and Korea to the study of race, citizenship, and immigration. I face questions ranging from the curious ("Why are there immigrants in East Asia?") to the confused ("You mean you study Asian immigrants to the United States?"). These questions reflect not simply lack of knowledge about migration to East Asia but broader assumptions—both among the general public and in academia—that migration necessarily flows from the Global South to the Global North or from East to West. In fact, intraregional and South–South migration are now the dominant forms of international movement.

By examining the linkages between immigration, citizenship, and racism through comparative, interdisciplinary research on East Asian industrial democracies, my work interrogates conventional understandings of phenomena commonly associated with Western classifications, on one hand, and probes culturalist assumptions about East Asian politics and society, on the other. By extending the boundaries of how and where we study immigration, citizenship, and racial politics, I aim to broaden our comparative lens to consider recurrent patterns of social, political, and cultural conflict not only in societies long deemed multiracial or traditionally considered sites for immigration but also in societies assumed to be racially and ethnically homogenous. My work thus explores immigration politics in countries that do not acknowledge the presence of immigrants, highlights racist discourses that circumvent direct references to race, and examines the citizenship practices of those excluded from formal membership in the state.

Thematically driven scholarship opens up opportunities to explore the changing character and categories of politics that methodologically driven work may take for granted. Instead of questioning the relevance of Asian cases to the theoretical frameworks and models of political science, productive interchanges between area studies and political science grapple with the puzzles that emerge from inter-area and interdisciplinary collaborations. By questioning our area-specific *and* disciplinary assumptions, we can be more attentive to emergent forms of politics, thus developing methodological tools and generating new research agendas that travel between disciplines and move beyond isolated cases.

Erin Aeran Chung is the Charles D. Miller Associate Professor of East Asian Politics in the Department of Political Science, the director of the East Asian Studies Program, and the codirector of the Racism, Immigration, and Citizenship (RIC) Program at the Johns Hopkins University. She is the author of *Immigration and Citizenship in Japan* (2010) and *Immigrant Incorporation in East Asian Democracies* (forthcoming).

■ NOTES

The author thanks Ryan Calder, Tina Chen, Daisy Kim, and Nicole Thornton for their insightful comments and suggestions.

1. See, inter alia, Cumings (1997) and Johnson (1994).

■ **WORKS CITED**

Blyth, Mark. 2006. "Great Punctuations: Prediction, Randomness, and the Evolution of Comparative Political Science." *American Political Science Review* 100, no. 4: 493–98.

Cumings, Bruce. 1997. "Boundary Displacement: The State, the Foundations, and Area Studies during and after the Cold War." In *Learning Places: The Afterlives of Area Studies,* edited by Masao Miyoshi and H. D. Harootunian, 261–302. Durham, N.C.: Duke University Press.

Hero, Rodney E. 2016. "American Politics and Political Science in an Era of Growing Racial Diversity and Economic Disparity." *Perspectives on Politics* 14, no. 1: 7–20.

Jaschik, Scott. 2010. "Should Political Science Be Relevant?" *Inside Higher Ed,* no. 8.

Johnson, Chalmers, and E. B. Keehn. 1994. "A Disaster in the Making: Rational Choice and Asian Studies." *The National Interest,* Summer, 14–22.

Rudolph, Susanne Hoeber. 2005. "The Imperialism of Categories: Situating Knowledge in a Globalizing World," *Perspectives on Politics* 3, no. 1: 5–14.

Schmitter, Philippe C. 2009. "The Nature and Future of Comparative Politics." *European Political Science Review* 1, no. 1: 33–61.

Smith, Rogers M. 1997. "Still Blowing in the Wind: The American Quest for a Democratic, Scientific Political Science." *Daedalus* 126, no. 1: 253–87.

The Study of Asian American Politics in the United States

JANELLE S. WONG

Is there a place for ethnic studies, and specifically Asian American studies, in political science? Ethnic studies is an interdisciplinary field that places race and racialization at its center. It strives to understand the ways in which racial categories are created and maintained and their consequences for representation, resource allocation, and identity. As such, the concerns of ethnic studies overlap with the concerns of political science and the study of governance, the state, and the institutionalization of social and economic power. Ethnic studies scholarship would argue, for example, that political institutions and the distribution of social and economic power reflect state-supported racial formations. Hence ethnic studies has advanced the concept of "the racial state" (Omi and Winant 2014). Asian

American studies is a subfield of U.S. ethnic studies, focusing on the experience of members of the Asian diaspora residing in the United States.

Over the course of my career, I have come to believe that there is, in fact, an important place for Asian American studies in political science. Importantly, Dr. Don Nakanishi, a Harvard-trained political scientist (PhD, 1978), played a central role in establishing both the subfield of Asian American politics and the multidisciplinary field of Asian American studies. He did this both through research and through institution building. For example, he was on the Executive Board of the Asian Pacific American Caucus of the American Political Science Association, eventually receiving the Lifetime Achievement Award from the association's Section on Race, Ethnicity, and Politics, and he served for twenty years as the director of the UCLA Asian American Studies Center, the oldest and largest Asian American studies center in the nation.

Nakanishi's research and field development created intellectual connections across political science and Asian American studies. In 1976, for instance, Nakanishi and several other scholars of the Asian American experience published a series of essays in *Counterpoint: Perspectives on Asian America* (Gee 1976). In this collection, several authors documented and analyzed the participation of Japanese, Korean, Indian, and Chinese immigrant communities in the United States in leftist and nationalist movements. The authors emphasized the development of a distinct Asian immigrant politics in the United States informed by both international affairs in the immigrants' countries of origin and the deep discrimination that Asian immigrants were facing in their daily lives in the United States in the era of Asian exclusion. In a chapter in this volume titled "Minorities and International Politics," Nakanishi (1976) forwarded a critique of the traditional political science international relations literature with a claim that while it addressed inequalities between nation-states, it failed to consider the fact of white supremacy. Similarly, he critiqued the literature on race relations in the United States because it failed to take into account power differentials between the United States and the home countries of Asians in the United States.

Over the course of the next forty years, the study of international politics, comparative politics, and, to some extent, U.S. politics developed along separate intellectual and methodological trajectories in many of the ways Nakanishi had anticipated. Race was not at the core of international or comparative politics, and the subfield of race, ethnicity, and politics was marginalized within the field of American politics. In a 2007 ranking of the most cited scholars in American government, very few of the "top" scholars on the list participated regularly in the race, ethnicity, and politics subfield (Masuoka, Grofman, and Feld 2007).

Still, Nakanishi continued to lay the groundwork for the study of Asian Americans in U.S. politics with the publication of several research pieces that highlighted challenges to electoral representation, citizenship, voter registration, and voter participation among Asian Americans. In addition, in 1976, he published, through the UCLA Asian American Studies Center, the comprehensive *Asian American Political Almanac,* which sought to document Asian American local, state, and national political representation in the United States. Nearly one hundred dissertations that focus on the topic of Asian American politics cite Nakanishi's early research in the field.[1]

In the late 1990s, scholars of Asian American politics, including Nakanishi, found an intellectual home in the American politics subfield of race, ethnicity, and politics. To some extent, they also claimed a space in Asian American studies. The methodological emphasis in both fields greatly influenced the study of Asian American politics. It has been, from the start, an interdisciplinary enterprise. For instance, in 1998, sociologist and ethnic studies scholar Leland Saito published *Race and Politics,* an ethnographic analysis of Asian American politics in the multiracial suburban context of Monterey Park, California. This work, although groundbreaking in its focus on intergroup relations with Asian Americans at its center, was very much in the ethnographic tradition of the field of ethnic studies. Political scientist Pei-te Lien published the earliest monograph on the topic of Asian American politics in 1997, drawing on publicly available regional data sets with large samples of Asian Americans in Southern California. At this point, methods that allowed researchers to study political behavior and attitudes through survey research were ascendant in American politics and in the subfield of race, ethnicity, and politics. Lien and her colleagues conducted the first multicity, multilingual, multiethnic survey of Asian American political attitudes and behavior in 2001 (Lien 2004) and published the findings in a 2004 book, *The Politics of Asian America: Diversity and Community* (Lien, Conway, and Wong 2004).

It is fair to say, however, that since the late 2000s, the dominant focus in the field of Asian American politics has been on the political attitudes and behavior of U.S. Asians, though the methods have expanded to include field experiments and a limited number of qualitative studies (cf. Geron et al. 2001; Wong 2005; Bedolla and Michelson 2012). Notable exceptions to this trend toward studying political attitudes and behavior among Asian Americans include Claire Jean Kim's (1999) seminal treatment of

Asian American politics as part of her work on *racial triangulation*. Asian Americans, Kim argues, have been racially "triangulated" vis-à-vis whites and blacks. Society valorizes Asian Americans relative to blacks (using model minority stereotypes) to reinforce blacks' subordinate position in society. But, at the same time, society constructs Asian Americans as "forever foreign" and unassimilable compared to whites and native minorities (black Americans). Intraminority conflict is encouraged by the state under the invisible umbrella of white supremacy. Kim's research is notable because, though it is grounded in an empirical case study of a 1990 boycott by black residents of a Korean immigrant–owned store in Brooklyn, New York, it is at its heart a theoretical treatment of contemporary race relations in the United States. James Lai's (2011) research on Asian American elected representation is also an exception. Lai's research is based on surveys and observations of Asian American elected officials, and political representation is its focus.

Political science methodologies have both constrained and opened up knowledge about Asian American politics. Much of what we know about Asian Americans in the U.S. political system is about specific kinds of political attitudes and behavior related to U.S. party identification, U.S. policy attitudes, and U.S. race relations and racial identities. Because data collection tends to be sporadic and nonlongitudinal, and to rely on standard questions, we know very little about the development of political identities over time, institutional influences on Asian American politics, or conflicting or unique Asian American political ideologies. At the same time, these methodologies have yielded a new understanding of Asian Americans in the U.S. political sphere. We know quite a bit about how the Asian American mass public evaluates the current president, policies ranging from gun control to the environment, and partisan leanings among different Asian national-origin groups. The lifting up of the voices of everyday Asian Americans through traditional political science research is, in my view, an important element of the Asian American community's democratic inclusion.

The field of Asian American politics continues to evolve along with its disciplinary anchors, political science and Asian American studies. With the transnational turn in Asian American studies, for example, scholars of Asian American politics began to look more closely at transnational ties and their effects on Asian American political attitudes and behavior (Collet and Lien 2009). To return to the question framing this essay, the place of ethnic studies in political science is revealed by the fact that as scholars of Asian American politics, we insist, along with our ethnic studies colleagues, that we cannot understand state power and the relationship between a people and their government without unwavering attention to race and racial minority status.

Janelle S. Wong is professor of American studies and director of the Asian American Studies Program at the University of Maryland, College Park. She is the author of *Democracy's Promise: Immigrants and American Civic Institutions* (2006) and the coauthor of three books on Asian American politics.

■ NOTE

1. Based on a search of the ProQuest Dissertation and Theses Global database.

■ WORKS CITED

Bedolla, Lisa García, and Melissa R. Michelson. 2012. *Mobilizing Inclusion: Transforming the Electorate through Get-Out-the-Vote Campaigns.* New Haven, Conn.: Yale University Press.

Collet, Christian, and Pei-te Lien, eds. 2009. *The Transnational Politics of Asian Americans.* Philadelphia: Temple University Press.

Gee, Emma, ed. 1976. *Counterpoint: Perspectives on Asian America.* Los Angeles: University of California, Los Angeles, Asian American Studies Center.

Geron, Kim, Enrique de la Cruz, Leland T. Saito, and Jaideep Singh. 2001. "Asian Pacific Americans' Social Movements and Interest Groups." *Political Science and Politics,* no. 3: 619–24. doi:10.1017/S104909650100097X.

Kim, Claire Jean. 1999. "The Racial Triangulation of Asian Americans." *Politics and Society* 27, no. 1: 105–38.

Lai, James S. 2011. *Asian American Political Action: Suburban Transformations.* Boulder, Colo.: Lynne Rienner.

Lien, Pei-te. 1997. *The Political Participation of Asian Americans: Voting Behavior in Southern California.* Rev. ed. New York: Routledge.

———. 2004. *Pilot National Asian American Political Survey (PNAAPS), 2000–2001.* ICPSR03832-v1. Ann Arbor, MI: Inter-university Consortium for Political and Social Science. doi:10.3886/ICPSR03832.v1.

Lien, Pei-te, M. Margaret Conway, and Janelle Wong. 2004. *The Politics of Asian Americans: Diversity and Community.* 1st ed. New York: Routledge.

Masuoka, Natalie, Bernard Grofman, and Scott L. Feld. 2007. "The Political Science 400: A 20-Year Update." *PS: Political Science and Politics* 40, no. 1: 133–45.

Nakanishi, Don. 1976. "Minorities and International Politics." In *Counterpoint: Perspectives on Asian America*, edited by Emma Gee, 47–62. Los Angeles: University of California, Los Angeles, Asian American Studies Center.

Omi, Michael, and Howard Winant. 2014. *Racial Formation in the United States*. 3rd ed. New York: Routledge.

Saito, Leland T. 1998. *Race and Politics: Asian Americans, Latinos, and Whites in a Los Angeles Suburb*. 1st ed. Urbana: University of Illinois Press.

Wong, Janelle S. 2005. "Mobilizing Asian American Voters: A Field Experiment." *The ANNALS of the American Academy of Political and Social Science* 601, no. 1: 102–14. doi:10.1177/0002716205278450.

Keeping Sight of the Big Questions When Navigating between Area Studies and Discipline

ERIK MARTINEZ KUHONTA

The central analytical problem faced by any comparative political scientist who is deeply committed to area studies is the question of how to speak to two different audiences: one that is more interested in general social theory and one that is more concerned with the details and events of a country. Emphasizing a parsimonious theory to a greater extent than is warranted is likely to lead to severe criticisms from area studies scholars that the work in question has not done justice to the countries and has in fact exploited the countries for the sake of fitting them in a procrustean manner into a predefined theoretical box. On the other hand, giving too much emphasis to the details of cases to the neglect of a general overarching theory runs the danger of having one's work ignored in the larger disciplinary literature because its overall theoretical argument is not articulated in a manner that can be easily grasped or recalled. In a profession that largely rewards contributions made to one's home discipline, it is not insignificant if one's work fails to speak to fellow political scientists.

This disciplinary–area studies tension is aggravated by the methodological battles in political science over qualitative and quantitative approaches. The conventional wisdom here is that those who are more quantitatively oriented are focused on contributions to the discipline, while those who are more qualitatively oriented are concerned with countries. At a superficial level, there may be some truth to this, especially if we scan the American Political Science Association flagship journal, the *American Political Science Review*, which overwhelmingly publishes quantitative work that is devoid of any concern with in-depth analysis of specific countries.

But one has to be careful about accepting this conventional wisdom too easily. As the editors and contributors to *Southeast Asia in Political Science: Theory, Region, and Qualitative Analysis* showed, scholarship that is founded on qualitative methods can contribute to both area studies *and* theoretical knowledge (Kuhonta, Slater, and Vu 2008). Area studies and theory can work in a synergistic manner to produce research that illuminates both fields, as long as the researcher knows how to frame his or her work. The issue at hand is ensuring that scholarship centered on a country or region speaks broadly to larger analytical themes within the discipline. In other words, much depends on the framing of the research puzzle.

Scholarship in Southeast Asian politics has played a significant role in linking area studies, qualitative methods, and social theory. John Furnivall's (1948) study of colonialism in Burma and Indonesia was foundational to a concept that has had a major impact in social science: the idea of the "plural society." James Scott's (1985) scholarship on peasant resistance has forced us to rethink our ideas of ideological hegemony, while also giving us in-depth analysis of class tensions in a Malay village in the Malaysian state of Kedah. Benedict Anderson, renowned for his original study of nationalism, *Imagined Communities* (Anderson 1991), actually conceptualized his idea of an imagined community through earlier, empirical work on Indonesia and Thailand. Indeed, if one reads carefully through Anderson's many articles, including "Withdrawal Symptoms" (Anderson [1977] 1998)—about the counterreaction against the democratic movement in 1970s Thailand—one finds already germinating in that piece ideas of "imagined" sociological collectivities.

More recent generations of Southeast Asianists have also employed qualitative methods and area studies effectively in generating theory. John Sidel's (2006) deeply sociological study of religion and violence in contemporary Indonesia made a distinct argument—paralleling the ideas of scholars of Islam in the Middle East—that the level of Islamist violence reflected the extent to which radical Islamists felt incorporated in the political system and specifically that acts of violence were an indication of declining political influence. This study provided a clear understanding of contemporary violence in Indonesia as well as a theory explaining the rise in violence and the reasons for different types of violence. Dan Slater's

(2010) study of authoritarian regimes and state building in Southeast Asia has given us both more insight into regime politics in the region as well as advancing a sophisticated theory of the relationship between contentious politics and institutional trajectories. My own research (Kuhonta 2011) has laid out a broad theoretical argument explaining how political institutions—especially political parties and state structures—can effectively address problems of inequality, while also analyzing different manifestations of inequality in four countries in Southeast Asia. In sum, scholarship on Southeast Asian politics has shown very clearly, and continues to show, that area studies, qualitative methods, and disciplinary theory can combine in such a way that all three research fields—region, method, and theory—enrich each other.

That said, this does not mean that conventional wisdom juxtaposing area studies to theory and the study of countries to quantitative methods is totally inaccurate or, more specifically, that there are not some very real tensions that scholars and especially younger graduate students face when confronting the discipline-area studies question in conjunction with the methodology question. After all, the above listing of scholarship in Southeast Asian politics might not be so easily "replicable"—a research practice that is increasingly, and very incorrectly, being used as a means for defining what constitutes science. For budding academics who are navigating the many options for building one's career, it will be extremely challenging to excel in all research fields—foreign language training for in-depth area studies, advanced quantitative methods that meet the standards of the discipline, and systematic understanding of qualitative methods, where ideas of causality, mechanisms, concepts, and cases are solidly grasped rather than superficially addressed.

How, then, might one address this tension where discipline and area studies collide and where discipline increasingly demands more extensive quantitative training? The recent push in political science toward multimethods training is one answer, where we now expect our younger generation of scholars not to dismiss any one particular tool kit or methodological approach but rather to absorb all of them. There is clearly some advantage to this strategy, but it is also too much of a goldilocks recipe that may end up designing a project that ticks all requisite boxes but that does not ultimately come together in any theoretical or ontological sense. Besides the actual challenge of achieving such a broad methodological feat, aggregating different methods and perspectives into one project may fail to add up to something analytically coherent.

I would rather suggest that the more interesting and feasible direction for scholarship of Southeast Asian politics is for scholars to do what earlier generations of social scientists like Karl Marx, Max Weber, Emile Durkheim, Gabriel Almond, Seymour Martin Lipset, Myron Weiner, Samuel Huntington, Robert Putnam—and indeed the late Benedict Anderson—did: ask the big questions that matter to social science and use systematic methods, concepts, and theories to answer those questions. This is a relatively simple point to make, but in the context of a discipline where there is an increasing emphasis on method above all else, this point is not inconsequential. An excessive concern with technique and methodology may lead the younger generation of scholars astray in terms of priorities. This does not mean that methodological training should be ignored; it shouldn't. But at the same time, if we are to concern ourselves primarily with producing valuable scholarship that is not motivated by the need to follow fashionable trends, it seems to me that the answer lies in asking foundational questions about politics and society and letting the methodological chips fall wherever they may fall. In other words, let the analytical puzzle precede the tool box, and not the other way round.

If the analytical puzzle lies at the heart of any research project, some contribution to theory—whether implicit or explicit—is likely to be made. And this ultimately is what should matter for the social sciences—not one's methodological proclivities but one's capacity to contribute to the ongoing debates that are at the heart of the academy and of real-world problems. Indeed, theory is likely to be of significant value for addressing real-world problems because it can provide a new lens from which to see pressing puzzles. If political science is to uphold its promise of engaging with the real world, it should seek to answer big questions that can aid in theoretical development as well as in making the world a more humane place.

Erik Martinez Kuhonta is associate professor of political science and associate member of the Institute for the Study of International Development at McGill University. His recent book, coedited with Allen Hicken, is *Party System Institutionalization in Asia: Democracies, Autocracies, and the Shadows of the Past* (2015).

■ WORKS CITED

Anderson, Benedict R. (1977) 1998. "Withdrawal Symptoms." In *The Spectre of Comparisons*, 139–73. London: Verso.

———. 1991. *Imagined Communities: Reflections on the Origins and Spread of Nationalism.* 2nd rev. ed. London: Verso.

Furnivall, John. 1948. *Colonial Policy and Practice: A Comparative Study of Burma and Netherlands India.* Cambridge: Cambridge University Press.

Kuhonta, Erik Martinez. 2011. *The Institutional Imperative: The Politics of Equitable Development in Southeast Asia.* Stanford, Calif.: Stanford University Press.

Kuhonta, Erik Martinez, Dan Slater, and Tuong Vu, eds. 2008. *Southeast Asia in Political Science: Theory, Region, and Qualitative Analysis.* Stanford, Calif.: Stanford University Press.

Scott, James C. 1985. *Weapons of the Weak: Everyday Forms of Peasant Resistance.* New Haven, Conn.: Yale University Press.

Sidel, John T. 2006. *Riots, Pogroms, Jihad: Religious Violence in Indonesia.* Stanford, Calif.: Stanford University Press.

Slater, Dan. 2010. *Ordering Power: Authoritarian Leviathans and Contentious Politics in Southeast Asia.* Cambridge: Cambridge University Press.

Disciplinary Quandaries: A Metacommentary on the Relationship between Political Science and the Interdisciplinary Study of Asia

LEELA FERNANDES

The relationship between disciplinary practices and the interdisciplinary study of politics, culture, and society has long been a site of intellectual contestation within the U.S. academy. Such contestation has been particularly vigorous when it has been imbricated within relationships of power marked by inequalities like race, ethnicity, and gender or by historically specific global relationships of power between countries and regions of the world (Szanton 2004). Taken together, the commentaries in this feature provide an important analysis of the possibilities, limits, and challenges that the discipline of political science holds for the study of Asia and Asian diasporic communities and a productive avenue for an exploration of questions of disciplinarity, power, and knowledge. However, if the relationship between disciplinarity and interdisciplinarity is to be fully addressed—both in relation to the study of Asia/Asian diasporas and in relation to the broader question of knowledge production—it requires an exploration of the ways in which interdisciplinary fields of analysis (and their institutionalized sites) may also become disciplined by the cross-disciplinary formations that are dominant within them (Fernandes 2013; Miyoshi and Harootunian 2002). As the commentaries cogently argue, the turn away from "area studies" has had an impact on the discipline of political science. However, the question that then arises is how this disciplinary trend has begun to impact the institutional presuppositions and conditions of knowledge production within the interdisciplinary study of Asia.

A central constraint that has shaped political scientific scholarship on Asia and Asian diasporas is the institutionalization of a set of dominant norms regarding "methodological rigor." The question of the effects of disciplinary methodological imperatives cuts across all of the commentaries on the state of the field. Whether they address the constraints of disciplinary norms that privilege quantitative scholarship (Lee; Wong), the devaluation of single-country "case study" research (Chung), or the formulaic dangers of mixed-methods approaches (Kuhonta; Lee), the commentaries point to the intellectual limits of a methodological rigidity and narrowness that produce chasms between political science and the study of Asia. The issue at hand is not that work that has drawn on quantitative or cross-national comparative approaches has not produced innovative and important scholarship on Asia or even that such approaches have not drawn on or contributed to in-depth understandings of Asia. Mixed-methods approaches in political science now often contain a fieldwork-based component that may include interpretive methods that draw on oral interviews, ethnography, or discourse analysis. However, the methodological doctrine of political science presumes a hierarchy of knowledge practices that are tied to the kind of methods being deployed. Thus, for instance, in the mixed-methods formula, interpretive methods are generally deployed to flesh out, extend, or deepen a research design that is defined by the foundational rigors of quantitative or cross-national comparative methods.

Such questions of methods are also fundamentally questions about intellectual legitimacy within the discipline. Methodological practices in effect become the disciplinary signposts of what kind of knowledge matters. Dominant conceptions of methodological rigor are inextricably bound up with epistemological judgments of what forms of knowledge are generalizable and therefore of significance to the discipline. However, the question of generalizability is itself encoded with long intellectual histories that have juxtaposed universal theories (historically coded as "Western" and "white") with particular cases, contexts, and groups (historically coded as non-Western or marked by race). Thus, whether we are speaking of the case of fields such as Asian American studies in political science or individual scholarly works that seek to analyze politics in single countries, these histories produce weighty intellectual obstacles to intellectual legitimacy. Consider Wong's striking observation that not a single article focusing on Asian American politics has been published in the three top-ranked American politics journals. Conforming to the dominant methodological norms of the discipline thus becomes an understandable route for scholars to gain intellectual legitimacy for their research.

The stakes in this cycle of knowledge production are high as they produce the epistemological boundaries that determine what is included and excluded in our understandings of Asia and Asian diasporic communities. That is, empirical, conceptual, and theoretical gaps accumulate over time to produce highly skewed, if not distorted, understandings of Asia. The central question that haunts such intellectual legacies is one that asks, what kinds of research agendas, theoretical questions, and empirical understandings are foreclosed by the weight of disciplinary practices? What are the cumulative implications for the way we understand Asia (and the world as a whole) when work that breaks with disciplinary norms is rendered marginal to the discipline through the mundane institutional practices and cultures that constitute disciplines? This may be in part an unanswerable hypothetical question, because it asks us to reflect not on individual scholars who may successfully navigate between political science, ethnic studies, and area studies but on generational training that shapes not just what kinds of questions are asked but the weighty legacy of questions that are not being posed by new generations of scholars. The silences of unasked questions are often the most critical markers of fields of knowledge.

The implications of the disjunctures between political science and the interdisciplinary study of Asia are not, however, limited to research agendas within the discipline. It is tempting to rest with a binary juxtaposition between a rigidly defined discipline and a textured, eclectic field devoted to context-specific understandings of Asia. However, a comprehensive and in-depth exploration of the important questions that frame this discussion requires a careful look at the ways in which the interdisciplinary study of Asia also becomes disciplined in subtle but significant ways. In other words, the drift of political science research agendas away from area-based work has an impact not just on the discipline but on the institutionalized interdisciplinary sites that are devoted to the study of Asia and Asian diasporas. How disciplinary practices creep into interdisciplinary sites will, of course, vary based on the field in question. My own consideration of this question stems from my observations about the field of South Asian studies.

The field of South Asian studies (largely focused on India) has had a long-standing tradition of political scientists who have shaped both area-based debates on politics and political economy and debates within the discipline. This has encompassed an eclectic range of scholarship, including the foundational work of Susanne Rudolph (a past president of the American Political Science Association) and Lloyd Rudolph on democratic politics; Atul Kohli's work on democracy, inequality, and poverty; and Amrita Basu's work on social movements. Political science scholarship on India has continued to use single-country analyses (often deploying comparative methods that compare states within India's federal structure) and often has a strong fieldwork-based component that includes both qualitative and quantitative aspects. As commentaries by Kuhonta, Lee, and Wong note, it is critical for discussions of the discipline to produce accurate intellectual genealogies that take into account variations of subfields and that do not erase the significant contributions that have been made by political scientists in both the discipline and the study of Asia. For example, as Kuhonta rightly notes, there have been major contributions of political scientists (such as James Scott and Benedict Anderson) whose work at the intersection of social theory, Asian studies, and political science transformed theories of nationalism and resistance and shaped generations of social science and humanistic research.

Despite this rich body of scholarship, political science has become an increasingly marginalized component of South Asian studies. Empirical markers of this can be seen in the relatively low numbers of applicants (and recipients) of area-based fellowships and the relatively low levels of participation of political scientists in area-based conferences. These trends have had a profound impact on the conditions of knowledge formation within South Asian studies. The declining presence of political scientific approaches within the field leads to a disciplining of area studies through the disciplines that are consequently dominant in the field (such as history, anthropology, and literature). While such forms of disciplinarity are often subtle, their cumulative effect is as significant as the more overt forms of disciplinarity in political science. At the micro level, this may take the form of intellectual cultural dispositions that construct particular approaches to the study of politics, culture, and society as intellectually valuable or meritorious. These normative disciplinary judgments (that may rest on anything from the kind of theoretical approach deployed to the type of methods used or the style of writing) become normalized as markers of "cutting-edge interdisciplinarity."

Constructions of political science scholarship as lacking in nuance, in this context, are not merely about methodological divides. That is, the exclusionary practices that creep into conditions of knowledge production within South Asian studies are not merely about a rejection of scholarship based on quantitative methods. In fact, any attempt to strengthen the social science components of fields such as South Asian studies by adding in political science work based on a checklist of methodological practices (for instance, trying to be inclusive of work that uses quantitative approaches) in fact simply reifies dominant conceptions of what counts as social science research and misses the pluralism and diversity of scholarly work that has and is being conducted by political scientists. The issue at hand rests with a much deeper set of disciplinary practices that become embedded in fields such as South Asian studies. What becomes foreclosed is an analytical terrain that falls somewhere between the "interdisciplinary" field of South Asian studies and the "disciplinary" field of political science (Fernandes, forthcoming). Consider just one set of examples of what is often shortchanged by divergences between the two fields. Both political science and South Asian studies have wide and deep literatures on questions of inequality, democratic politics, and state power. Yet what we see is a steep decline in analyses that speak to *systemic* explanations of the reproduction of socioeconomic inequality and the relationship between socioeconomic processes and cultural identities that depart from both the "disciplinary" normative advocacy of economic reforms in political science, on one hand, and "interdisciplinary" approaches that, on the other hand, assume that nuanced understandings of identity and inequality must rest on a diffused conception of power. "Interdisciplinary" studies of the state and democratic institutions within South Asian studies rarely (if at all) engage with the broad political science scholarship on such questions. Meanwhile, intellectual dispositions within South Asian studies (through the everyday practices that materialize fields of knowledge) tend to dismiss systemic explanations of inequality as outdated examples of structural functionalism. In the process, avenues for productive interdisciplinary exchanges are foreclosed and the accumulation of unasked questions continues, albeit in a different disciplinary mode.

For the conditions of knowledge production about "Asia" to be opened up and deepened will require a hard look at the cultural and institutional practices within fields, such as South Asian studies, that have increasingly begun to discipline the field. That is, if the task of this set of commentaries is to open up an analytical space that can encourage political science to learn from Asian studies, such an endeavor itself becomes a practice of disciplinary rigidity if it does not also ask what the study of Asia should learn from political scientists.

Of course, by way of a conclusion, it is worth remembering that this commentary on the production of knowledge about Asia is focused on institutional practices within the United States. Questions regarding the kinds of knowledge that matter may take a very different form when the

national and international geopolitical location of the intellectual shifts
are taken into account. That is perhaps one of the most important cautions for the need for intellectual humility that must be made in any of
the debates on knowledge production and in the claims of what counts
as creative, contextual, interdisciplinary knowledge about Asia and its
diasporas.

Leela Fernandes is the Glenda Dickerson Collegiate Professor of Wom-
en's Studies and professor of political science at the University of Michigan. She is the author of *India's New Middle Class: Democratic Politics in
an Era of Economic Reform* (Minnesota, 2006), *Transnational Feminism in
the United States* (2013), *Producing Workers: The Politics of Gender, Class,
and Culture in the Calcutta Jute Mills* (1997), and *Transforming Feminist
Practice* (2003) and editor of *Routledge Handbook of Gender in South Asia*
(2014). She is currently engaged in research for a new book project, *Public
Works in a Post-liberalization State: Urbanization, Inequality, and the Politics
of Water in India.*

■ WORKS CITED

Fernandes, Leela. 2013. *Transnational Feminism in the United States: Knowl-
edge, Power and Ethics.* New York: New York University Press.
———. Forthcoming. "Rethinking the 'Dominant Proprietary Classes':
India's Middle Classes and the Reproduction of Inequality." In *The
Political Economy of Development in India: Revisited,* edited by Elizabeth
Chatterjee and Matthew McCartney. London: Oxford University Press.
Miyoshi, Masao, and H. D. Harootunian. 2002. *Learning Places: The After-
lives of Area Studies.* Durham, N.C.: Duke University Press.
Szanton, David. 2004. *The Politics of Knowledge: Area Studies and the Dis-
ciplines.* Berkeley: University of California Press.

Interface

JAN CHRISTIAN BERNABE, CLARE COUNIHAN, AND SARITA ECHAVEZ SEE

Sea, Land, Air and the Center for Art and Thought

"FILIPINOS WORK EVERYWHERE." With those words, we launched the Center for Art and Thought's inaugural virtual exhibition *Sea, Land, Air: Migration and Labor* in summer 2013, and we established the curatorial and intellectual framework that guides all of our projects: a new kind of Philippine-centrism. As the curator, editor, and executive director of the Center for Art and Thought (CA+T), a web-based, nonprofit organization based in California, we take up this invitation from *Verge* to reflect on how and why CA+T takes the Philippines and Filipinos around the world as a point of departure—rather than a point of arrival—for bringing into focus and understanding other histories, spaces, and communities. *Sea, Land, Air: Migration and Labor* comprises artistic and scholarly works from thirty contributors, and our curatorial selection diversely reflects the Philippines's current role as what sociologist Robyn Magalit Rodriguez calls a "labor brokerage state," a country that "actively prepares, mobilizes, and regulates its citizens for migrant work abroad." With *Sea, Land, Air,* we wanted to capture Filipinos' and the Philippines's role in and experiences of global systems of (neo)colonialism, militarism, labor, and migration. This history, we argue implicitly through all our projects, provides a departure point from which to understand contemporary global processes: we look *from* the Philippines and Filipinos at home and abroad *toward* the rest of the world. Thus, we do not think solely about Filipinos; sometimes we use Filipino paradigms to understand, for example, the (de)racialization of American "craftivists" and crafting cultures in CA+T's virtual online exhibition *RaceCraft* or the intersection between food and colonialism in CA+T's exhibition *Food Worlds.* At the same time, we hope to

"

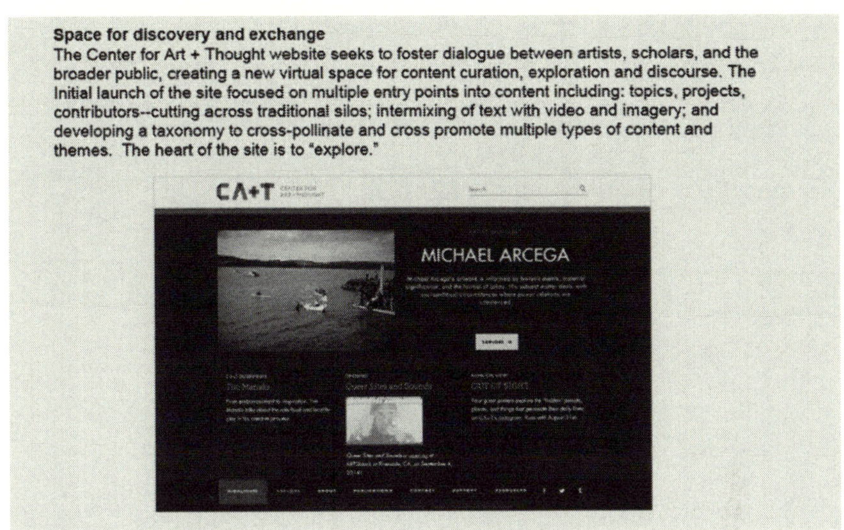

Figure 1. Screenshot of the Center for Art and Thought's website ("Space for Discovery and Exchange").

contribute a curatorially based approach to the study of Filipino mobilities and digital networks, an exciting field of scholarship that can range from communications studies scholar Fernando Paragas's research on migrant workers' experience of simultaneity, to historical anthropologist Deirdre de la Cruz's analysis of the relationship between mass media and the cult of the Virgin Mary, to American studies scholar Jan Padios's writings on the call center industry.[1]

We decided to open *Sea, Land, Air* with images of Jenifer Wofford's series of drawings *MacArthur Nurses* because the Filipino nurse has become an icon of the globalization of care. Wofford's nurses, alongside artwork, scholarship, poetry, interviews, and journalism from the other contributors, illuminate global processes of economic and psychic transformation that Filipinos—and all contemporary subjects—face. We posted these works serially, over the course of several weeks. Juxtaposing creative and scholarly works, this carefully sequenced, staggered launch makes the most of our digital platform. By releasing our virtual exhibitions over time, each new work (or two to three works by a single contributor) enjoys users' focused scrutiny, while we fulfill the demand for constantly new content. More importantly, users can interrogate each work individually while—over the course of the launch—interpreting and reinterpreting each work in light of previous and subsequent pieces. For example, in Catherine Ceniza Choy's essay "The New Face of Immigration: Flor de

Figure 2. Jenifer Wofford, *MacArthur Nurses (Descent)*, 2009. Ink and acrylic on paper. Courtesy of the artist.

Manila y San Francisco by Jenifer K. Wofford" engages Wofford's drawings, and both Wofford's and Choy's works are recontextualized by Wawi Navarozza's photographic series, *Perhaps It Was Possibly Because,* that blurs the lines between tourism, labor migration, and cynical travel. *Sea, Land, Air,* along with all of our other virtual exhibitions, we believe, shows how much the world has to learn from the globalized experiences and perspectives of Filipinos. At the same time, we strive to achieve a productive tension between the users' twinned desires to skim the surface and to dive deeply into content.

As the works in *Sea, Land, Air* capture the complexities of migrations across oceans and landmasses, CA+T itself has become an example of cultural digital mobility that challenges the segregation between "art" and "scholarship" and provides a crucial alternative to mainstream academic and art worlds. The digital realm has facilitated new and radical modes of connections and communications between users off- and online and between institutions and their constituents. CA+T participates in these disruptive—and yet productive—modes of digital exchange. Here we use *disruptive* to signal modes of digital communication, learning, and exchange that challenge normative (or analog) epistemic, creative, and communicative models, for example, knowledge production that is sanctioned within university walls or within art galleries or museums. CA+T's team live tweets conference panels. Users comment on works through the website's interface with Facebook and alert friends and colleagues to

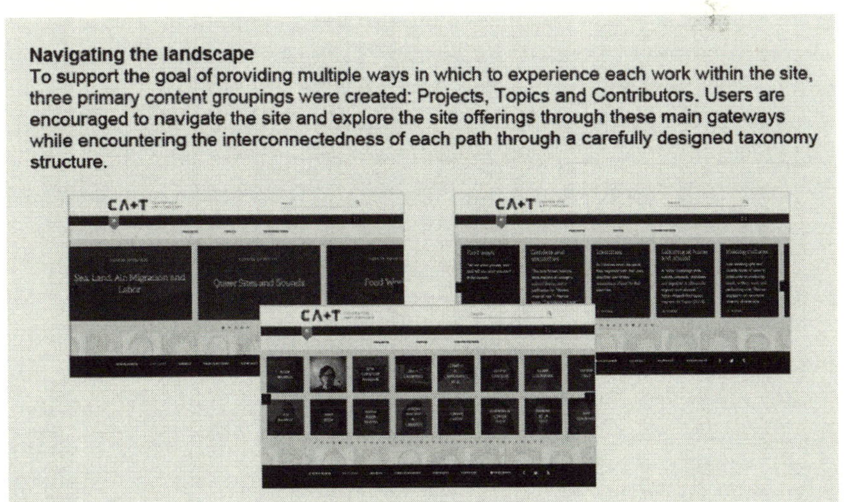

Figure 3. Screenshot of the Center for Art and Thought's website ("Navigating the Landscape").

other resources. Our Artist-in-Residence program invites users to engage directly with artists as they share their processes of creation and elaboration. Several faculty members have used CA+T to teach their courses. Digital exchange begins to look something like this: conversations start on the website, migrate to Facebook posts and private messages, move on to e-mail, and return to the website. Our content is free and our principles are not-for-profit, enabling us to move works into the same networks of global migration and labor as the people whose lives *Sea, Land, Air* traces. This confluence of people and knowledge reveals the systemic socioeconomic and historical circumstances shaping both—albeit via vastly different mechanisms. On a very practical level, we approach artists and scholars directly for permission to reproduce or republish their works on CA+T's website. We also commission new pieces, providing artists and scholars an alternative venue to share their work. Thus, CA+T desequesters creative and scholarly materials from behind the literal and virtual paywalls of art galleries and university libraries. In so doing, CA+T has emerged as a digital arts and culture hub that questions the authoritative and conventional processes of knowledge production, acquisition, and exchange. These acts of production, acquisition, and exchange are no longer exclusively the realm of institutionally and financially sanctioned actors; they are available to anyone with an Internet connection.

In the types of cultural and epistemic work that CA+T produces for an online global audience, CA+T's cultural digital mobility allows it to surpass what the organization could do if it existed solely as a brick- and-mortar organization. Not only are we *not* constrained by the storage space of a physical archive but users access CA+T's materials from (in order of number of users) the Philippines, the United States, Russia, Canada, and the United Kingdom, among other countries. This relationship between organization and constituent offers knowledge exchanges that, by their very nature, are unfixed spatially. That is to say, cultural production and the cultural work of CA+T are always already mobile online *and* accessible via networked devices and spaces. *Sea, Land, Air* and CA+T's subsequent projects make the relationship between art and culture and critical modes of thinking more accessible, responsive, and grounded in the realities of the im/migrant body in the digital age.

CA+T also calls into question the conventions of curatorial practice. The digital age necessitates new modes of curation that might be guided chronologically, thematically, or by completely different guidelines altogether. This, of course, holds true for exhibitions offline, but what makes digital curation different for CA+T is the ability to harness the digital for a deeper and quicker experience, to juxtapose more readily materials

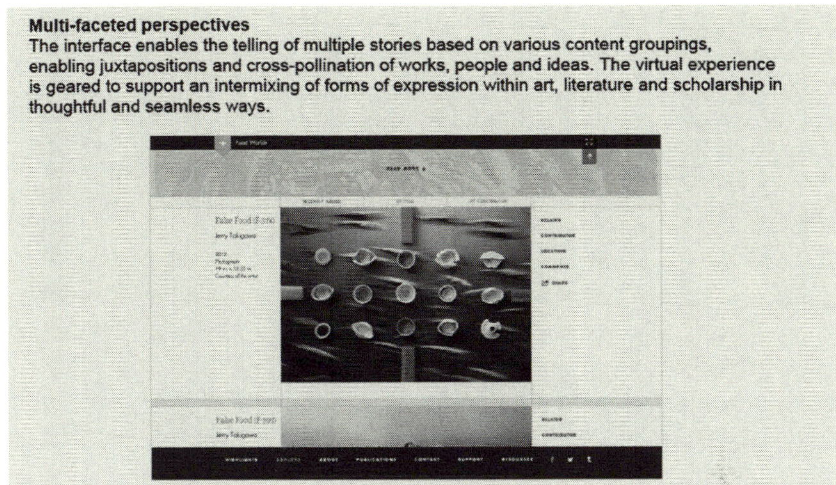

Figure 4. Screenshot of the Center for Art and Thought's website ("Multi-faceted Perspectives").

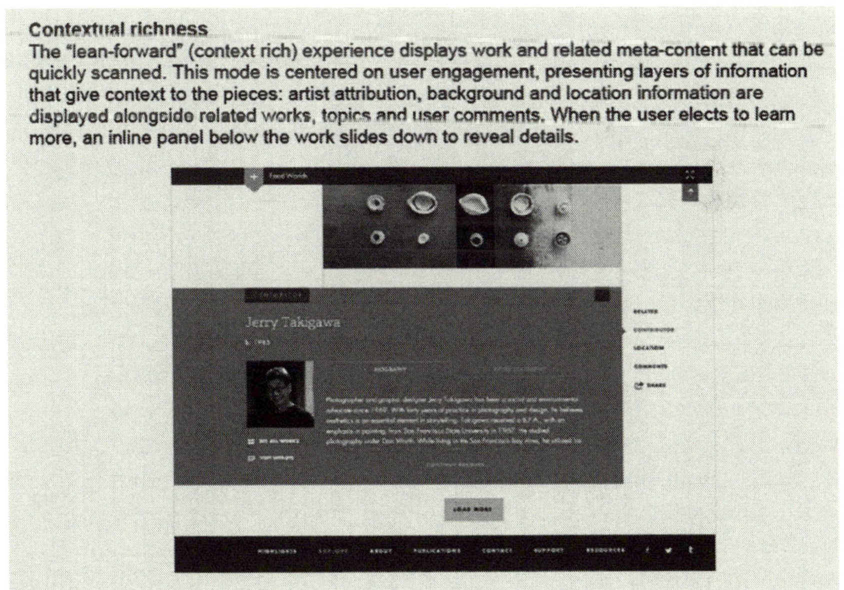

Figure 5. Screenshot of the Center for Art and Thought's website ("Contextual Richness").

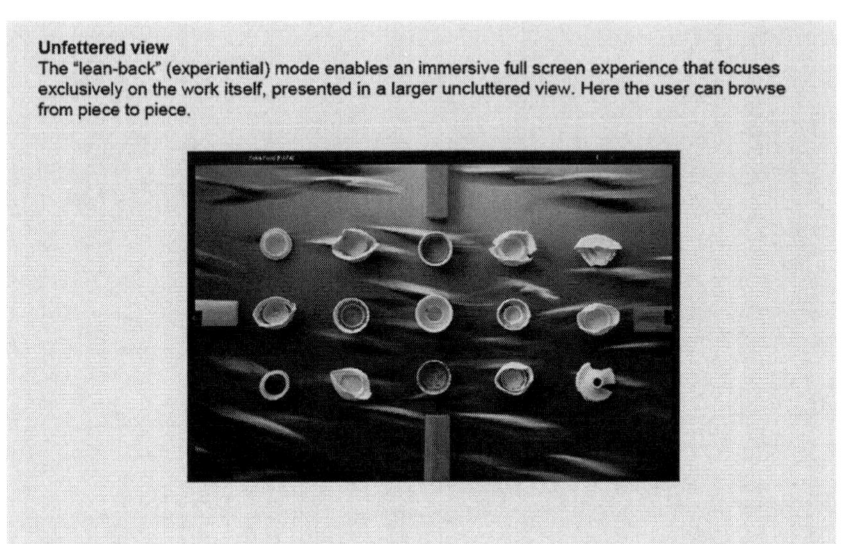

Figure 6. Screenshot of the Center for Art and Thought's website ("Unfettered View").

from different exhibitions. If we think of art images as nodal points, CA+T's digital curation exposes how these nodal points connect to other nodal points with a click of the mouse. Digital time and space produce rhizomatic exhibition experiences for CA+T's users. For example, a user might start with Wofford's *MacArthur Nurses* and wander, via Wofford's participation in the Mail Order Bride/MOB collective, to Thea Quiray Tagle's analysis of how their Manananggoogle project's "relocation of the Filipino demon to California's Silicon Valley provides a critical commentary on global circuits of political and economic exchange," and thence to Miguel Libarnes's *Settle I,* a video installation of the haunting of *Queer Sites and Sounds.* The ease of clicking from one work to another erases the separation implied by distinct virtual exhibitions, and the subsequent sequence constitutes its own virtual exhibition.

A disruptive digital art and culture hub, CA+T creates—and finds its strength as—an alternative space for thinking critically and creatively, away from institutional practices of knowledge production that can stifle rather than incite curiosity. In large part, this freedom and flexibility spring from our experiences creating (curating) virtual exhibitions. Our curators have learned how to use a content management system (or CMS) as a means to display works online and ultimately to archive the works themselves. We have also embraced the expansive possibilities of digital curation: the malleability of collecting, organizing, presenting, and molding content. For example, we very quickly realized—with our second virtual exhibition—that works and contributors would inevitably "speak" to and reread each other. Thus, Jenifer Wofford's ink and acrylic *MacArthur Nurses* images, from *Sea, Land, Air,* mean very differently when encountered through *RaceCraft*'s scrutiny of the role of "crafts" in making a racial (or deracialized) subject of the nation—and both are immediately available in CA+T's digital archives.

CA+T continues to model new modes of virtual curation, including exploring ways to integrate digital and physical realities. CA+T's 2014 collaboration with University of California, Riverside's ARTSblock, to stage an on-site exhibition of *Queer Sites and Sounds,* enabled the "live" encounter between works, artists, and audience to extend and nuance the conversations the exhibition inspired online. During the one-day symposium connected with the on-site exhibition at ARTSblock, the invited speakers Gina Osterloh, Ronaldo Wilson, Kiam Junio, and Jeffrey Songco engaged in a far-reaching, illuminating conversation with the audience about the racial and sexual politics of passing, performance, desire, and the photographic grid. The combination of virtual and on-site versions of *Queer Sites and Sounds* prepared and allowed for participants to engage with each other substantively, even if they were meeting face-to-face for the first time. During the closing roundtable panel, the poet Ronaldo Wilson observed that the creative process involves learning how to internalize constraints, poetic as well as technological, and figuring out how to "let your body unleash into this space of freedom," as he put it. CA+T aspires to create both the moment and the archive for that kind of unleashing to happen.

While not all of CA+T's virtual curated exhibitions are thematically queer—indeed, only *Queer Sites and Sounds* is explicitly "about" queer subject matter—CA+T itself is deliberately, organizationally, and epistemically queer. In both our curatorial practices and knowledge production, CA+T prefers nonnormative modes of inquiry and curation. The digital landscape—with its constantly changing technologies, interfaces, capacities, and ethics—means that CA+T will never find a static ground from which to proclaim mastery. Not only does the digital flux seamlessly between its "proper" purpose and infinite "mis"-uses but users' capacity to remake, immediately and repeatedly, the tenuous narratives CA+T does proffer perverts even the possibility of singular linear master narratives. While Edward Said's *Beginnings* (1975) debunked the primacy of endings, users' rhizomatic experiences also reveal the digital's erasure of "the beginning" as singular and portentous. In this digital rhizome, every user and every work represents a potential (an actual) beginning to multiple unique narratives. As CA+T creates exhibitions and an archive, we embrace the certainty that we are engaged in a process of co-production and co-creation with our users.

Jan Christian Bernabe is an interdisciplinary scholar of Asian American art history and visual culture, comparative race and ethnic studies, and queer cultural studies. He is the Center for Art and Thought's curatorial director and the coeditor of *Queering Contemporary Asian American Art* (2017).

Clare Counihan serves as CA+T's editor and development consultant. She also currently works at the University of North Carolina at Chapel Hill in the Carolina Women's Center.

Sarita Echavez See is cofounder and executive director of the Center for Art and Thought, and she is associate professor of media and cultural studies at the University of California, Riverside. She is the author of *The Decolonized Eye: Filipino American Art and Performance* (Minnesota, 2009) and *The Filipino Primitive: Accumulation and Resistance in the American Museum* (forthcoming) and a coeditor of *Critical Ethnic Studies: A Reader* (2016).

■ NOTE

1. The following list is far from representative of the field of Filipino mobilities and digital networks but indicates, we hope, the wide range of topic, approach, and method that has developed over more than a decade: Fernando Paragas, "Migrant Workers and Mobile Phones: Technological, Temporal, and Spatial Simultaneity," in *The Reconstruction of Space and Time: Mobile Communication Practices,* ed. R. Ling and S. Campbell, 39–65 (New Brunswick, N.J.: Transaction, 2009); Deirdre de la Cruz, *Mother Figured: Marian Apparitions and the Making of a Filipino Universal* (Chicago: University of Chicago Press, 2015); Emily Noelle Ignacio, *Building Diaspora: Filipino Cultural Community Formation on the Internet* (New Brunswick, N.J.: Rutgers University Press, 2004); and Jan Maghinay Padios, "Queer Confessions: Transgression, Affect, and National Crisis in the Philippines' Call Center Industry," Center for Art and Thought, 2013, http://centerforartandthought.org/work/item/queer-confessions-transgression-affect-and-national-crisis-philippines%E2%80%99-call-center-industry.

ANN SHERIF

Book Histories, Material Culture, and East Asian Studies

"NOT SURE *WHAT* THEY ARE. Some kind of old Chinese books maybe? Are you interested?" she asked uncertainly. Of course, I said yes. When the mysterious objects finally emerged from their dark space, I could see why even the librarian had struggled to identify them. It wasn't just the lack of cataloging information or the unfamiliar script. Most confounding about these paper things was their failure to resemble proper *books,* conveyers of civilization worthy of reading and protecting. Yet the library had kept them for more than a century.

Most of them were mere slender stacks of paper with flimsy covers and no spine at all, just thin thread stuck through a couple of holes along one edge. Who could guess that these were nineteenth-century Japanese translations of the Bible? Next on the shelf, there was a volume small enough to fit in the palm of your hand. Though it had Western binding, the tiny pages were covered with Chinese characters. Another book distributed by Protestant missionaries? No, this one was a popular edition of the Confucian Classics from the 1870s.

A series of interactions like this one involving unrecognizable books raised many questions for me about productive approaches to book studies and East Asian books. In the age of the digital object, book studies takes as a starting point the material book. This focus on the materiality of the book leads the student not only to engagement with the physical object but more broadly to theorization and historicization of books as material culture demanding our attention. But how can those of us in the field proceed if the "old Chinese books" present themselves as so unrelated to anything that we moderns recognize as books? Does it follow that their social and cultural weight has vanished, the worlds they were part of devoid of interest? And what if the Chinese books are Japanese? Or Korean? Or Vietnamese?

Book studies (or history of the book) is now a well-established multi- and interdisciplinary field of research and pedagogy internationally. With deep roots in a range of local bibliographic, historiographical, hermeneutic, and humanistic disciplines and practices, book studies describes and analyzes the production, consumption, preservation, and destruction of technologies, cultural modes, and even book worlds. Over the past two decades, the field of book studies has not only energized research and teaching in academia but also given rise to productive collaborations among scholars, librarians, authors, and a publishing industry that face rapidly changing digital and print technologies as well as new cultures of reading and writing.

To date, Euro-American research and practice on history of the book in Europe and the Americas have developed and elaborated so deeply and thoroughly on a regional basis that it is often taken as a universal model. In this essay, I offer an overview of contemporary approaches to book studies in East Asia. East Asian book studies challenges the privileged status and assumed universality of Western book history but at the same time remains deeply informed by the profound theoretical approaches and insights arising from that book world. My goal here is not to reject Western-born book history models, which remain alluring both because of their maturity and the controversial yet alluring linear history of the printing press as an agent of change—print culture leading the way to the Renaissance, to the Copernican Revolution, to print capitalism, to modernity itself, to our cherished freedom of speech and the press.

Back in my library, I ponder the challenge in identifying "old Chinese books." Is there no long regional (East Asian) book world around which a narrative of change and social transformation could be told? Should we conclude that the book histories, the book cultures of Asia, evolved on a nation-state basis? In fact, the book histories of China, Japan, Korea, and Vietnam in modern times *have* been told separately, as only vaguely related, with little sense of the merit in grasping them also in a regional East Asian sense, as a book world unto itself.

Although I focus in this essay on several recent key publications in book studies, my thinking has also been shaped by participation in a series of workshops at which China, Japanese, and Korean studies scholars gathered with the goals of clarifying (1) the nation-state-based frameworks that mold our scholarship and (2) the merits of being able to step beyond circumscribed, nationally based approaches and to articulate the dynamics of an East Asian book world. The first of these Book in East

Asia workshops highlighted innovative pedagogical approaches for incorporating East Asian print culture and books in the classroom within the undergraduate Asian studies curriculum. Given book studies' focus on books as material or digital objects, participants considered the types of collaboration possible among faculty, librarians, curators, and conservators as well as campus and online resources to support book studies in the curriculum. Subsequent workshops emphasized research approaches. These ongoing dialogues also take as objects of inquiry the entangled histories of books as a transregional and intraregional phenomenon, as objects and ideas spanning empire and colony, traversing trade routes and creating networks of dynamic ideas and narratives. Nonetheless, the nation-state-based approach still has a powerful draw for many scholars of the East Asian book and in the public imagination.

■ TECHNOLOGY TRANSFER AND NATIONALISM IN BOOK HISTORY: THE CASE OF KOREAN PRINTING

For every bureaucrat who seeks to banish physical books to remote sites, to digitize and discard space-occupying things bearing text, there is a digital native who goes out into the world to seek the technological transfers, local conditions, and social contexts from which these many book things sprung over the centuries. In 2015, Steph Rue, a twenty-two-year-old Fulbright grantee, traveled throughout South Korea looking for premodern Korean books and seeking to learn how those books were made. Over a few short months, Rue was able to apprentice with papermakers who use methods to produce *hanji* not unlike that of Cai Lun, said to be the inventor of paper in China in AD 105; she tried her hand at woodblock printing of the kind that dominated in East Asian book production for more than five hundred years. Her journey took her to vast libraries of woodblocks used for printing Confucian classical texts and Buddhist sutras.

Rue also observed the production techniques of Lim Inho, a craftsman who produces metal type in the manner of the thirteenth-century Koreans who may well have invented movable type. In her *Field Notes from Korea* blog post about the Cheongju Metal Type Training Center, Rue (2015) notes that "Cheongju is special because the first book ever printed with metal type, *Anthology of Great Buddhist Priests' Zen Teachings,* or *Jikji* for short, was produced at Heungdeok Temple, which was located in Cheongju. It was printed during the Goryeo Dynasty in 1377, 78 years prior to Gutenberg's Bible."

Rue's successful search for living examples of historical technologies of the book in Korea was made possible by complex currents of cultural and technological nationalism, colonialism, militarism, resistance, East

Asia as a region, and the dominance of Western models of book history. Nationalistic pride in Korean civilization's technological innovations—and specifically the invention of metal type—is evident in public and private museums and in the press; Korean scholars have written tomes that offer evidence for Korea's technological prescience on a global level, beating not only Gutenberg and the West but also China to movable type. In 2009, the South Korean government affirmed the value of Mr. Im's metal type skills to national identity and reputation by officially designating him an Important Intangible Cultural Property.

When Korean papermakers teach techniques for making the highly durable, beautiful, and infinitely useful *hanji* (Korean paper), part of the lesson includes the ways that *hanji* has long been a site of anti-imperial resistance. Drawing on the internationalist Wilsonian rhetoric of the Samil (March 1) 1919 Independence Movement, contemporary advocates for *hanji* tell of papermakers who fought to preserve indigenous *hanji*-making methods in the face of the Japanese colonial occupiers. The imperialist Japanese, it is said, tried to force colonized subjects to shift to *washi* (Japanese) papermaking methods, which differed subtly in terms of technique and materials but varied hugely in political and cultural terms.

On Rue's quest to discover the Korean book, she encountered in museums and workshops histories of the Korean book in exceptionalist terms, as strictly national achievements, with little acknowledgment of Korea as part of a regional book world. In fact, the formative influence of early technology transfer is glossed over—from the fact that the first writing system in the Korean peninsula came to Korea from China (only to be superseded centuries later by *hangul,* an indigenous phonetic alphabet), as did paper and other technologies and formats of the book. The centrality of Confucian and Buddhist texts in Korea can only be understood in the context of the dynamic movement of thought and religion across vast distances of Asia, often in textual form, over the centuries. Notions of reading, literacy, high regard for education, and textuality imply an emulation of, or rivalry with, achievement of those values in the East Asian hegemon, China—until the regional and global order changed.

Finally, Rue's sources on the significance of Korean metal type cite the standard chronology influenced by Western chronologies of print technologies that center on Gutenberg's innovations with movable type and the printing press in 1501 that have been credited with revolutionizing access to knowledge and information and thus changing the "world" forever. In terms of the premodern and early modern book worlds of Korea and East Asia, Gutenberg's "revolution," starting from innovations in publishing the Bible, and the role of the printing press in the Enlightenment

Figure 1. Metal type printing in Cheongju. Molten copper (twelve hundred degrees Celsius) is poured into the casting frame. Reprinted with permission from Stephanie Rue.

play a relatively minor role until the late nineteenth century. Yet the authority of the Western book studies narrative has been densely theorized and described, perhaps because its evolution coincided with the geopolitical hegemony of the West over the past half-century. As a result, scholars and bibliographers in Korea, China, and Japan have tended to define their national book cultures in relationship to this model rather than working toward an entangled history of the book in a regional East Asian framework.

The particular history of Korean books narrated by Ru in her beautifully designed and illustrated blog—along with the very fact of her successful quest, as a digital native, for these book things and the networks of people and histories that remember, revive, and sustain them—demonstrates the extent to which humanistic scholarship and frameworks that shape our understanding of book history East and West have permeated the broader public networks of national imaginations and identities. This essay seeks to explore contemporary theoretical and scholarly currents in book studies that inform such public discourses about material culture and cultural history. I will make reference especially to several recently published works on book history that call into question the silos of national book histories in East Asia as well as the often unchallenged universality of the Gutenberg chronology and other dominant theoretical models. These, at least, were some of the issues that first motivated me to organize the 2012 workshop at my home institution of Oberlin College, and I continue to wrestle with them through a continuing series of collaborations with other scholars in the rapidly emerging field of East Asian book history.[1]

■ BOOK THINGS, THEORY, AND METHOD

Studies of material culture often focus on everyday objects and the ways that the production, consumption, and reception of those physical objects, and the social life of those material objects construed as "actors," lead to discoveries about the workings of society and culture. A thing, according to scholar Bill Brown, is "less an object than a particular subject-object relation"; things are "what is excessive in objects, as what exceeds their mere materialization as objects or their mere utilization as objects— their force as a sensuous presence or as a metaphysical presence, the magic by which objects become values, fetishes, idols, totems" (Brown 2001, 12). Things structure human relations and networks, and it is "our very being to devour things," as we are "only human through things" (Hodder 2014, 34).

But what happens when the objects of our study are book things, text-bearing objects, text–image things? Isn't it text and images—in other words, the apparent *content* of those things—that appeal to and construct knowledge? Content, it is said, can easily be provided; content is now so simply transferred as strings of text, as image in digital form from one technology to another. Scholars of the book challenge us to situate books as made objects in the context of material culture rather than to define them, and dismiss them, as content-bearing objects that take up space deserved by digital tools and mechanical things. The "history of the book" is a misnomer because the field is multi- and interdisciplinary, spanning economic history, social history, aesthetics, psychology (cognition, literacy, and reading), government, and technological history. Grounded in bibliographic practices, book studies proposes widely accepted yet contested theoretical models for the field, such as Robert Darnton's communication circuit, a historically grounded analysis that emphasizes economics and social forces in the "life cycle" of the production, circulation, and reception of books. Nicolas Barker and Thomas R. Adams's influential critique of Darnton's model shifts the focus of analysis to the book itself, rendering the social networks and processes secondary. Those who critique these dominant models find fault with the overemphasis on mechanical type and the printing press as well as on the marketplace, which excludes significant and persistent scribal practices, other printing technologies and book formats, oral traditions, and still-common practices of noncommercial production, circulation, and reception of books.

The Gutenberg chronology lends itself to the framework of the marketplace and technological change that expands literacy and knowledge, an ultimately liberatory and linear concept of history and society. In Europe and America, even critics of late Elizabeth Eisenstein's hugely influential and often contested *The Printing Press as an Agent of Change* did not reject the author's assertion that the printing press and its apparent introduction of "typographical fixity" spurred social and political change in the Enlightenment but rather mainly debated the *extent* to which it did so. The field of book history "has its origins in the liberal Western Enlightenment and its global spread, a process that is not ending but intensifying under twenty-first century globalization" (Loughran 2015, 51).[2]

In all models, the established field of book studies (or history of the book) proposes the physical book—and not only its contents—as embodying values and beliefs, art and narrative; the book's material form informs reading and hermeneutic practice; the physical book is deeply enmeshed in the major currents of technological, social, and economic change. Along a dynamic range of methods and analytical approaches in the multidisciplinary field of book studies, one widely shared methodological assumption is the importance of experience with handling and studying the objects. In short, the physical book—and not only its contents—embodies values and beliefs, art and narrative.

■ EAST ASIAN BOOKS AS THINGS

And that is why I, and a number of other colleagues, decided to organize a second East Asian Book History workshop, this time to be convened at the University of Pennsylvania. We wanted to continue to provoke and to cultivate a scholarly conversation focused on East Asian books as things, as material objects that embody value, belief, art, and narrative and that transmit and become the occasion for social and cultural practice.

Led by co-organizers Patricia Sieber and Young-Kyun Oh and supported by an ACLS grant, the team aimed to accomplish two tasks: first, to articulate the book cultures of China, Korea, and Japan from the thirteenth to nineteenth centuries as an East Asian regional phenomenon, and second, to propose productive methods for scholars to engage in the materiality of the book through the development of common methods and a shared terminology for analyzing the East Asian book as object. More than anything, we wanted to facilitate dialogue among Chinese studies, Korean studies, and Japan studies scholars of the book—exchanges that happen too rarely, despite our shared interests.

Through the process of drafting the various grant application narratives, we needed to arrive at a sense of the state of the field of book studies vis-à-vis East Asian materials. Accordingly, we began to craft a set of guiding principles that would frame our discussions. These principles were further refined over the course of the workshop and are still a work in progress. I take as my fundamental point of departure, however, the dictum that analysis of the East Asian book as object (paper, binding, print, the page, and format) yields information about production, use, interpretation, and reception.

In English-language East Asian studies, the book's material form informs reading and hermeneutic practice; the physical book is deeply enmeshed in technological, social, and economic change. Historians such as Cynthia J. Brokaw, Lucille Chia, and Elizabeth Berry and art historians such as Maggie Bickford and Julie Nelson Davis propose the study of the page itself and paratexts—devices that guide readers, such as page layout and commentary—in sixteenth- to twentieth-century Chinese books as a means of exploring reading practices for a range of widely circulated printed texts, from the Confucian classics and missionary writings to books for children. Charlotte Eubanks and other scholars of religion and literature encourage us to conceive anew of the relationship between printed objects and the body and the possibilities of bodies embodying texts. Richard Rubinger (2007) and Matthias Hayak and Annick Horiuchi (2014) focus on the book object in educational contexts.

In East Asian scholarship, an unquestioned adherence to the very concepts of book studies as it has evolved in the West sometimes leads to unproductive and reductive questions, such as why Chinese society, despite its invention of movable type and paper, adhered to supposedly regressive technological printing technologies such as xylography (woodblock printing), which dated back to at least the eighth century. As Roger Chartier, Christopher Reed, and others point out, certain book history assumptions are guided by notions that equate movable type and industrial printing with progress and modernity—and even civilization and the project of enlightenment—and, conversely, see the centuries-long employment of xylographic printing in all of East Asia as a sign of barbarism or a lack of civilization (Chartier 1996; Brokaw and Reed 2010; Reed 2007).[3]

Among recent work that advances appropriate frameworks and theoretical approaches for East Asian book histories, I have found the collection *The Book Worlds of East Asia and Europe, 1450–1850: Connections and Comparisons,* edited by Joseph P. McDermott and Peter Burke, to provide some of the most productive frameworks. The volume brings into conversation these two long and rich strands of book history from the fifteenth through the nineteenth centuries as the "book worlds" of East Asia and Europe. Partly due to their close continental proximity and interchange, scholars of Europe have deeply researched the local and regional book histories that composed a European book world, one that until the recent past was often spoken of as the sole book world. The theoretical and methodological paradigms in the field of book studies evolving around European and American objects and histories will only be invigorated by comparison with another major book world. How can we ascertain what is universal and what is a local affair without such a comparative approach? For example, a robust proto-print capitalism and a sense of a public sphere arose in parts of East Asia despite the dominance of xylographic printing and the absence of discourses of democracy and individualism. How can we account for this by recourse solely to European models?

The question I kept coming up against in the course of grant narratives, workshop organizational statements, and e-mails to intrigued colleagues was, how do we bring the long and rich history of East Asian book cultures to light in terms that non-Asianists can find meaningful? Roger Chartier, among others, warns us against the hazards of a mechanically comparative approach, which often drones on about differences and likenesses without contextualization. A comparative approach also may propose one culture as the standard, which in turn suggests a normative, hierarchal relationship.

Again, I found myself inspired by the material in the McDermott and Burke edited volume. Rather than a strictly comparative approach to these two complex book worlds, McDermott, Burke, and contributors to their anthology advocate for analysis of the ways book histories and cultures are linked (entangled) *(histoire croisee)* through the intersection of distinct book cultures and processes of transformation and interaction rising from exchange of material culture, social formations, aesthetics, and ideas (McDermott and Burke 2015, 5). Such a vantage point allows scholars outside of the field glimpses of an East Asian book world that evolved distinctly, in complicated processes of reference to and engagement with a Sinitic worldview, values, and social orders. The lenses of "technology transfer, knowledge transfer, and the history of 'news'" lead to exploration of the ways technologies invented in Asia, such as paper and movable type, moved across the Eurasian continent and found places in cultures that mobilized them for political and economic ends.

McDermott and Burke conceive in regional terms the task of analyzing, documenting, and theorizing the East Asian book world during the early modern period at least. They focus on the fifteenth to nineteenth centuries because those centuries coincide with the dominance of print culture in Ming–Qing China and in Europe (though not necessarily coinciding with print capitalism). Because of the rise of early modern social formations such as urbanization, rise in literacy rates, and spread of education and leisure, McDermott and Burke, building on the work of Arthur Danto and Howard Becker, employ the notion of a "book world" to frame analyses in terms of "the network or system of people and institutions that supported and sometimes restricted the production, diffusion, and consumption of books: scriptoria, printer's workshops, book peddlers, bookshops, libraries public or private, large or small, etc." (9). The author–reader relationship, still dominant among some literary scholars especially, in this model becomes yet one element in a broader social and material process through which books circulate and create cultural and social meanings.

So far, so good. But the workshops I had in mind were more ambitious in their geographical and temporal range. I wanted to, and still want to, build a conversation that is more regional in nature, that encompasses the broader East Asian cultural sphere and does not rely solely on reference to the Western case. To varying degrees throughout early modern East Asia (especially early modern Japan and Ming–Qing China), the emergence of commercial printing shared many characteristics (such as competition for readers and consumers fueling new book formats and conceptions, and development of readership) with that of early modern Europe because of comparable social and economic processes, but differed significantly in the elaboration on the advantages of xylographic technologies (rather than movable type) and ideological and political contexts. In that sense, East–West comparison can be tremendously productive. However, articulating various historical manifestations of Chinese, Japanese, Korean, and Vietnamese book cultures within the framework a regional East Asian regional book world has proven, as one might suspect, a less than straightforward task. Since the mid-twentieth century, these national book cultures have been studied mainly in isolation from each other. The geographical vastness of the eastern Eurasian continent and Pacific archipelagos is but one reason for the separation into nation-state book cultures. We also note the political and military conflict based in war and empire among China, Korea, and Japan since the nineteenth century, and more recent nationalist enmity. From this side of the Pacific, divisions among country-based area studies in the United States and beyond have only encouraged rifts among these related East Asian book histories.

Combined, these factors contribute to separate national book histories that obscure shared aspects of book cultures throughout pre- and early modern East Asia. These shared characteristics and currents include common or overlapping print technologies; book formats, materials, and reading practices; dynamic networks of book circulation within the region; and intellectual, political, and aesthetic currents and values. However, even when scholars have studied the flow of books and knowledge within the region (such as Japanese scholars' explorations of the influence of Ming–Qing Chinese books on early modern Japan), these engagements have tended to be one-sided and overshadowed by narratives of national exceptionalism in the context of shifting global hierarchies of power. A range of preexisting East Asian bibliographical and historical approaches to the book have built a solid foundation for new generations of book historians, many of whom have gravitated toward the compelling and growing coherence and dominance of book history made in the West.

In the 2015 *Cambridge Companion to the History of the Book*, Sydney Shep notes a similar nation-focused emphasis among European book historians but advocates for newer approaches that "increasingly looked beyond the nation state as the unit of analysis and beyond the notions of national exceptionalism that drove the proliferation of large-scale national book history projects" (61). She optimistically agrees with scholars who describe the social networks that make up the book trade world as characterized by "a series of fluid and elastic interconnections between agents—producers and consumers of books—that are non-hierarchical, decentred and multidirectional" (61). In contrast with the majority of anthologies or companions of book history over the past decade that have treated non-European/non-American book cultures as minor traditions that can be accounted for in a chapter or two, the editor of the 2015 *Cambridge Companion* created one of the first volumes in the English-speaking world to move toward decentering the Gutenberg chronology and the Western book world and to encourage "new models" for book history. Whether these proposed models, which are complexly engaged with postcolonial theory, new imperial histories, *histoire croisee*, transnational frameworks, and concepts of intersectionality, will be able to generate viable new theories and methods for the history of the book remains to be seen. Certainly the *Cambridge Companion*'s goal of challenging "the distinction and hierarchy implicit in the spatial binaries of centre/periphery or metropole/colony" (61) is a worthy one in relation to book studies.

We also need to take seriously Trish Loughran's challenge, in that same volume, to the tendency in Anglo-European book studies to focus on "the relation between print capitalism and today's nation state system," because its notion of a "print-based (and highly modern) 'imagined community' minimizes all other book cultures that flourished both before and after the coming of the hand press" (44–45). If that same chronology pivots on Gutenberg's innovations and the printing press as agents of change and social improvability, then we also need to articulate the *agency* of East Asian book technologies and cultures. Historian Cynthia Brokaw has evaluated the impact of the distribution of "imprints" in eighteenth- and nineteenth-century China and the tendency for a "relatively high degree of uniformity and stability," whether in popular literature imprints or civil service examination textbooks. In her chapter in the McDermott and Burke volume and elsewhere, Brokaw vividly proposes the complex ways this vital and vast book culture tended to have an "integrative" function rather than setting the groundwork for radical social change. Brokaw also challenges readers to study the extent to which late imperial Chinese book cultures relate to or shape "common Chinese culture" in the twenty-first century (Brokaw 2015, 228, 234–35).

In *The Book Worlds of East Asia and Europe,* McDermott and Burke emphasize Chinese studies—and its object, China—as the principal sites of knowledge production about "book history and such core issues as canon formation, manuscript culture, text transmission methods, cultural integration, and access to knowledge" in East Asia. Undeniably, the depth and breadth of book historical topics in Chinese studies have resulted in situating the book and book cultures in a position "central to the study of China's cultural history" (McDermott and Burke 2015, 3–4).[4] The prominence of book historical approaches finds its roots in Chinese-language scholarship as well as in the profound authority of the material manifestations of the book (in the very broadest sense of text-bearing objects) and in relevant social networks and cultural meanings in Chinese concepts of governance, ritual, visual cultures, religion, and economy for countless centuries. Indeed, it would be difficult for Chinese studies scholars in premodern and early modern society in virtually any disciplinary field—from intellectual history (Benjamin Elman) to art history, social history (Cynthia Brokaw; Lucille Chia; Kai Wing Chow), popular literature, elite literatures, and drama (Ann McLaren; Christopher

Nugent)—to avoid book history. In China, as in Europe, books were "objects viewed as worthy of possession"; these things need to be understood in the most intimate and in the broadest contexts of "possession and exchange," whether as part of the marketplace or governance, public or private (Raven 2015, 179).

The high quality of English-language Chinese studies scholarship of the book—along with its sheer volume and range of disciplinary approaches—has resulted in growing awareness of the richness, complexity, and longevity of China's book world on the part of non-Asianists. This is a good thing, but Asian scholars must advance with caution, lest the book world of East Asia remain defined solely in relation to *Chinese* book cultures. In other words, the book history of China needs further entanglement with the regional book world of East Asia. Korea, Japan, and Vietnam all developed rich, stable book cultures based not only on a core thread of Sinitic book and textual values, among others, but also on many shared material cultural conceptions and practices. Entangled and comparative perspectives will help to advance knowledge about the regional East Asian book world and especially studies on the social and economic dynamics of publishing; approaches to reading and literacy; conservation and transmission of books by the state; schools, libraries, publishers, and individuals; the construction of authorship and copyright; modes of commentary (official and subversive); and the format and design of books in these areas of East Asia.

■ WHERE DO WE GO FROM HERE? POINTS GLEANED

Though this conversation about book histories in East Asia remains a dynamic and exciting work in progress, my explorations thus far suggest several potential take-home points. First, working toward a regional framework demands careful research on various historical manifestations of East Asian regional book culture, thus taking us beyond our primarily nationally specific analyses to date. These characteristics include, among others, regionally recognized writing systems; shared canons; systems to express vernacular language in text (local vernacular, constructed vernacular); patterns of reading; shared philosophical, political, religious, and literary texts; continuity in printing and binding technologies; text–image relations; books not intended to be read; persistence of scribal cultures; hermeneutic traditions; and a long and rich commercial and amateur market for books. Fundamentally, East Asian cultures have placed a high value on the written word, and books in East Asia have, over millennia, created abundant meaning.

Second, one common thread in workshop discussions focused on the need for scholars to recognize and characterize further distinct dynamics between the state and the book throughout East Asia, both at a national and at a regional level. Young-Kyun Oh's (2013) study of a premodern Korean moral primer, for example, makes clear the relations between the Korean court's entrance as a Confucian state into the Chinese imperial order in the fifteenth century, the state's mobilization of books to ensure desired social order, and the state's strategic use of metal type in its publishing projects. At the regional level, Patricia Sieber has noted that the lopsided nature of the interest in books (Japanese and Korean interest in Chinese books) needs to be properly theorized as something distinct from the European "Republic of Letters" and from an East Asian "Tributary World Order." Furthermore, the relationships between book cultures can not only be understood as a country-to-country dialogue but need to be placed into a context of multilateral mediation. In short, current scholarship aims at generating the regionally interrelated yet locally distinctive book cultures of East Asia and their points of intersection and divergence.

Third, the complex relationship of text and image in East Asian books demands that we ask questions about the ways the pictorial and textual elements shape the experience of reading and interacting with the book. Art historians such as Julie Nelson Davis and Maggie Bickford have interrogated the visual vocabulary of the printed book in East Asia, whether in the privately appreciated painting scroll formats or in the side-stitched books with densely printed text–image formats that were available to a broader reading public. Bickford interrogates the status of word- and-image manuscript scrolls from eleventh- to twelfth-century Song China to understand the "bookness" of these objects. Though they have been classified in modern institutional settings as "art," Song period bibliographers assigned them to the elevated category of books *(shu)*. Contemporary writers and readers, furthermore, constructed meaning "by integrally working images and words" in ways fundamental to their "ingrained habits of reading" (Bickford 2013, 53–56). Nelson's exploration of eighteenth- and nineteenth-century networks of "artist, publisher, carver, printer, and viewer" of sophisticated color woodblock single sheet prints proposes the need to look at the images along with xylographic books because these "kinds of printed things were equally part of that system of production and reception" and because (quoting Craig Clunas) "every act of viewing" of either book or print was "also an act of social interaction" (Davis 2015, 17, 192).

Fourth, I would like to see the field move to recognize patterns of circulation, charting how various book technologies have moved between and among various East Asian cultures. In common throughout the region, we see the long dominance of xylography and the transition to letterpress and lithographic printing, changing modes of mechanical industrial printing from the late nineteenth to the twentieth century, electronic commercial and personal printing, and digital objects. Current scholarship emphasizes the historical concurrence of print and scribal culture in East Asia. Rather than one technology of writing replacing another, scribal culture persisted because handwriting or copying suited certain social contexts, such as transmission of secret teachings, as Peter Kornicki and others have demonstrated. The communication circuit does not transpire solely in the marketplace; handwritten texts, furthermore, are not always meant to be read. Rather than transmitting texts, we see, for example, the practice of copying sutras aimed at gaining religious merit. Moving closer to the present, productive forays into digital humanities approaches to twentieth-century publishing and literary history are being undertaken by Hoyt Long, the National Institute for Japanese Literature's International Collaborative Research project, and others.

An East Asia regional book history will continue to interrogate how and what kinds of books circulated widely through East Asia, such as Buddhist texts, mathematics primers, medical books, Confucian moral primers, classical works of prose fiction and poetry, painting manuals, and examples of books distinctive to certain localities. The formats range from hand scrolls and hanging scrolls to albums and bound books. Many contemporary scholars have shown interest in the points of contact among readers, writers, and texts as books traveled throughout East Asia (and Vietnam). Remarkably, the material book also accommodated a range of significant linguistic differences and gave rise to an accessible literary language. However, these scholarly efforts for the most part have framed the circulations of books from national perspectives.

■ DIGITAL NATIVES, DIGITAL TOOLS, AND THE FUTURE OF BOOK STUDIES

"The essential characters of books is their mobility," notes Sydney Shep (2015, 61). Commerce and individual travelers are not the only reasons for such vigorous movement of hard copy and digital books. Their multiple institutional settings are also important factors. Books from East Asia over the past several centuries have traveled around the world, and some have been protected and conserved, studied in museums, universities, libraries, and private collections. Large-scale projects of digitizing premodern books create another means of mobility. The ongoing emphasis on digitization of premodern books, as well as the increasing focus on their physical status as part of special collections, in the library, in the university, and in other institutional settings, presents a range of challenges and opportunities that we should grapple with collaboratively.

The abstract notion of a book culture regarded as a "premodern particular" starts to fade away with exposure to the physical object, which in turn gives rise to numerous questions: What is this book? Why does it look this way? Who were the intended readers? and so on. It is digital natives who will inherit the countless unique collections of "rare" physical books from centuries and millennia past. Will these scholars and students of the future find as compelling the book as physical object and continue to theorize these *things* as embodying the social networks, intellectual and spiritual discourses, and knowledge that scholars of book studies theorize? Whether in vast libraries of rare books or in diminutive sets, special collections of books offer present-day libraries and archives the opportunity to distinguish themselves at a time when digital collections render libraries more and more alike. Scholars are increasingly using these collections in research and teaching. Premodern East Asian books and printing blocks also show up for purchase on eBay and other social media.

In contrast to libraries' and archives' rush to digitize collections of print objects—thereby overcoming the physical challenges of access—useful digital tools that aid the reader in identifying, contextualizing, and rendering legible the digitized objects have emerged slowly. Thanks to the efforts of libraries and archives, thousands of high-resolution digitized early modern books await readers. Yet, illegible calligraphic writing and printing deter many readers, and librarian professionals may not have the scholarly training or knowledge to fully identify the objects. Digital humanities funding can facilitate learning through the development of digital tutorials in reading calligraphic and cursive characters. As in the past, however, it is not the digitization itself or the software that makes these books legible but the hard work of students with advanced training in language and disciplines and the research and analysis of experienced area studies scholars.

Of late, we can take advantage of more sophisticated digital tools, with visuals and examples of digital humanities tools, such as "glass view" or "firefly view," that allow the user to see legible readings of often difficult-to-decipher scribal characters. However, absence of adequate contextual information on many websites continues to plague students of the East Asian book. Though digital humanities leaders debate the importance of contextualization and metadata, many working in critical digital historiography advocate for descriptive practices that have evolved as part of scholar–archivist collaborations and that include thorough accounting for metadata and provenance (collection context). Again, scholars are the ones who contextualize the texts, such as historical background, metadata, videos of manipulation of the physical object, and analysis of the meanings of the texts and images. Experienced scholars, furthermore, are well aware of another limitation of digitized archives: only a fraction of all books can be accessed in digitized form. These best practices in advancing the use of premodern books, whether in physical or digital form, emerge at the intersection of scholarly, archival, musicological, and archeological method and theory (Hering 2014).

Contemporary East Asian cultures have paid great attention to protecting, conserving, researching, and digitizing collections of premodern and early modern books (special collections). As in the case of Korea, these book things come to symbolize a highly valued current of the past—the culture's long-standing book world—and, less often, that of the region as a whole. Partha Chatterjee (quoted in Loughran 2015, 47) argues that the "postcolonial nation state 'accepts the claim to universality of this "modern" framework of knowledge' at the expense of its own history, its own tradition and its indigenous material (book) cultures, which forever after can and often are consigned to the realm of the premodern particular." States, museums, archives, and scholars have actively mobilized their own book cultures through book histories and the objects themselves to make them part of contemporary national identity and imaginary. It is our job as scholars to investigate more fully the complex networks of books among East Asian societies.

Ann Sherif is professor of East Asian studies at Oberlin College. She is author of *Japan's Cold War: Media, Literature, and the Law* (2009).

■ NOTES

I am indebted to Aimee Lee, Stephanie Rue, Young-Kyun Oh, Charlotte Eubanks, Cynthia Brokaw, Peter Kornicki, Soren Edgren, Ed Vermue, Ray English, Xi Chen, Amy Margaris, Wendy Hyman, Laura Baudot, Sandy Zagarell, Julie Nelson Davis, Tina Chen, Leland Tabares, and an anonymous reader. Workshops were made possible by the generous support of the Henry Luce Foundation, the Andrew W. Mellon Foundation, ACLS, and the Chiang Ching-kuo Foundation for International Scholarly Exchange.

1. For scholars and students working outside of East Asia, other notable workshops and collaborations taking place in Europe and the Americas that focus on the book in East Asia include the journal *East Asian Publishing and Society,* the European Association of Japanese Resource Specialists, and the Council on East Asian Libraries.

2. Loughran (2015, 45) somewhat misleadingly describes the trajectory of Chinese print as not needing to "be linked at all to the rise of the global nation-form."

3. In the contexts of global climate change and sustainable futures, one could resituate xylographic printing in discourses of "appropriate technologies" that are low cost, require a degree of human labor to work, are energy efficient, and use easily available resources, regarded as low tech and culturally appropriate.

4. The large number of distinguished scholarly works listed in the useful bibliographical essay in the same volume demonstrates the centrality of the book in Chinese studies in the English-speaking world and Western Europe. Many of these scholars build on the work of scholars working in China and Japan. Although rigorous and groundbreaking book studies research by top scholars can be found in Japan studies and Korean studies as well, book history does not occupy the same dominant position as in Chinese studies. At present, Shawn McHale and Peter Kornicki are among the few scholars to make available the book history of Vietnam in Western languages.

■ WORKS CITED

Berry, Elizabeth. 2006. *Japan in Print: Information and Nation in the Early Modern Period*. Berkeley: University of California Press.

Bickford, Maggie 2013. "*Tu* and *Shu*: Illustrated Manuscripts in the Great Age of Song Printing." In *The History of the Book in East Asia*, edited by Cynthia Brokaw and Peter Kornicki, 53–73. Burlington, Vt.: Ashgate.

Brokaw, Cynthia J. 2015. "Empire of Texts: Book Production, Book Distribution, and Book Culture in Late Imperial China." In *The Book Worlds of East Asia and Europe, 1450–1850: Connections and Comparisons*, edited by Joseph P. McDermott and Peter Burke, 181–235. Hong Kong: Hong Kong University Press.

Brokaw, Cynthia J., and Christopher A. Reed, eds. 2010. *From Woodblocks to the Internet: Chinese Publishing and Print Culture in Transition, 1800 to 2008*. Boston: Brill.

Brown, Bill. 2001. "Thing Theory," *Critical Inquiry* 28, no. 1: 1–22.

Chartier, Roger. 1996. "Gutenberg Revisited from the East." *Late Imperial China* 17, no. 1: 1–9.

Davis, Julie Nelson. 2015. *Partners in Print: Artistic Networks and the Ukiyo-e Market*. Honolulu: University of Hawai'i Press.

Hayak, Matthias, and Annick Horiuchi, eds. 2014. *Listen, Copy, Read: Popular Learning in Early Modern Japan*. Boston: Brill.

Hering, Katherine. 2014. "Provenance Meets Source Criticism." *Journal of*

Digital Humanities 3, no. 2. http://journalofdigitalhumanities.org/3-2
/provenance-meets-source-criticism/.

Hodder, Ian. 2014. "The Entanglement of Humans and Things: A Long-
Term View." *New Literary History* 45: 19–36.

Loughran, Trish. 2015. "Books in the Nation." In *The Cambridge Companion
to the History of the Book,* edited by Leslie Howsam, 36–52. Cambridge:
Cambridge University Press.

McDermott, Joseph P., and Peter Burke, eds. 2015. *The Book Worlds of
East Asia and Europe, 1450–1850: Connections and Comparisons.* Hong
Kong: Hong Kong University Press.

Oh, Young-Kyun. 2013. *Engraving Virtue: The Printing History of a Premodern
Korean Moral Primer.* Leiden: Brill.

Raven, James. 2015. "Distribution: The Transmission of Books in Europe
and Its Colonies: Contours, Cautions, and Global Comparisons." In
*The Book Worlds of East Asia and Europe, 1450–1850: Connections and
Comparisons,* edited by Joseph P. McDermott and Peter Burke, 47–179.
Hong Kong: Hong Kong University Press.

Reed, Christopher A. 2007. "Gutenberg and Modern Chinese Print Culture:
The State of the Discipline II." *Book History* 10: 291–315.

Rubinger, Richard. 2007. *Popular Literacy in Early Modern Japan.* Honolulu:
University of Hawai'i Press.

Rue, Steph. 2015. "Metal Type Printing in Cheongju." *Field Notes from
Korea* (blog), October 19. https://stephruejournal.wordpress.com/2015
/10/19/metal-type-printing-in-cheongju/.

Shep, Sydney. 2015. "Books in Global Perspectives." In *The Cambridge
Companion to the History of the Book,* edited by Leslie Howsam, 53–70.
Cambridge: Cambridge University Press.

Portfolio

CURATED BY **CATHY J. SCHLUND-VIALS**

Art, Activism, and Agitation: Anida Yoeu Ali

> If you encounter the Red Chador, will you fear her or walk with her? Would you help her across the terrain or would you block her path? Would you take a moment to notice her? Would you care at all?
> —*The Red Chador*, exhibit brochure, Trinity College, December 2015

> This is a time when presidential candidates can make extremely Islamophobic comments and not be challenged or criticized, and even applauded for it. . . . The entire world is currently engaged in this conversation: What are the Muslims doing to us?
> —Anida Yoeu Ali, quoted in "'The Red Chador': Trinity Exhibit Chronicles an Artist's Walk Through Hartford," *Hartford Courant*, November 2015

DENOTATIVE OF an "intense dislike or fear of Islam, especially as a political force," and indicative of an exaggerated "hostility or prejudice towards Muslims," "Islamophobia" as apprehensive phenomenon and divisive discourse is very much thriving in a contemporary, post-9/11, "War on Terror" imaginary.[1] To that end, the global fight against terror—despite claims of nationalistic liberation, assertions about regional stabilization, and objectives concerning international securitization—has more often than not intersected with disconcerting attacks against what has been monolithically labeled the "Islamic World." These racially inflected confrontations and religiously based hostilities are rendered conspicuous in the wholesale profiling of Arabs and South Asians at airport security checkpoints and widespread federal surveillance of Muslim communities. They are analogously at the forefront of domestic calls to "shut the door" on Muslim immigrants and Syrian refugees in France, Britain, and the

United States (among other countries). As significant, these essentializing characterizations are concomitant with disastrous U.S. foreign policy directives in the Middle East. Marked by a collateral pursuit of radicalism via drone attack and distanced warfare, such turn-of-the-twenty-first-century militarized initiatives have resulted in a disproportionate number of civilian casualties, problematically furthered extremist agendas, and—most recently—fomented the rise of the Islamic State (ISIS).[2]

Situated within a vexed context in which terrorism is synonymous with Islam, it is not surprising that Islamophobia has emerged as an established political fixture in the United States and Europe. Nor is it startling that anti-Muslim hate crimes have increased exponentially when "terrorist" is tantamount to being "Muslim." Illustratively, the Council on American–Islamic Relations (CAIR) and the University of California, Berkeley's Center for Race and Gender reported that in 2015 alone, anti-Islam bills became law in ten U.S. states. Such state-sanctioned Islamophobia was matched by vehement anti-Muslim sentiment at the local and community levels: seventy-eight mosques in the United States were targeted by domestic hate groups, the largest number reported since CAIR began tracking anti-Muslim incidents in 2009 (see Rathod 2016). Following a spate of high-profile shootings and bombing attacks (in January and November 2015), hate crimes in France against Muslims tripled in 2015 from 133 reported incidents in 2014 to 400 (Chazan 2015). The statistics concerning growing Islamophobia were equally alarming in Britain, which witnessed a 300 percent increase in anti-Muslim bias crimes (Johnson 2015). As Nader Hashemi, director of the Center for Middle East Studies at the University of Denver, somberly summarizes, "the political climate in Europe and in the U.S. has taken it to the worst in terms of the level of anti-Muslim bigotry. It has never been this bad" (*RT* 2016).

Hashemi's observation that anti-Muslim prejudice has "never been this bad" evocatively intersects with Anida Yoeu Ali's pointed assertion in the opening epigraph. As the artist/activist notes, contemporary political discussions about immigration and debates over difference time and again encompass the question of "what Muslims are doing to us." Such accusatory interrogations, which pivot on a bifurcated reading of domestic victim and foreign perpetrator, correspondingly lay bare the growing precariousness of Muslim selfhood in the United States and around the globe. These anxieties—built on the stereotypical comprehension of Muslim subjectivity through perceived threat along with an interpretation of Islamophobia via false assumption—foreground Ali's *The Red Chador*, an affectively driven performance/installation piece commissioned by the Palais de Tokyo (see Figure 1).

Figure 1. *The Red Chador,* publicity/brochure image. Photograph by Masahiro Sugano. Courtesy of Studio Revolt.

A transnationally conceptualized project, *The Red Chador* was originally envisioned as a series of provocative durational performances wherein Ali (in traditional Muslim dress) ambled through Parisian streets and occupied the city's public spaces; Ali's overall artistic aim in *The Red Chador* was to elicit spontaneous public responses, which were photographed, filmed, and subsequently curated. Such civic enactments were part of curator Kahiruddin Hori's *Secret Archipelago,* an exhibition that featured more than forty Southeast Asian and diasporic Southeast Asian artists (March 27–May 15, 2015). Programmatically, *Secret Archipelago* was connected to the Singapour en France-le festival, which was intended to celebrate Singapore's Gold Jubilee and fifty years of French–Singapore diplomatic relations. A multidisciplinary enterprise and interdisciplinary undertaking, *Secret Archipelago* incorporated "installations, videos, sculptures, sound works, and random pop-up performances" that traversed multiple geopolitical and sociopolitical imaginaries (quoted in Forrest 2015). Such diverse movements included past colonial histories alongside more recent militarized pasts (e.g., the American War in Vietnam), politicized reclamations of indigenous culture, and contemplations of globalization (particularly with regard to migration and the resultant fusion of cultural affiliations). In turn, these traversals were aesthetically refracted in works by artists who had "received basic training in Western art yet retaine[ed] a strong connection to their indigenous heritage and spiritual and cultural practices." Consistent with the exhibit's titular engagement with the undiscovered and multisited, *Secret Archipelago* was conceptualized as "a bridging of the gap between past and future" and signaled "the creative tension between memory . . . tradition . . . and contemporary Western influences" (quoted in Forrest 2015).

Such multivalent interweavings are consistent with what Hori ultimately characterizes as *Secret Archipelago*'s overriding premise, which concerns the "osmosis between the cultures of the archipelago [Southeast Asia] . . . and the erasing of eras" (quoted in Forrest 2015). Reminiscent of porosity, flexibility, and the unconscious assimilation of ideas, "osmosis" proves (as will subsequently be clear) an admittedly complicated descriptor for Ali, a self-described "Cambodian American Muslim transnational" whose work as an "artist, scholar, and global agitator" consistently foregrounds a personal history of forced migration and brings to light an enduring preoccupation with globally inflected identarian politics. These histories and preoccupations are embedded *in* and at the forefront *of* Ali's *The Red Chador,* a blended performance work that confronts the complex interplay of race, gender, and religion vis-à-vis Islamophobic optics and (anti)assimilationist logics. Accordingly, such emphases—which marry the personal to the political and the private to the public—emblematize the artist's long-standing negotiation with boundary crossing, permeability, and refugee-ness. As a further contextualization of Ali's "agitative" oeuvre and a concluding close reading of *The Red Chador* accentuate, these specific thematics emerge from and are attributable to the artist's distinct location as a 1.5-generation Cambodian American Muslim refugee.

■ CAMBODIAN AMERICAN MUSLIM TRANSNATIONAL: ANIDA YOEU ALI

Anida Yoeu Ali was born in Battambang, Cambodia, in 1974.[3] Soon after her birth, on April 17, 1975, the Khmer Rouge entered Cambodia's capital city (Phnom Penh), signaling the start of what many outside Cambodia refer to as the "Killing Fields era" and those in-country term "Pol Pot Time." The Khmer Rouge was particularly wary of individuals who ostensibly bore the most "prerevolutionary" memory and those who were allegedly "tainted" by Western imperialism. To eliminate such "threats," the Khmer Rouge executed teachers, university students, lawyers, doctors, civil servants, military personnel (from the previous Lon Nol regime), artists, and religious minorities (specifically Muslims). As Cambodian Muslims (the Cham), Ali and her family struggled to survive during the disastrous Khmer Rouge regime, which—over a three-year, eight-month, twenty-day period (1975–79)—claimed the lives of an estimated 1.7 million Cambodians due to starvation, forced labor, torture, disease, and execution. Ali and her family left Cambodia soon after the January 7, 1979, Vietnamese invasion of the country and takeover of Phnom Penh, which ushered in the end of the Khmer Rouge's reign of terror. After making their way to a Thai refugee camp, Ali and her family briefly migrated to Malaysia, where they stayed with relatives, awaiting asylum sponsorship from the United States. They eventually resettled in Chicago, Illinois. Chicago would serve as Ali's primary artistic hub until 2011, when she was awarded a Fulbright fellowship and traveled to Phnom Penh, Cambodia.

Ali would spend the next four years, 2011–15, in Cambodia. It was in Phnom Penh that Ali became a collaborative member—with her husband, Masahiro Sugano—of Studio Revolt, an independent artist-run media lab that produces films, videos, installations, and performance projects.[4] In 2015, Ali returned to the United States as a 2015–16 McGill Visiting Assistant Professor in International Studies at Trinity College (Hartford, Connecticut). Ali is the recipient of multiple grants and fellowships, and her work has been exhibited at numerous festivals, including the aforementioned Palais de Tokyo, the Fuikuoka Asian Art Museum, Musee d'arte Contemporain (Lyon, France), Southeast Asia Artsfest (London), the Malay Heritage Centre, the Singapore International Photography Festival, and the eighth Asia Pacific Triennial of Contemporary Art (Brisbane, Australia). Awarded the 2014–15 Sovereign Art Prize, Ali is presently a lecturer in the School of Interdisciplinary Arts and Sciences at the University of Washington, Bothell.

Despite the interdisciplinary richness suggested in this brief biographical overview, Ali's initial forays into art by and large took lyrical form. Soon after graduating from the University of Illinois (Urbana-Champaign) with a bachelor's of fine arts in 1996, Ali cofounded (along with Marlon Esguerra, Emily Chang, and Dennis "Denizen Kane" Kim) the Asian American spoken-word ensemble I Was Born with Two Tongues. Between 1998 and 2003, the award-winning quartet gained national prominence for its hard-hitting critiques of U.S. imperialism, militant appraisals of American racism/xenophobia, and blended use of hip hop/slam poetry. While a member of I was Born with Two Tongues, Ali also collaborated and toured with the multimedia, Chicago-based feminist collective Mango Tribe, founded in 2000. Whereas Ali's work with I was Born with Two Tongues was intimately connected to her experiences as a racial minority (e.g., as an Asian American), her association with Mango Tribe was decidedly more intersectional with regard to race and gender. Ali recollects,

> I noticed that [there] was an absence [of] the voices of Asian American women. I felt like there really needed to be this collective of Asian American women [who would come together] to put our stories on stage. And so Mango Tribe was born with the specific intention of doing collaborative work for the stage. Whether it was theatrical or performance poetry, it was sort of whatever we wanted to do as a collective. But it was a little bit more experimental than just reading a poem. That's how Mango Tribe came into being. (Levine 2009)

Ali's artistic politics, fixed to collaborative engagements and collective concerns, were by no means limited to spoken word and performance; such interactions and agendas were also at the forefront of Ali's growing arts activism and increased community organizing. Two years after the formation of Mango Tribe, Ali founded Young Asians with Power! (a creative space for Asian Pacific Islander American youth to explore community focused issues through "writing, reflections, and making a ruckus"). Ali was also instrumental in the development of the Asian American Artists Collective–Chicago, an alliance network dedicated to creating intersections between "art, audience, and activism" through "artistic development, support, and empowerment."[5]

Whereas Ali's early career was very much rooted in vocalized performance and community-based arts activism, her more recent artistic endeavors are considerably more multidisciplinary, indicating Ali's stated desire to engage new ways of "seeing" and "speaking" via tactical shifts in medium, milieu, and movement. Notwithstanding her considerable success as a slam poet and despite her status as an acclaimed theatrical performer, Ali became progressively discontented with the limitations of spoken-word forms; she accordingly pursued playwriting and trained in Butoh to expand her artistic vocabulary. Concurrent with increased artistic experimentation, Ali's focus also shifted and involved more overt engagements with refugee/Muslim subjectivity. To clarify, whereas Ali's earlier work was very much indicative of a politicized Asian American selfhood (as emblematized by poems concerning Asian American stereotypes and model minoritization), her later ouevre became decidedly more international after 2004, when she "returned [to Cambodia] for the first time in nearly twenty-five years." Ali reiterates,

I came back as an invited artist to participate in the Mekong Project Artist Residency, which brought together fourteen artists from Southeast Asia and two diasporic artists from the U.S. to exchange thoughts, skills, artistry and create cross-cultural connections and new regional networks. This return and immersion amongst was the best way for me to experience a contemporary Cambodia that would inspire me to make more trips and eventually relocate there in 2011.[6]

This particular comingling of Southeast Asian and diasporic artists proved a pivotal moment in Ali's career insofar as she witnessed firsthand the limitations of verbal speech. In remembering her first return to Cambodia during a December 2015 talkback for *The Red Chador,* Ali admitted that she was unable to adequately communicate to audiences whose first language was not English and who were by and large unfamiliar with certain genres (namely, spoken word, "Western" drama, and American theater).[7]

Four years after her first Cambodian return, in 2008, Ali began a master's degree in fine arts at the School of the Art Institute Chicago (which she completed in 2010); it was while a graduate student that she expanded her oeuvre vis-à-vis multimedia installation, performance, and textiles. Such artistic capaciousness is evident in two works completed in rather quick succession during this time period: *Palimpsest for Generation 1.5* (2009) and *The 1700% Project* (2010). As a deeper investigation underscores, at stake in *Palimpsest for Generation 1.5* and *The 1700% Project* is a connective yet nonetheless differing contemplation of refugee personhood. On one hand, such subjectivity is, as Ali's familial past confirms, necessarily born out of the artist's forced migration to the United States, symptomatic of her experiences as a racialized U.S. subject, and symbolic of transnational engagements with both the country of origin (Cambodia) and the nation of settlement (the United States). On the other hand, and equally important, such dislocation lays bare the "unmooring" of Muslim selfhood in a post-9/11 U.S. body politic. As another point of convergence, these refugee-oriented meditations, as the next section highlights, utilize a mixed media/performance format that to varying degrees and relevant ends anticipates Ali's *The Red Chador.*

■ TEXTILE TESTIMONIALS: *PALIMPSEST FOR GENERATION 1.5 AND THE 1700% PROJECT*

On December 11, 2009, *Palimpsest for Generation 1.5* premiered at Chicago's Betty Rymer Gallery (see Figures 2 and 3). An austere installation, *Palimpsest for Generation 1.5* features Ali in an unembellished white dress. With face turned to the wall, back bare and exposed, Ali's hair is pinned up. The whiteness of Ali's dress, along with the strategic placement of

Figure 2. *Palimpsest for Generation 1.5.* Photograph by Masahiro Sugano. Courtesy of Studio Revolt.

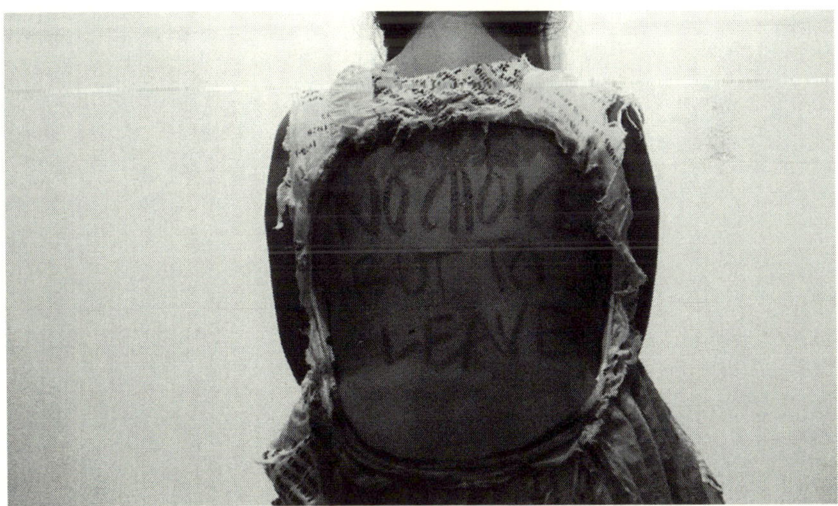

Figure 3. *Palimpsest for Generation 1.5.* Photograph by Masahiro Sugano. Courtesy of Studio Revolt.

her hair, purposefully recalls a building covered in hanging vines and suggests a long passage of time. According to Ali, *Palimpsest for Generation 1.5* was initially "inspired by a scene in Maxine Hong Kingston's *The Woman Warrior.*" As Ali successively notes,

> [the installation] includes inscriptions written onto my back along with the gesture of washing them away. Text pulled from my family's memories and histories related to Cambodia are inscribed in ink on my back. As a result of the act, ink and water drip onto my back and stain the dress. When the gestures end and the body leaves the installation, detached roots, a disembodied dress, and faint traces of a performed history remain.

Evocative of a tablet upon which earlier writing has been erased, a "palimpsest" underscores on one level a layering of the past that, despite seeming invisibility, nevertheless remains. On another level, such sedimentary traces—indicative of a polyvocal "performed history" that hinges on "detached roots"—emerge from Ali's familial experiences with and individual recollection of forced migration and statelessness. On the whole, these remembrance-oriented frames, which potently undergird *Palimpsest for Generation 1.5*'s tactical use of written recitation and minimal curation, render palpable through ritualized performance the work's enduring focus on a Cambodian American refugee past.

Like Kingston's Fa Mu Lan protagonist, Ali's back—which faces the gallery audience—becomes a canvas upon which intergenerational grievances are inscribed and summarily erased. Another woman, also dressed in white, performs the writing/erasing ritual, which occurs at timed intervals; she wears a headdress reminiscent of that worn by the Cham, accentuating Ali's own location as a Cambodian American Muslim. Over the course of the installation, the following inscriptions appear:

> "Father School Teacher" / "Nixon Orders Bombings" / "Khmer Rouge Regime" / "90% Artists Killed" / "Family Trip: Refugee Camps" / "Family Trip: Chicago" / "Family Trip: First Home" / "Family Trip: Malaysia" / "Family Trip: Niagara Falls" / "Family Trip: Distant Cousins" / "Family Trip: Hawaii" / "From Somewhere Else" / "Father PTSD Panic Attacks" / "Return After 15 Years" / "Return After 25 Years" / "Return After 30 Years" / "Never Returned" / "Site of Tourism and Atrocities" / "Sugar Palm Trees" / "Graceland Chapel"[8]

As these captions reveal, central to Ali's performance is the historicized articulation of various migrations, returns, traumas, and losses that span Cambodia and the United States. Notwithstanding these cartographic coordinates, key to *Palimpsest for Generation 1.5* is a negotiation with a series of "absent presences" that converge on the Killing Fields era and its multiple aftermaths. These absent presences are in the end intertextually and thematically linked to an intergenerational reading of 1.5-generation Cambodian selfhood. As a self-identified member of the stateless 1.5 generation, Ali imagines and remembers a series of events and locations that answer vexed questions of "who" one is, "how" one left, and "how" one got here. In so doing, *Palimpsest for Generation 1.5* enunciates, by way of inscription and performance, a complex sense of Cambodian personhood.

Such "textile testimonials" and selfhood deliberations are revised and rescripted in Ali's *The 1700% Project*, another installation project that utilizes a similar staining/cloth technique as a means of articulating the experiences of a particular group. Whereas *Palimpsest for Generation 1.5* is metaphysically concentrated on the absent presence of past war, genocide, and trauma, *The 1700% Project* is squarely focused on the hyperpresence of present-day Islamophobia. Inspired by the post–September 11 percentage increase of hate crimes against Arab and Muslim Americans, *The 1700% Project* was conceived as "a collaborative project utilizing art as intervention" that would "challen[ge] monolithic stereotypes of a 'Muslim' identity while acknowledging the significance of historical persecution."[9] A wide-ranging, interdisciplinary installation, *The 1700% Project* is a multiphased endeavor comprising spoken-word poetry, video, audio recordings, and performance; these modes are strategically layered, replicating by way of artistic form the intricate contours of *Palimpsest for Generation 1.5.*

Even more allusive is *The 1700% Project*'s centerpiece, titled "Otherance," an ensemble performance comprising five individuals (including Ali) who identify as Muslim American. With stained wet rags, each participant ritually washes over a white wall with embossed lettering (see Figure 4). As the pieces of damp cloth methodically move over the letters, words such as "Kill all Arabs," "You foreigners caused all this trouble," "LEAVE TOWN," and "Sikh mistaken for Muslim" are gradually revealed; these particular phrases are excerpts from Federal Bureau of Investigation and police reports filed by South Asian American, Arab American, and Muslim American victims of hate crime violence. The text for "Otherance" also serves as the basis for an accompanying performance poem titled "1700%." The poem takes the form of a cento, a hundred-line lyrical work entirely composed of verses or passages from other authors. Despite its use of "found text," "1700%" remains in its indefatigable rehearsal of anti-Muslim acts and bias crimes incontrovertibly connected to its original source (e.g., state documents that underscore widespread Islamophobia and pervasive prejudice).

Figure 4. *1700% Project,* "Otherance." Photograph by Masahiro Sugano. Courtesy of Studio Revolt.

While *The 1700% Project* was intended to raise awareness about Islamophobia and engender support for those targeted by racist, anti-Muslim attacks, the installation's "Otherance" centerpiece was the source of unexpected controversy. Expressly, soon after its completion, the wall was vandalized with anti-Muslim slurs. Despite the unequivocally biased nature of the vandalism, the School of the Art Institute of Chicago remained largely silent. In response to the incident, Ali wrote the following blog post on the installation website:

My work as a performance/installation had a course, a direction, an aesthetic, and conceptual framework—all of which has been disrupted and ruptured because of a vulgar act of defacement. . . . I feel assaulted and violated. I feel strongly that this is not just an assault on me, but an attack on entire communities for which the work speaks. . . . The attack is an act of silencing. . . . My installation has been thrown off course and now I am forced to incorporate the mark of hate (aggressively created by someone else) into my work. . . . My work is about the refusal to end in violence and if I didn't so strongly believe in that, then I would not be able to pick up the pieces and make this into something more empowering. For me, art is a transformative agent. This is the theory that propels the work.

On one hand, Ali's response to the vandalism accesses from the outset a profound sense of vulnerability; this vulnerability—born out of systemic violence, redolent of religious-based prejudice, and indicative of the exclusionary logics of the contemporary "War on Terror"—underscores a disconcerting ubiquity and troubling normativity vis-à-vis post-9/11 Islamophobia. On the other hand, Ali's "refusal to end in violence," along with her concluding statement that "art is a transformative agent," reconfirms a decidedly agentic location as an *agitative* arts activist. Such arts activism—inclusive of Ali's position as both precarious subject and empowered practitioner—figures keenly in her most recent work, *The Red Chador.*

■ REHEARSING, RESTAGING, AND REHEARSING ISLAMOPHOBIA: *THE RED CHADOR*

To recapitulate, *The Red Chador* premiered almost four months after the January 7, 2015, Charlie Hebdo shootings on April 18, 2015; it was subsequently restaged thirty-five hundred miles away and six months later in Hartford, Connecticut, at Trinity College's Widener Gallery. Thematically reminiscent of *The 1700% Project, The Red Chador* was guided by Ali's desire to directly confront, challenge, and confirm Islamophobia in public spaces and places. In that vein, *The Red Chador* was first and foremost an "agitative" piece meant to elicit unplanned and unscripted audience responses. While press releases about the two-day work were issued in conjunction with the *Secret Archipelago* exhibit, no contextual explanations were given "on-site." Such agitative solicitations are likewise embedded in the work's central conceit: Ali chose the chador precisely because it was so closely and controversially identified with a homogenizing reading of "Muslim-ness." Within the dominant imagination, the chador has a particular history with fundamentalism, specifically with regard to Iran. Prior to the 1978–79 Islamic Revolution, black chadors were used for funerals and during periods of mourning. By contrast, lighter-colored chadors were reserved for everyday wear. Following the late-1970s overthrow of Mohammad Rez Sha Pahlavi, the installation of the Grand Ayatollah Ruhodollah Khomeni, and the concomitant establishment of the Iranian Islamic Republic, the chador—like its textile counterpart, the hijab—became a problematic metonym for Islamic fundamentalism despite geographic specificity (to Iran) and everyday use.

Ali amends the somber scripts associated with the chador via dramatic

Figure 5. *The Red Chador.* Subway. Photography by Masahiro Sugano. Courtesy of Studio Revolt.

color, gleaming fabric, and theatrical draping: composed of ostentatious red-sequined cloth, Ali's chador is both spectacular and a spectacle. Intended to be playful and provocative, Ali's chador refuses easy assimilation into crowds: the costume is visually anomalous and tactically conspicuous. As indicated by title and substantiated by performance, the chador Ali donned assumed the conflated registers of religious costume, identifiable character, and autobiographical subjectivity (as a Muslim American). On the first day, Ali, dressed in the chador, "took to the streets of Paris" with photographer and videographer in tow; as The Red Chador, Ali strolled through famous Parisian tourist sites such as the Eiffel Tower, explored the city's subways, made her way into churches, and sat in various cafés (see Figure 5).[10] As The Red Chador, Ali took on a silent persona and limited her communication to slight gesticulations and measured expressions; this economic treatment with regard to performance and affect furthered the work's emotional agenda, which in its desire to generate responses privileged audience reactions over Ali's Red Chador character. As Ali made her way through the city, she interacted with tourists and Parisians and

Figure 6. *The Red Chador.* Protest. Photography by Masahiro Sugano. Courtesy of Studio Revolt.

was inadvertently part of a peaceful protest involving Muslim women and antiwar activists (see Figure 6). While friends and colleagues had warned her of increased anti-Muslim sentiment, Ali—in stark contrast to *The 1700% Project*—encountered no resistance, nor did she experience hostility from those she met. Instead, "inadvertent" audience members (who, to reiterate, were largely unaware that this was part of a larger performance work) repeatedly asked if she required assistance, offered curious glances, and provided polite greetings.

The following day, on April 19, Ali once again assumed the guise of The Red Chador via a performance/installation piece titled *Beheadings.* Over a twelve-hour period, Ali sat at a white table, which was located in the main lobby area of the Palais de Tokyo. Armed with a cleaver, Ali would periodically grab a French baguette (painted white) from a pile (see Figure 7). After placing the baguette on a cutting board, Ali would issue an ultimatum that contained a specific task. As The Red Chador, Ali threatened to "execute" the baguette if her demands were not met; those who chose to answer The Red Chador's directive were given an hour to fulfill the demand (which was timed). To be sure, Ali's Red Chador propositions were tactically outrageous: these included asking schoolchildren to bring "all the flags of the French empire"; requisitioning the *Mona Lisa*'s smile;

Figure 7. *Beheadings.* Concept and performance by Anida Yoeu Ali. Photography by Masahiro Sugano. Courtesy of Studio Revolt.

demanding that all school lunches comply with Muslim doctrine; requesting that all girls be renamed "Fatima"; and commanding that all museum visitors be nonwhite French subjects. When the alarm sounded, The Red Chador would solemnly announce whether or not her requests had been fulfilled. If the demand was met, then The Red Chador would spare the baguette; if the mandate remained unfulfilled, Ali would ceremoniously behead a white baguette, and the process would begin anew (see Figure 8). While many audience members took The Red Chador's requests literally, Ali would defy expectations and occasionally accept creative responses. For instance, in response to the aforementioned "flag" request, Ali accepted drawn representations in lieu of actual banners. Taken together, Ali's *The Red Chador* strategically combines humor and absurdity in order to, as the artist summarizes, "build off the tension and fear of the other."[11]

On one hand, this constructive tension, which assumes form in hyperbolic performance, exaggerated gesture, and noncurated audience response, satirically replicates the irrational parameters of Islamophobia and anti-Muslim loathing.[12] On the other hand, the very setting for Ali's

Figure 8. *Beheadings*. Concept and performance by Anida Yoeu Ali. Photography by Masahiro Sugano. Courtesy of Studio Revolt.

The Red Chador—Paris—accretes meaning when situated adjacent to the extreme bloodiness of the French Revolution, the violence of French colonialism (in Africa and Asia), and more recent domestic attacks. These histories and politics are most evident in the *Beheadings* section, wherein Ali draws upon the terror of the guillotine and the cultural imperialism of the baguette. Both the guillotine and the baguette were exported to the colonies as a means of establishing—to varying degrees and to very divergent ends—French colonial hegemony through violence and assimilation.

Notwithstanding the historical, political, and cultural significations embedded in *The Red Chador*'s Parisian setting, it is arguably the reception it received in the United States that renders most visible the disconcerting pervasiveness of Islamophobia in the contemporary moment. As mentioned previously, Ali restaged *The Red Chador* in Hartford, Connecticut, while she was a visiting faculty member at Trinity College. In contrast to Paris, this iteration of *The Red Chador* was primarily ambulatory: Ali as The Red Chador journeyed through the New England capital's main avenues, side streets, churches, and neighborhoods; she would also stage

Figure 9. *The Red Chador: What Do You Fear?* Photography by Masahiro Sugano. Courtesy of Studio Revolt.

walk-ins at Trinity College (see Figures 9 and 10). Despite the diversity of setting, what remained constant was the hostility Ali encountered as The Red Chador. For instance, Ali's documentary film crew had to intervene when the artist was threatened while waiting at a city bus stop; likewise telling is the response *The Red Chador* received on Facebook after Ali had performed the work in a Trinity College dining hall on October 21, 2015:

"OMG! What the fuck is that? Why is she looking at me?"

"Anyone get the eyes from red cloak lady today? She must have seen some shit 'cause when I looked into her eyes I saw the reflection of one thousand dead baby koalas."

"Her clock building eyes."

"Plot Twist: Red Cloak Lady Packs a Paintball Gun"

"What's going on? I'm so scared."

As was the case with *The 1700% Project,* these negative reactions and problematic statements were incorporated into *The Red Chador*'s larger artistic imaginary; in particular, Ali included these comments as part of

Figure 10. *Red Chador, Sanctuary (The Red Chador: What Do You Fear?).* Concept and performance by Anida Yoeu Ali. Hartford, Connecticut, October 22, 2015. Documentation by Pablo Delano. Courtesy of Studio Revolt.

a cumulative photographic/video exhibit titled *The Red Chador: What Do You Fear?* staged in Trinity's Widener Gallery. The anxiety contained in these specific reactions, coupled with the hostility Ali endured while assuming the Red Chador persona, lays bare the vehemence of Islamophobia along with its profoundly violent potential. Such affective responses, born out of a confrontational arts practice, in the end cohere with Ali's larger oeuvre, which consistently and tirelessly endeavors to critique systemic oppression via an identifiable agitative artistic politics.

Such agitative artistic politics were most recently at the forefront of a controversy involving *The Red Chador* and the Smithsonian Institution's Asian Pacific American Center (APAC) in Washington, D.C., which hosted a Memorial Day weekend exhibit in its Arts and Industries building (May 28–29, 2016). Titled *Crosslines: A Culture Lab on Intersectionality,* the exhibit was envisioned by APAC organizers as a progressive platform through which to "engage topics of racism, sexism, colonization, and religious discrimination" via live performances, art installations, and interactive

Figure 11. Triptych from D.C. series: *Red Chador, Furies, and Muses (The Red Chador: Thresholds)*. Concept and performance by Anida Yoeu Ali. Crosslines Culture Lab at Smithsonian Arts and Industries Building. Washington, D.C., May 28–29, 2016. Documentation by Les Talusan. Courtesy of Smithsonian Asian Pacific American Center.

artist/audience spaces (see Waters 2016). Featuring forty artists, *Crosslines* was, according to acting APAC director Jeanny Kim, intended to "illustrate the rich diversity of the Asian Pacific American story" and "show how these stories are threaded throughout the fabric of American life and how they intersect with numerous categories of identity" (Smithsonian Institution 2016). Notwithstanding these broad-minded aims and objectives, *Crosslines* proved a politically vexed experience for Ali.

After being invited by APAC to participate in the exhibit, Ali proposed a revised installation/performance version of *The Red Chador* that involved ninety-nine American flags painted white and featuring the Arabic word for peace *(salaam)*. As The Red Chador, Ali would ritualistically manipulate the flags to intermittently highlight both sides, symbolically reflecting her own subject position as a Muslim American; as Ali explains, "it's talking about the Muslim identity and the American identity being a kind of palimpsest that cannot fully be erased. To me it was very poetic; it was never about anything that was going to be a defacement or a disgrace" (quoted in Waters 2016). Despite APAC support, Smithsonian officials rejected the proposal on the grounds that it was too political and divisive. Ali subsequently suggested a "filibuster" wherein The Red Chador would read passages from the Bible and Koran until she was exhausted; this too was censored.[13] In the end, Ali staged an installation wherein she—as The Red Chador—stood silently and was surrounded by American flags.

Notwithstanding controversy and forced revision, Ali's final staging of *The Red Chador* was ultimately consistent with the artist's agitative artistic politics. Indeed, while the final product strayed quite dramatically from Ali's original vision, the censorship that led to its creation was explicitly revealed in accounts that appeared in the *Huffington Post* and became integral to *The Red Chador*'s latest iteration. Faced with profound pushback from a U.S. governmental entity (the Smithsonian), and driven by an overriding sense that the "personal" is in fact "political," Ali nevertheless maintained her initial intent via the stark juxtaposition of patriotic emblem and religious dress. This juxtaposition, wherein Muslim and American identities are comingled, intermingled, and conjoined, evocatively corresponds to Ali's overall oeuvre, which, in its indefatigable contemplation of complex identarian politics, unfailingly returns to a hybrid location as "Cambodian American Muslim transnational."

Cathy J. Schlund-Vials holds a joint appointment as professor in the Department of English and the Asian and Asian American Studies Institute in the College of Liberal Arts and Sciences at the University of Connecticut. She is the author of *Modeling Citizenship: Jewish and Asian American Writing* (2011) and *War, Genocide, and Justice: Cambodian American Memory Work* (Minnesota, 2012).

■ **NOTES**

1. *Oxford English Dictionary*, s.v. "Islamophobia."

2. According to a joint report by Physicians for Social Responsibility, Physicians for Global Survival, and International Physicians for the Prevention of Nuclear War titled "Body Count: Casualty Figures after 10 Years of the 'War on Terror,'" an estimated 1.3 million lives have been lost in Iraq, Afghanistan, and Pakistan since the 9/11 attacks. This represents a conservative estimate. See Lazare (2015).

3. There is slight dispute as to Ali's birthdate (which is alternatively listed as December 1973 and 1974). The latter date reflects the one used in the artist's publicity materials.

4. Studio Revolt's first feature-length film, *Cambodian Son,* was released in 2014; the documentary focuses on Kosal Khiev, a deported Cambodian American slam poet. Studio Revolt also produced *My Asian Americana,* which similarly focused on Cambodian American deportees (which Ali terms "exiled Americans"). This was submitted to the White House's Initiative on Asian Americans and Pacific Islanders' "What's Your Story

Video Challenge." Though a finalist, the video was ultimately not selected.

5. Asian American Artists Collective, http://www.chicagoartistsresource .org/resource-links/asian-american-artists-collective?discipline=All/.

6.http://discover-cambodia.com/drenched-in-imagination-anida-yoeu -ali/.

7. "Talkback: *The Red Chador*," Trinity College, Hartford, Conn., December 8, 2015.

8. For a more in-depth analysis of Ali's *Palimpsest for Generation 1.5,* please see Schlund-Vials (2012).

9. See *1700% Project* (artist website), https://1700percentproject.word-press.com/.

10. Publicity materials/press release, *The Red Chador* (provided by the artist).

11. E-mail exchange with the artist, May 15, 2016.

12. Ibid.

13. Ali was not the only artist who faced censorship by Smithsonian officials. Gregg Deal, an Indigenous artist who belongs to the Pyramid Lake Paiute nation, received notification from the Office of Public Affairs that the mention of the Washington Redskins in his work was too politically charged.

■ **WORKS CITED**

Chazan, David. 2015. "Hate Crimes against Muslims and Jews Soar in France." *Telegraph,* December 30. http://www.telegraph.co.uk/news /worldnews/europe/france/12075018/Hate-crimes-against-Muslims -and-Jews-soar-in-France.html.

Forrest, Nicholas. 2015. "Palais de Tokyo's Secret Archipelago of Southeast Asian Art." April 9. http://www.blouinartinfo.com/news/story /1131458/palais-de-tokyos-secret-archipelago-of-southeast-asian-art.

Johnson, Henry. 2015. "Hate Crimes against Muslims in the U.K. on the Rise." November 23. http://foreignpolicy.com/2015/11/23/hate-crimes -against-muslims-in-the-u-k-on-the-rise/.

Lazare, Sarah. 2015. "Body Count Report Reveals at Least 1.3 Million Lives Lost to U.S.-Led War on Terror." March 26. http://www.common dreams.org/news/2015/03/26/body-count-report-reveals-least-13-mil lion-lives-lost-us-led-war-terror.

Levine, Tymothy. 2009. "Anida Yoeu Ali Interview." Asian American Art Oral History Project, Depaul University. May 29. http://via.library.de paul.edu/cgi/viewcontent.cgi?article=1000&context=oral_his_series.

Rathod, Sara. 2016. "2015 Saw a Record Number of Attacks on U.S. Mosques."

June 20. http://www.motherjones.com/politics/2016/06/islamopho
bia-rise-new-report-says.

RT. 2016. "Political Climate in Europe: 'Worst Level of Anti-Muslim Bigotry Ever.'" March 23. https://www.rt.com/op-edge/336929-brussels
-muslims-hysteria-attacks/.

Schlund-Vials, Cathy J. 2012. *War, Genocide, and Justice: Cambodian American Memory Work.* Minneapolis: University of Minnesota Press.

Smithsonian Institution. 2016. "Smithsonian Debuts 'CrossLines: A Culture
Lab.'" May 17. http://newsdesk.s.edu/releases/smithsonian-debuts
-crosslines-culture-lab.

Waters, Rachel. 2016. "Crossing the Line: The Smithsonian's Most Recent Censorship of Artists Hurts Us All." *Huffington Post,* June 22.
http://www.huffingtonpost.com/rachel-waters/crossing-the-line
-the-smi_b_10607330.html.

Essays

STEVEN YAO

Oceanic Etymologies: Shanghai and the Transpacific Routes of Global Modernity

■ PORT OF DEPARTURE: NEW YORK

Undomesticating Asian American Literature

In a characteristically taut lyric from his 1981 volume *Broken Off by the Music,* Chinese American poet John Yau makes an evidently playful, eponymous reference to the city of Shanghai. Yet, in the ensuing ten lines of this poem, the Chinese metropolis makes what is at best a nebulous appearance, barely registering, if at all, behind a stubbornly opaque curtain of interwoven verbal strands. In its steadfast refusal of any conventional legibility, "Shanghai Shenanigans" flouts the prevailing testimonial conventions for Asian American literary expression. In sharp contrast, Yau's poem exhibits the characteristic traits of an alternative poetic mode that would come to gain recognition during the 1990s and which I have termed *ethnic abstraction* (see Yao 2010, 15ff.). It does so by pointedly declining to communicate individual (though implicitly representative) experience through the vehicle of personal testimony and the familiar operations of normal linguistic reference and grammaticality. Deftly employing the intricately casual manner of his mentor(s), John Ashbery and the New York School poets more generally, Yau's poem instead foregrounds the artifice of its own medium, not least by underscoring the capacity of language to obscure as much as to clarify. Accordingly, the Chinese city mentioned in the title remains remote. It serves no recognizable material or historical function within the body of the poem itself, operating neither as an obvious physical setting nor as a direct referential impetus for the chain of surrealistic images:

The moon empties its cigarette over a row of clouds
whose windowsills tremble in the breeze

The breeze pushed my boat through a series
of telephone conversations started by perfume

Perfume splashed over the words of a nomad
who thought it was better to starve than to laugh

To laugh at the administration's most recent mishap
will make the guests stay until the party

Until the party is bundled in chatter
I will count the pearls lingering around your neck (Yau 1989–94, 106)

While details such as "the moon," a "cigarette," a "boat," "perfume,"
the "administration," and a "party" suggestively reference and perhaps
even successfully conjure visions of life in an international metropolis in
China, the poem repeatedly frustrates definitive placement in either space
or time. Each couplet begins to establish the barest outlines of a setting,
only to have the succeeding stichic unit change direction. Such disconnection creates the effect that any narrative drive in the poem seems to
lurch back and forth or spin about rather than move discernably forward.
Indeed, the resulting absurdist scenario that unfolds discontinuously
seems aimed at suspending narrative progression and resolution altogether, or at least subordinating these values in favor of a sonic principle
of cohesion and development. This auditory logic manifests most overtly
in the phrasal repetition that crisscrosses the poem and seems to hold the
stanzas together in the absence of other, more traditional binding forces,
such as a decipherable narrative arc or a recognizable speaker. Hence the
final arrival of the poem at a moment of suspended desire rather than
closure in the image of the hanging pearl necklace; and hence, too, even
the refusal of grammatical completeness in the fourth and penultimate
couplet of the poem along the way.

Instead of identifying an actual place or physical location, then, the
"Shanghai" in the title seems primarily to designate a sequence of sounds,
one resembling that in the vernacular term "Shenanigans," meaning,
variously, according to the *Oxford English Dictionary (OED)*, "trickery,
skullduggery, . . . 'kidding,' nonsense; (usu. *pl.*) a plot, a trick, a prank,
an exhibition of high spirits, a carry-on."[1] The strong sonic resemblance
between these terms only further emphasizes the idea of a playful nonsense that disrupts or violates sanctioned protocols of expression. Thus

this work employs a Chinese place-name (or at least its Anglicization) for sonic, rather than clearly referential, purposes. In "Shanghai Shenanigans," the verbal signifier for the international (and once partially colonized) Chinese metropolis functions mainly as a phonemic sequence only vestigially attached to its signified or referent. As I discuss later, Yau is far from unique in his act of verbal piracy committed under the sign of "Shanghai." Rather, he stands at the recent end of a deep and expressly "transpacific" literary archive wherein "Shanghai" has served as both the verbal token and historical impetus for experimentation with prevailing conventions of literary form and their associated protocols of legibility in various languages and locations around the Pacific Ocean. In charting this terrain, I hope not only to broaden the geographic and linguistic dimensions of "Asian American literature" as a cultural formation but also to help clarify its complex relation to modernist literary traditions and practices across Asia.

For based upon the individualist, cultural nationalist logic that continues to determine the main assumptions and conceptual horizons of contemporary Asian American literary studies, Yau's poem stands out as virtually illegible.[2] One might begin to make some vague sense of "Shanghai Shenanigans" within that hermeneutic regime, which has until recently focused overwhelmingly on works that employ conventional reference and realism as primary expressive modes.[3] But such an understanding requires the selective application of biographical information about the author and his family as well as a willingness to ignore the explicit statement of the poem (however elliptically given) in favor of a set of interpretive possibilities defined by the intersection between authorial experience and ethnic stereotype.

As it happens, Shanghai is the original hometown of Yau's parents, who immigrated to the United States from mainland China earlier in the twentieth century, probably in flight from the chaos generated by war with Japan and the ensuing struggle between the Nationalist and Communist Parties for control of the country. As Yau has discussed in different interviews, his parents spoke Shanghainese as their native language, but Yau himself never learned the dialect (see, e.g., Foster 1990). Such linguistic estrangement from his ethnic heritage offers one plausible biographical explanation for why "Shanghai" might be employed in the poem more for its sonic value than for its function as a name. For in doing so, it evokes the constitutive mysteries of ethnic identity formation and the productive dissonances of linguistic difference. In this interpretive scenario, the poem dramatizes the playful results of Yau's "hybridized" development as an Asian American writer, one conditioned (but not entirely constrained) by a simultaneous disconnection from both dominant American culture and his heritage ethnic traditions.[4]

However plausible (or not), the reading I have just presented leaves something to be desired on several counts. Most immediately, it rests almost entirely on a negative foundation. That is, the poem gains its significance in this view for what it does not or what it refuses to say. Furthermore, this reading remains comfortably bound by the ethnonationalist assumptions that have dominated Asian American studies over the history of its rise as an oppositional academic formation in the United States. In doing so, it limits the significance of "Shanghai," as well as of the poem more broadly, to a strictly domestic sphere that reaches only as far as Yau's immediate family as a synecdoche for Asian Americans more broadly. Lastly, and most importantly, such an interpretation overlooks entirely the more prominent formal features in evidence, namely, the peculiar repetition of key words and phrases and the couplet structure. In what follows, I want to cultivate a more expansive approach to texts like Yau's, an approach that will enable readings of "Shanghai Shenanigans" and other works that similarly operate beyond the prevailing domestic norms of ethnic (and especially Asian) American signification in more positive and explicitly transnational terms.

To do so, I want to establish an expressly "transpacific" lineage for Yau's poem. More particularly, I want to follow back in time, as well as back and forth across the physical and psychic expanse of the Pacific Ocean, the signifying chain that connects his verse as a poet of Chinese descent living in the United States to a larger historical archive of writings undertaken in various languages from around and across the physical and cultural terrain of the Pacific Rim that also variously employ "Shanghai" as a mechanism to both reflect and reflect on the condition of modernity in its uneven spread around the world. For "Shanghai Shenanigans" stands at the recent end of an extensive history of material, cultural, linguistic, artistic, and myriad other forms of expressly "transpacific" exchange that has itself helped to determine the establishment and particular expression of the "modern." As a crucial distribution node in the emergent system of global capital that at once propelled and received peoples, goods, and ideas back and forth across the Pacific Ocean, the city of Shanghai has naturally figured in numerous crucial ways and moments in both the material establishment and imaginative representation of a global modernity. As we shall see, this concern with Shanghai as a politico-economic hub for various global forces and transpacific flows stretches across a range of distinctive historical, cultural, and linguistic contexts. In its hemispheric scope, such an archive illustrates the remarkable variety, breadth, and duration of the effort to come to grips with the shifting terrain of an ever increasingly global commerce that in its turn has served as the material and conceptual matrix within and against which a new, "modern" imagination has taken shape across the space of the Pacific Ocean.

Accordingly, then, I want here to use Yau's poem as a vector that points toward larger patterns arising within the history of the "transpacific" as a geocultural formation at once constituted by and deeply constitutive of global modernity. More particularly, I want to follow the historical itinerary of this internationalized traveling signifier, "Shanghai," as it has disseminated across time and space as well as across different languages, grammatical functions, and literary and cultural traditions over the course of the twentieth century. As I will discuss, this signifier has achieved over the last 150 years or so the status of a figure or trope that condenses the intuited but as yet not fully decipherable flows of transnational commerce and interrelation enabling and accompanying the rise of global modernity. It also therewith has served in different instances as an imaginative effort to grasp by neologism and other formal explorations the increasingly complex web of evolving connections among people and nations as well as other more fluid formations that together make up such a global condition. Hence this trope also testifies to the importance of the "transpacific" as a crucial dimension in the historical unfolding of that modernity in the shape of the corollary aesthetic and cultural category of the "modern." For the trope or topos of "Shanghai" also gets consistently associated in these same and other works with the kinds of formal experimentation and disruptions of prevailing aesthetic conventions that have been understood under the rubric of "modernism" in various locations and literary traditions.

Put another way, I am concerned here with Shanghai not mainly as a geopolitical locus where national and international forces converge to shape the physical and psychic landscape of the city under the compressed conditions of an ongoing global modernity, though to be sure that ample subject continues to warrant its own dedicated discussion (see, among many others, Shih 2001; Lee 1999; Hansen 2000; Knight 2003; Hansen and Kong 2009; Zhang 1999). Rather, I am concerned with "Shanghai" (as well as 上海) as a polylingual verbal sign that appears in literary works from around the Pacific Rim as a figure or trope for the increasingly global scale of interactions that together make up economic and cultural modernity—and which, thereby, also consistently (though not exclusively) co-occurs with assorted forms of general aesthetic experimentation, in particular the disruption of prevailing formal conventions and their associated protocols of legibility, whatever those happen to be at any given moment in any particular national and/or linguistic literary tradition. As we shall see, writers from the United States, China, and Japan all responded in their own distinctive yet still usefully comparable ways to the collective challenges of global modernity and the transformations of space and time, not to mention of representation, taking place around and across the world as a result of that modernity.

In undertaking such a journey, I seek to contribute to a deeper theorization of the "transpacific" as a critical geography that brings into focus certain dynamic aspects of global modernity. This emergent notion has been cultivated over the last fifteen years or so by scholars, including Yunte Huang, Jonathan Stalling, Naoki Sakai, and Janet Hoskins and Viet Nguyen (2014), among others, and in its particular conception of a global view, this approach seeks to create a productive conversation among two powerful strands of inquiry that have remained separated in our current disciplinary arrangements: first, the study of Western Orientalism, which reached a kind of height or tipping point with regard to East Asia in particular during the early twentieth century, particularly in its formative role in the development of canonical Euro-American modernism; and second, a parallel inquiry in the arena of Pacific Rim studies into the importance of flows and local agencies as part of an effort to reverse the conventional directions of material and epistemological priority under the old model of Western domination. Dedicated to testing the nature and coherence of the "Pacific Rim" as a geocultural formation, scholars in this parallel formation have been grounded in the social scientific competencies of area studies, most especially a recognition of the asymmetrical economic relations underwriting interactions around the space of the Pacific as a theater for the interconnected tragedies of modernity throughout Asia.[5]

Understood in part as the evolving intersection between these related critical strands, the "transpacific" also affords an opportunity to rethink the cultural and physical dimensions of Asian American studies beyond the boundaries of the domestic United States. Lisa Lowe (2012, 71) has recently noted that "transpacific Asian migration disrupts disciplinary practices for the study of 'Asia,' 'America,' and even the 'Asian American' that emerged in U.S. universities since the 1970s. To the extent that this new object exceeds the contours of the earlier paradigms, it may force a shift in the methods and objects of Asian Studies, American Studies and Asian American Studies." As early as 2002, Yunte Huang set out the initial formulation in the idea of "transpacific displacement," which he defined in primarily literary terms as "a historical process of textual migration of cultural meanings, meanings that include linguistic traits, poetics, philosophical ideas, myths, stories, and so on" (3). Later, Huang (2008, 2) broadens his conception and employs "the phrase 'transpacific imaginations' to refer to a host of literary and historical imaginations that have emerged under the tremendous geopolitical pressure of the Pacific encounters." Stalling (2010, 4) "cautiously employ[s] the term 'transpacific' to demarcate the historically specific cultural and textual pathways across which various philosophical, literary and aesthetic discourses travel, specifically from China (often by way of Japan) to America" from the late nineteenth century onward. Expanding the scope of the term, Sakai and Yoo (2012, 6) "place the complicity of the old and the new empires, the new alliance of Japan and the United States as the focal point of our conception of the trans-Pacific imagination." For them, "trans-pacific Studies . . . is a demand to invent the new meaning of East Asia through interrogations into the idea and practice of nation and nationalism informed by the regional and global condition" (31).

Broadening the focus still further, I want to draw attention to the material and human infrastructure that necessarily underwrites existing conceptions of the "transpacific" as an arena of cultural dissemination (and political hegemony) through textual and other channels. No less than their counterparts in the realm of the imagination, these histories of (uneven) material and human exchange across the physical space of the Pacific Ocean at once reflect and even constitute the shifting conditions of politico-economic modernity in its steady advance around the world. To be sure, scholars, not to mention bankers, merchants, laborers, bureaucrats, and sailors, have all long since recognized and reinforced the importance of Shanghai as a crucial node in the global circulation of financial, material, human, cultural, and other forms of capital. For their part, attempting to reckon the full impact of socioeconomic modernization upon their own respective lives and locations, imaginative writers from different cultural and literary traditions across the terrain of the Pacific Ocean have variously reflected upon the (sign for the) Chinese metropolis and its generative role in the establishment and operation of the manifold distribution networks that together make up the infrastructure for modernity as a global condition. That "transpacific" literary and cultural history shall be the subject of the discussion that follows.

■ PORT OF CALL: HOLLYWOOD

Transpacific Embarkations
Needless to say, perhaps, Yau's concern in "Shanghai Shenanigans" lies elsewhere than with the actual international metropolis and financial

center located in the People's Republic of China. Instead, his more direct interest remains centered on its history as an object of discourse across various media over time, that is, on "Shanghai" as both a verbal sign and an historically overdetermined figure or topos for the problem of representation more broadly. In other words, Yau focuses in this poem not on the city of Shanghai as a political entity or physical space but rather on its repeated deployment as a supercharged token within a larger semiotic and discursive system that itself reflects the accumulated effects of a manifold history of complex transpacific negotiations.[6] From his larger body of verse, we know that Yau has consistently found inspiration for some of his most biting work in the tradition of Hollywood Orientalism and its assorted depictions of Asian racial identity, culture, and (to a lesser extent) geography, most especially during the so-called Golden Era of the 1930s–50s.[7] And indeed, with its "cigarette," "windowsills," "boat," "party," and "pearls," the imagery, or perhaps more accurately image fragments, and surreal but decidedly stock scenarios of "Shanghai Shenanigans" seem pointedly, if obliquely, engaged with the visual and narrative idioms of that tradition. Accordingly, the Shanghai to which this "Shanghai" most immediately refers is the "Shanghai" coming out of Hollywood during the first half of the twentieth century. This cultural geography not only illustrates the scope of Yau's influences as a poet. It also locates an important site of his engagement specifically as an Asian American writer with the broader tradition of Western Orientalist fantasy. Bringing us from New York City, the site of both his physical residence and his most direct poetic influences, to the threshold of the Pacific Ocean, the Hollywood connection links Yau's poem to a much wider and deeper history of transpacific negotiations that have taken shape at once through and under the sign of "Shanghai."

Not surprisingly, as the main port for Western powers in China and itself partially divided among various European nations, the United States, and Japan, the city of Shanghai has for obvious reasons figured prominently across a wide range of efforts in various languages to come to grips with the question of modernity in Asia and its world historical consequences. Indeed, from the 1930s through the 1950s, questions of this sort became especially acute as military violence around and then on the Pacific engulfed the planet and once again reordered existing political alliances and prejudices. The causes of this increased conflict include, most spectacularly, the interconnected traumas of national revolution in China, imperial expansion across the Pacific by Japan and the United States, and the resulting friction between these empires in the struggle for dominance over territory and resources in Asia, as well as the world war that followed on as part of these processes. For its part, Hollywood at this time demonstrated a fascination with the city as a synecdoche, stage, and sign for questions relating to modernity in Asia and its global implications as well as the related issue of Asian racial identity. During the so-called Golden Age, in particular, nearly one movie per year appeared featuring the name "Shanghai" in the title, with spikes during crucial periods, such as 1937–38, when the Japanese army invaded China and Japan became an explicit threat to American interests in the region. Spanning the range from comedy to spy drama to noir thriller, these works routinely trafficked in various exoticist racial stereotypes, such as Asian sexual depravity, inscrutability, cunning, and intelligence, in constructing their visual narratives. Titles include, in reverse chronological order, *Shanghai Chest* (1948, a Charlie Chan movie), *The Lady from Shanghai* (1947, starring Orson Welles and Rita Hayworth), *The Shanghai Cobra* (1945, another Charlie Chan film), *Halfway to Shanghai* (1942), *The Shanghai Gesture* (1941), *North of Shanghai* (1939), *Shadows over Shanghai* (1938), *Daughter of Shanghai* (1937, with Anna May Wong), *Exiled to Shanghai* (1937), *West of Shanghai* (1937, featuring Boris Karloff), *Charlie Chan in Shanghai* (1935), *Shanghai* (1935), *Shanghai Madness* (1933), *The Shanghai Express* (1932, starring Marlene Dietrich and Anna May Wong), *The Ship from Shanghai* (1930), *Shanghai Rose* (1929), *Shanghai Lady* (1929), *Back from Shanghai* (1929), *Shanghai Bound* (1927), and *Streets of Shanghai* (1927).[8] Some of these films are topical dramas about historical events with obvious implications for the political and commercial interests of the United States, as in *North of Shanghai,* about the Japanese invasion of Manchuria. In others, Shanghai merely serves as a point of generic reference to signal the type of exoticism being purveyed, as in *West of Shanghai,* which features Boris Karloff as warlord General Wu Yen Fang, or as in the three Charlie Chan movies. Furthermore, as with Yau's poem, works such as *The Lady from Shanghai, Halfway to Shanghai,* and *Daughter of Shanghai* have only the slimmest of connections to their eponymous city at the level of character, setting, or plot.

More than any particular plotline or historical episode depicted, the sheer abundance and variety of these films together indicate the importance of "Shanghai" as both site and sign for the global reach of modernity in Hollywood's transpacific imagination at this time. In his own turn, Yau mocks the racist absurdities of this discourse through his canny surrealism in "Shanghai Shenanigans," which highlights the arbitrariness of Shanghai as a sign that bears no obvious relation to the content that follows.[9] And in doing so, he flaunts the instability of semantic reference as part of undercutting essentialist identity claims. Indeed, Hollywood

Orientalism in general inspires the visual atmosphere and narrative conceits for some of Yau's most sustained poetic interrogations of ethnic (and specifically Asian American) identity. These include the extended "Genghis Chan: Private Eye" sequence and the Hollywood Asians section of *Forbidden Entries,* especially in their more noirish aspects.[10] Such a chain of influence highlights the transpacific logic of Yau's specifically "ethnic" writing as an Asian American. And in doing so, it underscores the need for a hermeneutic frame that reaches beyond the horizon of the nation, even or most especially when addressing work by racialized writers of Asian descent in the United States. For this linkage connects his verse via Hollywood and the tradition of modernist American Orientalism to a larger, multilingual archive of expressly transpacific literary and popular texts in Chinese and Japanese from the early twentieth century. As we shall see, in this archive, "Shanghai" serves an overdetermined function as both topos and figure not only for examining the effects and implications of the spread of socioeconomic modernity throughout Asia but also for exploring the shifting logic and politics of representation under the pressure of such a volatile global condition.[11]

■ PORT OF CALL: SHANGHAI, CHINA

Transpacific Modernity, Chinese Modernism, and Mu Shi Ying (穆時英)'s "The Shanghai Foxtrot (a Fragment)" (上海的狐步舞-一個端片) (1932)

The next leg of our transpacific itinerary takes us to actual historical China of the 1930s and, in particular, to the site of Mu Shi Ying's famous short story "The Shanghai Foxtrot (a Fragment)." First published in 1932, this work has attained iconic status within the canon of modern Chinese literature, though it was only recently made available in English (Macdonald 2004).[12] Despite (or perhaps precisely because of) its brevity, at only eight pages in its original form (as well as in English translation), this text has enjoyed an outsized reputation. Here Shanghai is famously depicted as the modernist city par excellence, its headlong embrace of flashing signs and the glittering surfaces of unbridled capitalism anxiously celebrated and lamented by turns. In "The Shanghai Foxtrot," we glimpse the web of transpacific commercial and political relations that underlie the rise of cultural modernity in China. And in doing so, we also witness an earlier instance of the enduring association of "Shanghai" (both the city itself and the name) with that modernity as well as with a formal experimentalism that departs in significant ways from established protocols and conventions of literary representation.

As Shu-mei Shih (2001, 329) notes, "Mu's Shanghai is caught at the very moment of the traumatic encounter with technological modernity, which simultaneously assaults and fascinates the subject who is as yet unable to develop a psychic shield to ward off the onslaught of stimuli it brings." In its concern with these stimuli and their effects, the story ambivalently reflects and reflects upon the extent to which global and especially transpacific phenomena like commerce and imperialism shape the dimensions of the modern city in both material and psychological terms:

> NEON LIGHT reaches colored fingers writing large words in the blue ink of night's void. An English gentleman stands there, wearing coattails, carrying a cane under his arm, walking with a lively stride. Written underneath his feet: "JOHNNY WALKER STILL GOING STRONG." At the roadside the real estate utopia of a small grass lot, above it a Chesterfield smoking American looks on as if to say, "What a shame this lilliputian utopia; is that big lot too small for me to put my foot down in?" (801)

Shanghai's historical importance as a financial and cultural capital and semicolonial international metropolis finds expression in this multilingual description of billboards promoting British and American consumer products.

Above and beyond its thematic preoccupation with the transpacific routes of global modernity in urban Shanghai, this text aggressively pursues a formal experimentalism that accords with Western notions of modernist stylistic innovation in its fragmentary, repetitive, impressionistic, stream-of-consciousness narration. Thus translator Sean Macdonald (2004, 798) declares that "The Shanghai Foxtrot" "is truly a modernist gem of description and form, a cinematic arc light illuminating the exoticized fragments of 1930s Shanghai." The story opens famously with a disembodied narrative voice presenting a sequence of interrelated images of the city in a way that clearly seeks to emulate the visual grammar of cinematic montage. Strikingly, this opening anticipates the imagery of the moon, the night sky, and perhaps even the cigarette that make up Yau's initial couplet in "Shanghai Shenanigans":

> Shanghai. A heaven built on hell.

> West Shanghai, *the bright moon climbing the sky, illuminating the wasted sprawl. Ashen* sprawl, blanketed with silver-grey moonlight, then inlaid with deep grey tree shadows and heaps of village shadows. On top of the sprawl, iron rails draw an arc that reaches along the sky and goes down there beneath the horizon. (Macdonald 2004, 798–99, emphasis added)

Subsequently, a train hurtling down the tracks in darkness generates the emblematic rhythm of modernity that inspires the story's title, which itself enacts a transpacific appropriation through the mechanism of a calque in Chinese (狐步舞 parses into "fox step dance") from the original term in English, almost certainly via the historical mediation of Japanese:[13]

> Rumble of iron rails, railroad ties centipede-like creep forward in the beam, telephone poles appear and disappear in the pitch black, the belly of the "Shanghai Express" shoots out, da da da, to the beat of a foxtrot, bearing the night's pearl, dragon-like whipping by, rounding that arc. (799)

This concern with conveying the sensory texture of modern life and the rhythms of the city reverberates throughout the story and shapes its formal dimensions. Just as in Yau's contemporary poem in English, a carefully modulated repetition serves in Mu's Chinese story to draw attention to the material properties of language as a medium, thereby helping to achieve the abstraction that signifies modernist form. In another instance, the story combines the multilingual textuality that we have already seen in use to represent the visual landscape of Shanghai with a disjointed sequence of images that culminates in moment of self-reflexivity via the appearance of a figure for Mu himself, who cultivated a habit of spending time in nightclubs with pen in hand and drinking coffee as part of his very successful public persona:

> Azure dusk envelopes the space completely, a SAXOPHONE reaches its neck, opens up a pair of lips, whoowhoo pounds them shouting. In the middle of that polished floor, whirling skirts, whirling cheongsam slits, exquisite shoe heels, shoe heels, shoe heels, shoe heels, shoe heels. Fluffed hair and male faces. Male white shirt collars and female smiles. . . . The smell of alcohol, smell of perfume, smell of English ham and eggs, smell of cigarettes . . . a confirmed bachelor sits in corners taking hits of black coffee to stimulate his nerves.

Less than a page later in the text, this same sequence of images appears in reverse, partly signifying the swirling, disorienting experience of the dance hall:

> A confirmed bachelor sits in corners taking hits of black coffee to stimulate his nerves. The smell of alcohol, smell of perfume, smell of English ham and eggs, smell of cigarettes. . . . Male faces and fluffed hair. Exquisite shoe heels, shoe heels, shoe heels, shoe heels, shoe heels. Whirling cheongsam slits, whirling skirts, in the center a polished floor. Whoowhoo pounds them

shouting, that SAXOPHONE reaches its neck, opens up a pair of lips. Azure dusk envelops the space completely. (802)

This moment of self-reflexivity leads to even more extravagant meta-fictional gestures, as the mysterious writer figure who appears in these mirrored descriptions subsequently employs details of Mu's own life in the process of describing an internationalist aesthetic arising out of a global literary traffic made possible through the mechanism of translation and determined by the power of world literary prestige: "China's tragedy is here perfect material for a novel 1931 is my age *The Eastern Novel, North Star,* every month a special issue Japanese translations Russian translations translations from every country Nobel prize–winning great and rich" (804).

A celebrated (and notorious) figure in his own time, Mu Shiying enjoyed international recognition as a member of the *xinganjuepai* (新感覺派), or the New Sensationist school among the Shanghai modernists. In their efforts to define the terms of a "modern" literary idiom in Chinese, the writers associated with this informal group pursued a linguistic and cultural cosmopolitanism that freely incorporated both Japanese and Western languages and techniques of stylistic experiment.[14] Mu in particular responded to the linked questions of modernity in China and Chinese modernism by pursuing an artistic vision grounded in the concepts of fractured subjectivity, aesthetic autonomy, and the intrinsic value of formalist experimentation and "technique."

And as we have seen, "The Shanghai Foxtrot (a Fragment)" exhibits those ideals clearly and even defiantly in light of the precarious situation faced by writers in China at the time. For Mu and his fellow Chinese writers occupied a deeply fraught political and cultural landscape. Especially in the semicolonized Shanghai of the early twentieth century, a place where the question of Chinese sovereignty remained an open one, writers from across the political spectrum at once confronted and exerted on one another considerable ideological pressures from both the left and right to put their work in the service of the nation as defined by Communist or Nationalist party agendas. Not surprisingly, neither of these parties valued Mu's stance of aestheticist detachment. In fact, he was killed by a Guomindang agent in June 1940 for what was thought to be his collaboration with the Japanese imperial government in its invasion of China and the puppet regime of Wang Jingwei.[15] This last historical fact alludes to the complexities of Mu's various personal negotiations across and around the geopolitical theater of the Pacific Ocean. And in doing so, it underscores the extent to which "The Shanghai Foxtrot (a

Fragment)" and Mu's cosmopolitan vision together grow unmistakably out of various interlinked transpacific networks of influence and circulation, ranging from the specifically literary to the more broadly cultural to the full military and bureaucratic apparatus of imperial domination.

Within the literary sphere in particular, Mu was hardly the first writer in Asia to take up Shanghai as both an emblem for the condition of global modernity and, as such, an occasion for formal experimentation under the sign of "modernism."[16] In fact, the most immediate influence upon Mu Shiying and upon the *xinganjuepai,* or Chinese "New Sensationists" more broadly, were the *shinkankaku ha,* or the Japanese "New Sensationists," including most especially the canonical Japanese writer Yokomitsu Ri'ichi, who was a founding member of this aesthetic and literary movement.[17] Indeed, Mu's depiction of Shanghai as the modern city par excellence in "The Shanghai Foxtrot (a Fragment)" finds an earlier precedent and direct model in Yokomitsu's canonical modernist novel in Japanese, 上海 *(Shanghai),* a work that affirms the historical importance of Shanghai as both site and sign for the transpacific circuits of global modernity.[18]

■ PORT OF CALL: TOKYO, JAPAN

Transpacific Networks of Influence, Japanese Modernism, and Yokomitsu Ri'ichi's *Shanghai*

In his brief story, Mu depicts a semicolonized urban space riven by competing national and imperial interests, with the general sensory and especially visual effects of the struggle for domination necessitating new, multilingual protocols of signification to register their complexity. More than a year before the appearance of "The Shanghai Foxtrot (a Fragment)" in 1932, the Japanese writer Yokomitsu Ri'ichi completed the initial publication of his novel 上海 *(Shanghai),* which first appeared serially in the literary magazine *Kaizo* between 1928 and 1931. As translator Dennis Washburn explains, Yokomitsu similarly "uses Shanghai as both a historical site and an imaginary cityscape onto which his characters project their desires. And by relating the personal desires of his characters to political and social realities, Yokomitsu attempts to achieve the aesthetic aim of getting at unmediated experience through imagistic writing and the politically charged aim of resolving the conflicted historical consciousness of modern culture" (Yokomitsu and Washburn 2001, 237). With its unconventional grammar and overtly cinematic approach to narration, the famous opening scene stages in an especially clear way the connection between modernist formal experimentation and the demands of representing the Chinese metropolis, most especially the variety and complexity of international relations contained therein. Again looking ahead in remarkable ways to Yau's contemporary poem in English, the novel begins with a grammatically disconnected sequence of fragmentary images. In Yokomitsu's novel, these images together serve the function of an establishing shot in film:

> At high tide the river swelled and flowed backward. Prows of darkened motorboats lined up in a wave pattern. A row of rudders drawn up. Mountains of off-loaded cargo. The black legs of a wharf bound in chains. A signal showing calm winds raised atop a weather station tower. A customs house spire dimly visible through evening fog. Coolies on barrels stacked on the embankment, becoming soaked in the damp air. A black sail, torn and tilted, creaking along, adrift on brackish waves . . .
>
> One of the hookers turned her head toward Sanki. She spoke to him in English. (3)

As various scholars have already discussed, in *Shanghai,* Yokomitsu develops a narrative idiom that combines fragmentary, imagistic sentences that seek to mimic the effects of filmic presentation.[19] Conceiving of this style under the term *shajitsu* (realism), Yokomitsu sought to achieve direct representation of the turbulence and novelty of modern sensory experience. In an earlier formulation of the idea of the New Sensation from 1925, Yokomitsu makes clear the array of Western influences that contribute to this aesthetic doctrine: "Futurism, Three-dimensionalism, Expressionism, Dadaism, Structuralism, Surrealism—all of these I recognize as belonging to the New Sensation School" (Yokomitsu and Washburn 2001, 222).[20]

In its obvious and particular engagement with an array of Western movements and aesthetic doctrines such as imagism, symbolism, surrealism, and others, movements that were themselves influenced by (their own construals) of classical Japanese and Chinese aesthetics, Japanese New Sensationism underscores the transpacific routes of (asymmetrical) engagement and emulation in the rise of modernism on a global scale. Hence, quite apart from any evidence of direct influence, the common concern over the protocols of cinematic representation and/of Shanghai displayed by Yau, Mu, and Yokomitsu collectively validates some level of mutual contemporaneity among recent Asian American literary expression and both Chinese and Japanese New Sensationism.[21] And in doing so, this common concern testifies to the analytic utility of the transpacific as a critical geocultural formation vital to the establishment of global modernity.

At the level of theme, Yokomitsu's *Shanghai* pays especially close attention to the spread of economic modernity and its consequences for existing relations of power between East and West. Reading the novel from our current historical juncture under the shadow of the neoliberal trade agreement known as the Trans-Pacific Partnership, Yokomitsu's descriptions of the way global economic relations shape the rhythms and even possibilities life in the city of Shanghai exhibit a startling prescience. Again and again, the novel draws attention to the reach of economic globalization and the resulting interconnectedness of physically remote points of the world:

> The speed of the Mongolian ponies pulling those carriages moved the currency markets in New York and London. . . . The brokers who used these carriages were almost entirely Westerners, who ran from bank to bank armed with smiles and nimble wits. Their trading margins, . . . were the wellspring of activity between West and East. (34)

Even more significant than the familiar compression of physical space brought on by modernity, perhaps, the demands of global capital even encroach upon the terrain of individual desire by shaping the conditions of possibility for personal relationships:

> It had never occurred to Kōya that the British government's declaration lifting export limits on rubber would so quickly affect his search for a wife. Of course, he knew Britain had to repay its war debts to the U.S. And that it had been relying for some time on tin and rubber from Singapore to do so. Thus, the Singapore market was now in a panic, and the lumber trade halted. And for that reason he would probably have to put off looking for a wife. (35)

In an essay published in 1939, some eight years after the initial serialization of *Shanghai*, Yokomitsu elaborated upon his fascination with the Chinese city as both a concrete location and a manifestation of the "problem" of global modernity and its various conceptual and political challenges. Though it may have the feel of a "revisionist justification for the earlier work of fiction," this essay, titled "Shinakai" (The China Sea), nevertheless presents "an extension of the political and aesthetic ideology that had already found its first and fullest expression in his novel" (Yokomitsu and Washburn 2001, 228):

> [Shanghai is] the birthplace [故郷, *kokyō*] of the problem that ever occupies my thoughts. . . . The problem of the International Settlement is one of the most perplexing in the world. At the same time this location also represents the problem of the future. To some extent it is a very simple thing, but there is no other place on earth that so manifests the quality

[性質, *seishitsu*] that constitutes the modern [現代, *kindai*]. What is more, there exists no where in the world except the Settlement a site where all nations have created a common city. To think about this place is to think about the world in microcosm.

Unlike his Chinese protégé Mu Shiying, then, Yokomitsu Ri'ichi did not undertake his *Shanghai* as a technical exercise or simple literary experiment. Rather, in developing more immediate, New Sensationist techniques of representation, the Japanese writer sought nothing less than to help resolve the historical crisis of global modernity by providing an accurate portrayal of the problem as embodied in the city of Shanghai at a moment when Japan was prosecuting its own expansionist project with fresh vigor and beginning to compete openly and successfully with the West for world hegemony.[22] Such enormous stakes help to explain Yokomitsu's seemingly counterintuitive conception of his work under the designation of *shajitsu,* or realism.

Indeed, *Shanghai* has long been recognized as an apologia for Japanese imperialism and incursion into China, and this agenda certainly shapes the transpacific vision set forth in the novel.[23] So, for example, one of the main protagonists, Sanki, conflates individual bodies with national territoriality in such a way as to make imperial expansion an inevitable by-product of human migration under the conditions of economic modernity:

> People who had had their livelihoods taken from them in their native countries had gathered here and were creating an independent state unique in the world. . . . Even people who were idle, unemployed, or simply aimless could be thought of as an expression of patriotism simply by their mere presence in Shanghai. Sanki laughed at the thought . . . because he was in Shanghai, the space his body took up was always a territory of Japan. (44)

Eliciting praise and condemnation ever since the initial serial publication of *Shanghai* beginning in 1929, such ideological complicity with the project of Japanese empire has been integral to the recognition that Yokomitsu's novel has received over the years. However ambivalent, such acclaim merely underscores the transpacific significance of Shanghai as topos and figure for reckoning the global spread of modernity. Furthermore, as we have seen, for Mu Shiying and Yokomitsu Ri'ichi in particular, Shanghai not only served as a vehicle for examining the effects of modernity around and across the terrain of the Pacific. It also thereby inspired formal innovation under the sign of the "modern" to depict its manifold complexities.[24] As we shall see presently, the effort to reckon global modernity by way of "Shanghai" was not limited to elite literary formations like the *xinganjuepai* or the *shinkankakuha*. In fact, this phenomenon finds even earlier expression in a Japanese popular adventure tale from 1925 wherein "Shanghai" functions as a translingual verbal token signifying both the global spread of modernity and the corrosive effects of that process on the established lineaments of personal and national identity.

■ PORT OF CALL: KOBE, JAPAN

Transpacific Migration, Vernacular Modernism, and Tani Jōji's "The Shanghaied Man" (上海された男) (1925)

Accompanying the heightened flows of material commodities, commercial goods, cultural products, and financial capital, a dramatic increase in the movement of human bodies around and across the space of the Pacific Ocean also helped to constitute the rise of global modernity. Historically, this increased movement was driven by a number of distinct but interconnected forces: imperial expansion across the region on the part of various nations (most notably Japan, Russia, and the United States); unprecedented levels of international trade enabled by various technological advancements; and widespread political turmoil and economic hardship in nonindustrialized agricultural areas like the Pearl River Delta of Guangdong Province in southern China, which caused various displacements and large-scale coerced emigration over a sustained period. To be sure, this expanded transpacific circulation of human capital developed as a consequence of asymmetrical political, cultural, and financial relations among many separate, competing national interests from at least the early nineteenth century onward. And as we have already seen in the famous depictions of the city by both Mu Shi Ying and Yokomitsu Ri'ichi, these asymmetrical relations left their marks on the variegated physical and psychological terrain of urban Shanghai itself.

At the same time, however, the increase in transpacific human traffic also exerted its own unique pressures on those established relations through the social and economic turbulence generated by its very motion. These pressures threatened to destabilize the boundaries believed (and actively maintained) at the time to distinguish nations from one another, boundaries of culture, language, and "race," among others. Mounting repeated but ultimately benighted efforts to police both their physical and cultural borders, various national governments sought to control human traffic across the Pacific through legal and diplomatic means.[25] Despite these and numerous other efforts to stem its tide, the swell of transpacific human migration under the conditions of global modernity has left its own expansive, if still necessarily partial, documentary and cultural record of that collective experience.

Among the countless and still mostly anonymous contributors to this diverse and multilingual archive (the great majority of which has yet to be properly reckoned), the figure of Tani Jōji warrants particular attention for his popular adventure tales about the experience of transpacific migration and its various transformative cultural effects. In particular, his "Merican-Jap" (*meriken jappu*) stories appealed to an emergent audience of newly educated Japanese youths eager for tales about international adventure and economic opportunity abroad in the early decades of the twentieth century. These stories appeared in *New Youth* (新青年, *Shin seinen*), a popular culture magazine made famous by the mystery writer Edogawa Rampo. Moreover, they feature a series of transpacific migrant Japanese protagonists living as hobos in America who confront, and typically overcome, various challenges deriving from the discriminatory economic and racial order of the United States. Tani Jōji was the pseudonym of Hasegawa Kaetaro, the most commercially successful writer in Japan at the time of his sudden death in 1935, whose prolific and lucrative career was cut short by a heart attack due to overwork at the age of thirty-five.[26]

Earlier in his life, Hasegawa himself had spent four years wandering about the United States as a casual laborer, working short stints in restaurants and state fairs after dropping out of Oberlin College, where he had enrolled as a foreign student in 1920. Upon returning to Japan in 1924 by way of the boiler room on a freighter, Hasegawa began to publish fictionalized accounts of his life abroad. Indeed, over the next decade, according to translator Kyoko Ōmori, he "wrote under three pseudonyms simultaneously: Tani Jōji, for his sketches of American life; Maki Itsuma, for mystery fiction or romance novels; and Hayashi Fubō, for period works such as his series on the fictional samurai hero Tange Sazen, a master swordsman with only one good eye and arm" (290). Ōmori continues, "As a writer who popularized literature in the mass media, he wrote in the genres of mystery, period, and romance fiction (*tantei, jidai, katei shōsetsu*) that were created by Japanese modernists. He was [also] among the first to have his works appear in the commercial cinema when his Tange Sazen series was adapted to the silver screen in 1928" (290). Accordingly, based upon its specific generic vehicles, as well as on the technology of its popular dissemination, Hasegawa's collective oeuvre exemplifies what Miriam Bratu Hansen (2000, 10–11) has termed "vernacular modernism," a notion emphasizing popular or mass, rather than elite, culture as "a cultural counterpart and response to technological, economic and social modernity." Hasegawa offered perhaps his sharpest insights as a vernacular modernist into the transpacific dimensions of global modernity in a story given the expressly translingual and neologistic title *Shanhai sareta otoko* (上海された男), or "The Shanghaied Man."

Based very loosely on Hasegawa's own experiences, the plot of this mystery yarn revolves around the misadventures of one Mori Tamekichi, a maverick hero who is obliged to flee authorities as the prime suspect in an overnight murder case. Though initially innocent, Tamekichi ironically becomes the murderer he is originally merely suspected of being. The story thus anticipates by some fifty years the use of a narrative device generally considered a hallmark of Western modernist and even postmodernist detective fiction as it thematizes the corrosive effects of transnational commerce and global modernity on traditional moral economies and regimes of cultural and national identity.[27] Even more significant, perhaps, the story adumbrates its own brand of modernist formal disruption via "Shanghai" by incorporating through various plot devices both English and even Morse code into the very semiotic fabric of the text.

From the outset of the story, the protagonist finds himself alienated from his fellow Japanese citizens due to his own international experiences:

> Tamekichi heard the man was a third-rank engine boiler back in port after working the SS Toyo'oka, a transport ship that plied local waters. The two men had nothing in common because Tamekichi was a deckhand who specialized in long distance voyages. Perhaps that explained why he decided not to worry when the man continued to groan through the night. (291)

Longing to get back to the freedom of the ocean on board a ship, Tamekichi is stymied by the suspicions of a police officer who wants to question him in connection with the disappearance of his groaning roommate from the seaman's inn the previous night.

As he is being taken to the police station, Tamekichi decides to become a fugitive in a bold attempt to return to the deterritorialized state of the sea. Explaining this seemingly irrational desire actually to violate the law while merely under suspicion, the narrative rather pointedly resorts to the clichéd metaphor of maternity in an effort to validate a new logic of identity formation: "The sea was calling him. Tamekichi had left Naoetsu Bay in Niigata at the age of nine. He had sailed under flags from all over the world for twenty-some years. The sea was his home. It was like the bosom of a loving mother" (295).

Rather than being anchored to the site of his nativity, Tamekichi develops an "oceanic" sense of himself based on his extensive transpacific experience on different commercial vessels. Like the protagonist, these ships are formally registered under a particular national affiliation; but in reality, they conduct their trade on a global stage, only nominally observing the limits of national boundaries. To employ the familiar terminology of canonical European modernism, Tamekichi becomes a kind of oceangoing cosmopolitan, a "thalassapolitan," if you will.

Indeed, these experiences have not only broadened his horizons. They have also honed his perceptions and augmented his abilities. In a remarkably prescient detail that seems to anticipate the linguistic infrastructure of contemporary global commerce, one of those augmented abilities turns out to be knowledge of English. Indeed, this seemingly incidental fact of Tamekichi's character history not only plays a crucial role in the continuation of the plot; it also serves to call attention to the very semiotic coding of the story itself. It does so by thematically displacing Japanese from its presumed centrality as the standard for universal communication, a position implied by its role as the operative language of the text. The first manifestations of this displacement happen after Tamekichi flees authorities and forces his way on board the foreign ship. Importantly, he does so by way of a feat that the text goes to the trouble of noting explicitly:

> It was Tamekichi's fluent English that saved him. Moreover, he spoke a brand of English understood the world over only by men who sail the seas. He knew all the slang that sailors used. (295)

The ship that Tamekichi boards to escape the authorities neatly condenses into one polyvalent image global flows of culture, labor, and capital unmoored from any single national authority or interest. Not only does this "Norwegian" "tramp steamer" ironically boast the name of a famous character from Russian literature; it also charts an expressly transpacific itinerary in the service of global capital, which communicates its directives via the wonders of modern technology. Starting in Kobe, the ship plans to take on "a load of guano at Thursday Island" and from there set sail for "Hawai'i," subsequently heading "for Grace Harbor" to "take on a supply of lumber" before heading to the Klondike. The *Viktor Karenina* "was ready to go anywhere in the world—even at the behest of a telegram" (297).

Thus apparently escaping the short arm of Japanese law enforcement, Tamekichi enters into a semihallucinatory state wherein his grasp on both reality and morality becomes tenuous: "he found himself caught in a perverse state of mind in which he truly believed he had committed the crime of which he was accused" (298). Tamekichi continues to follow this unusual train of thought, soon falling asleep to the low-pitched "lullaby" of the ship's propeller. Not yet completely beyond the reach of the law, however, he awakes to find that the ship has been called back to port in Kobe, with officers due to arrive on board any minute to retrieve him. In an apparent display of occupational solidarity, one that underscores a shared disregard for existing legal protocols and national regimes of authority, the first mate offers to hide Tamekichi. In another revealing plot detail, the "Norwegian" first mate summons "Midnight Boston" from the bowels of the ship, and "pretty soon, a black man, who was nearly seven feet tall, came lumbering into the room with an oily rag in his hand" (299). Affirming a specifically transpacific racial economy among the international crew, this obviously stereotypical figure speaks somewhat comically (not to mention illogically) in perfectly idiomatic Japanese: "Get on top of the donkey boiler and crawl down into the space by the watertight bulkhead. You've no time to lose" (300). Significantly, the original text employs the parallel Rubi script to "spell out" the technical term 停泊用釜 as ドンキ・ボイラア.

Waiting out the police search in this cramped space, Tamekichi is surprised by "a sound . . . like someone scratching a piece of metal" (300). He listens further:

> Tap, tap, tap, scraaatch, scratch [given in Japanese hiragana onomatopoeia].
> All of a sudden, Tamekichi understood what he was hearing. It had to be the telegraphic code of the wireless, the universal ABC code by which every nation communicated. (300)

At this climactic recognition, the narrative again asserts the primacy of English as a medium of global exchange and the de facto linguistic standard for modern communication technologies like Morse code. This time, however, the very semiosis of the text expands. Tamekichi responds to the SOS distress signal tapped from within the boiler; and the exchange that ensues between the two sailors exhibits a modernist verbal density and linguistic range, though admittedly one that appears aimed more at popular adventure than cultural diagnosis or critique:

> "W-H-A-T I-S T-H-E M-A-T-T-E-R? . . ."
> Tap, scraaatch, tap, tap, tap, scraaatch.
> "S-H-A-N-G-H-A-I . . . ," came the reply.
> Shanghai?
> "W-H-A-T I-S T-H-A-T?" He tapped on the pipe again.
> "H-A-V-E B-E-E-N S-H-A-N-G-H-A-I-E-D."
> Shanghaied?! To kidnap a man on the street by force. To cart him off to a ship. And once the ship left port and there was no more contact with land, to make him work at hard labor. (301)

The kidnap victim imprisoned in the donkey boiler turns out to be none other than "Shintaro Sakamoto—the man [Tamekichi] was supposed to have murdered" (301). But rather than focus on the relief and joy brought on by this exculpatory discovery, Tamekichi feels "enraged" (無性に怒らせた). And in a fit of homicidal mania, he ends up actually murdering Shintaro, killing him with the very penknife that had earlier been used as damning circumstantial evidence in the original investigation. Thus ironically departing from the narrative formulas of the conventional detective story, "The Shanghaied Man" does not conclude with the restoration of social order through the application of justice. Rather, in a carefully measured and dispassionately voiced coda that delicately counterpoises the different identities at play and inverts the traditional values of the genre through nonjudgment, the story ends on a morally ambiguous note. Despite the various crimes committed (both real and imagined), the closing sentence formulaically proclaims the subsequent adherence to an extranational code of conduct on the part of the two main characters that appears finally to justify their subsequent respective fates:

> Following the time-honored custom that is the unwritten code among seamen the world over, neither Sakamoto Shintaro the "shanghaied man" nor Sakamoto Shinataro "the man who shanghaied himself" ever stepped foot on land again. (302)

Like Mu Shi Ying's experimental "The Shanghai Foxtrot (a Fragment)" or Yokomitsu Ri'ichi's canonical novel *Shanghai*, Tani Jōji's popular mystery story "The Shanghaied Man" undertakes to represent the manifold disruptions of global modernity via "Shanghai." It does so, notably, by hijacking the term *to shanghai* and employing it not as a topos but as a translingual verbal token that signifies the global spread of modernity via specifically transpacific flows of labor, capital, and culture as well as the disruptive effects of these flows on established regimes of personal and national identity. As the story helpfully explains to its Japanese readers, the meaning of this neologism based on the name of the Chinese city refers directly to extralegal human trafficking around and across the economic geography of the Pacific Ocean. In fact, though the story does not bother to explain it, the etymology of the neologism itself charts an expressly transpacific course of emergence. According to the *OED*, "to shanghai" originated as a term of American nautical slang, specifically meaning "to drug or otherwise render insensible, and ship on board a vessel wanting hands." For the initial appearance of the word, the *OED* cites a usage from 1872 by the apparently Dutch observer Schele De Vere, which is collected in his volume *Americanisms*: "And before that time they would have been drugged, shanghaied, and taken away from all means of making complaint" (347). Interestingly, elsewhere in the volume, another statement confirms the vision put forth in "The Shanghaied Man" of the sailor as transnational vernacular modernist, a figure who has discovered the terms of a truly global idiom: "the sailor is emphatically a cosmopolitan, and his speech the same in every harbor of the world" (341).

■ COMPLETING THE TRANSPACIFIC CIRCUIT: SHANGHAI (SHENANIGANS) SLIGHT RETURN

Having followed the historical transpacific itinerary of "Shanghai" as topos, figure, and polylingual verbal sign for the spread of global modernity and its effects, we are now perhaps better positioned to find in Yau's "Shanghai Shenanigans" something more than simply an act of refusal undertaken through a stuttering sequence of opaque images that dramatizes the contradictory experience of an American ethnic subjectivity. Coming back full circle, we can now expand our interpretive horizons beyond the physical, cultural, and conceptual boundaries of the domestic United States and instead consider this poem in light of a deeper historical archive of global modernist literary production from across the cultural terrain of the Pacific Ocean. I have already observed the striking resemblance between the images of Yau's initial couplet and the "bright moon" and "ashen sprawl" that appear in the famous opening scene of Mu Shiying's "Shanghai Foxtrot." Without any possibility of direct influence, by itself this resemblance might simply be written off as a happy, but isolated, coincidence. Yet, as I mentioned earlier, Yau's poem in its own fashion and moment also reiterates the interest shared by both Mu and Yokomitsu Ri'ichi in the visual aesthetics of film as an expressly modern medium in their respective New Sensationist literary treatments of "Shanghai" and its various complexities. In light of these prior achievements, Yau's own fragmented presentation of Orientalist visual and narrative absurdities not only expresses his individual critique of Hollywood racism during the 1930s–50s in the United States. Such presentation also therewith reflects and invites reflection on the historical durability and global reach of the *association* between "Shanghai" as a topos, figure, and verbal token with the various technologies of modernity. From this angle, Yau's lines call attention to the range and variety of verbally inventive "shenanigans" (another multivalent American neologism of obscure nineteenth-century origin) that "Shanghai" has inspired, as well as undergone, over the history of its transpacific circulation as a polyglot site, sign, and signifier.

Building on this foundation, we might now also find in the resonance between the Morse code that plays such an important role and receives such elaborate textual attention in "The Shanghaied Man" and the mention of "phone conversations" in the second stanza of Yau's poem additional evidence of a common concern with the technological infrastructure of global modernity. For both of these communications technologies are not only unmistakably rooted in modernity; as with film, each also at once directly facilitates and arguably marks a specific historical stage in its global propagation. We might further find another such echo in the similarity between the migrant sailor protagonist of Hasegawa's story and the "nomad" mentioned in the third stanza as paired avatars of the "transpacific" human migration that quite literally underwrites these diverse feats of global modernist literary production from China, Japan, and the United States.

In addition to its historical significance as modern technology, "phone conversations" evokes the parlor game Phone Call, which helps to clarify the particular type of "shenanigan" (in the sense of "prank" or "exhibition of high spirits") being perpetrated here. This latent allusion in turn offers at least some kind of internal rationale for the fragmentary repetition that structures the poem, which, as I have already discussed, lacks any sustained narrative or an obvious speaking subject. In the parlor game, accidental variations and modifications upon an original phrase accumulate through a relay of typically whispered verbal transmissions. The amusement lies in the magnitude of transformation wrought upon the original phrase or statement, which frequently has been made unrecognizable by the final turn. Comparably, in Yau's poem, the closing phrase or word of each successive couplet repeats as the opening of the next. But instead of continuing or developing any sustained narrative line, each successive couplet initiates its own scenario that ends with equal abruptness, thus creating the effect of repetition without continuity. In doing so, the poem seems to dramatize the intrinsic instability, and hence mobility, of words as verbal tokens that migrate through and across different grammatical functions and, by extension, even languages, "Shanghai" and its transpacific etymology in English being a particularly vivid example. We can now perhaps understand the resulting crisscross pattern generated by the staggered repetition of phrases in "Shanghai Shenanigans" as a structural registration of the historical circulation of material, human, and cultural capital around the Pacific Ocean that has been crucial to origins of the translingual term "Shanghai" and that has enabled the global spread of modernity. Much more than simply a willful gesture of refusal, however meaningful or evocative of ethnic identity, Yau's poem participates in and draws attention to a long-standing conversation among writers from across the Pacific Ocean about "Shanghai" (as figure, sign, and topos) and the expressly transpacific routes of global modernity.

Steven Yao is Edmund A. LeFevre Professor of Literature at Hamilton College in Clinton, New York. He is the author of *Translation and the Languages of Modernism: Gender, Politics, Language* (2002) and *Foreign Accents: Chinese American Verse from Exclusion to Postethnicity* (2010). He is also coeditor of *Sinographies: Writing China* (2007) as well as *Pacific Rim Modernisms* (2009) and *Ezra Pound and Education* (2012).

■ NOTES

1. The full entry for "shenanigans" includes the following information: "Shenanigan, n. Etymology: Origin obscure. orig. U.S. Trickery, skullduggery, machination, intrigue; teasing, 'kidding,' nonsense; (usu. *pl.*) a plot, a trick, a prank, an exhibition of high spirits, a carry-on."

2. In fact, it is only fairly recently that Yau's work has been discussed in any focused or sustained way, much less in relation to the category of "Asian American literature." For such discussions, see Park (2008), Yu (2009), Yao (2010), Jeon (2012), and Wang (2013).

3. For a very interesting recent effort to recuperate the critical potential of realism, see Esty and Lye (2012).

4. In subsequent poems, Yau has invoked "Shanghai" as part of his own interrogation and critique of testimonial poetics based on the notion of individual identity and biological descent, such as in "Autobiography in Red and Yellow" from *Borrowed Love Poems* (Yau 2002) or the introduction to *Paradiso Diaspora* (Yau 2006).

5. Scholars exploring the logic and ideology of the "Pacific Rim" include Chris Connery, Arif Dirlik, and Rob Wilson, among others. Scholars of later nineteenth- and early-twentieth-century Western Orientalism include Chris Bush, Eric Hayot, Colleen Lye, and R. John Williams (2014).

6. At least since the middle of the nineteenth century, these multidirectional negotiations have spanned the full range from missionary evangelism to formal and informal migration among different Pacific nations to imperial expansion to total war to, most recently, "cooperative" trade and cultural exchange.

7. See, e.g., the "Hollywood Asians" section of *Forbidden Entries* (Yau 1996), which contains poems such as "Peter Lorre Improvises Mr. Moto's Monologue," "Peter Lorre Dreams He Is the Third Reincarnation of a Geisha," and "Peter Lorre Confesses His Desire to Be a Poet."

8. Films listed on IMDb at http://www.imdb.com/find?q=shanghai &s=tt.

9. For more on Yau's use of surrealism, see Leong (2014).

10. Other poems in this section include the sequence of poems voiced in the persona renowned actor Peter Lorre. See *Forbidden Entries* (Yau 1996, 77–91). For a discussion of these poems and others reflecting Yau's critique of Hollywood's Orientalist racism, see Jeon (2012).

11. Hollywood's own figurative and repeated passage through "Shanghai" during its golden era takes place alongside other American transpacific engagements. Most notoriously, perhaps, Ezra Pound's interest in Confucian texts at this time stands out in the literary realm as a comparable instance of a generative modernist Orientalism.

12. Sean Macdonald's translation was the first appearance of this text in English. For the sake of convenient discussion here, I quote this text. For the original text in Chinese, see Mu Shiying's "上海的狐步舞" in the November 1932 number of the Chinese literary journal 现代 *(Xiandai),* or *Les Contemporains,* as they rendered it at the time.

13. For a discussion of Japan's mediating role in the spread of ideas about modernity in Asia, especially literary modernism, see Liu (1995).

14. Other writers associated with this literary school or movement include Liu Na'ou, Tao Jingsun, and Guo Jianying. For more on this movement, see Shih (2001, 257–68).

15. An air of mystery continues to surround the circumstances and reasons for Mu's assassination. For more on Mu Shiying and his short but eventful life and career, see Shih (2001, 306–16). Also see Zhang (2006).

16. As Lippit (2002, 85) discusses, several Japanese writers had already written about "Shanghai as Asia's most cosmopolitan city." For further discussion, see 85–87.

17. Other Japanese writers connected with this brief movement include the solidly canonical figures Kawabata Yasunari and Kataoka Teppei.

18. In his own time, Mu was referred to as the "Chinese Yokomitsu Ri'ichi."

19. See, e.g., Washburn in his "Translator's Postscript" (Yokomitsu and Washburn 2001, 232) as well as Lippit (2002, 254).

20. In a more expansive definition of *kankaku,* or "Sensation," Yokomitsu elaborates: "The general concept I call Sensation [*kankaku*] refers to the surface signs [or symbols, *hyōchō*] of perception; it refers to the intuitive triggering mechanism [*shkuhatsubutsu*] of subjectivity that strips away the external aspects of nature and merges with an object. . . . The concept of Sensation as it is used in literature is, to simplify, perception transformed to surface sign." As cited in Yokomitsu and Washburn (2001, 223).

21. Given Yau's own stated linguistic abilities, it is implausible that he has read Mu Shiying or Yokomitsu Ri'ichi, or, for that matter, Tani Jōji.

22. Most relevant here are the historical events referred to as the Manchurian Incident of 1931 and the Shanghai Incident of 1932.

23. Among others, see Shih (2001, 257–62) and Lippit (2002, 83–98).

24. Of course, this formulation necessarily simplifies things somewhat. In addition to its renowned formalist experimentalism in the opening scene, Yokomitsu's *Shanghai,* as Donald Keene (as cited in Lippit 2002, 83) has observed, "seems to combine aspects of both proletarian literature and popular fiction." Though these modes developed in opposition and contrast to one another in the West, in Japan, all three arose together in nonidentical opposition to classical Japanese literary values.

25. Notoriously, for example, the U.S. Congress initially passed the Chinese Exclusion Act in 1882. Similarly, the Gentleman's Agreement negotiated between the Japanese and American governments formalized the interests of both parties in preventing the emigration of "laborers" from Japan to the United States.

26. For more on Tani Jōji, see Ōmori (2002; 2004).

27. For example, American postmodern detective fiction writers employing this trope include Paul Auster and others.

▓ WORKS CITED

De Vere, M. Schele. 1872. *Americanisms: The English of the New World.* New York: Charles Scribner.

Esty, Jed, and Colleen Lye. 2012. "Peripheral Realisms Now." *Modern Language Quarterly* 73, no. 3: 269–88.

Foster, Edward. 1990. "An Interview with John Yau." *Talisman* 5 (1990): 31–50.

Hansen, Adam, and Belinda Kong. 2009. "Shanghai Biopolitans: Wartime Colonial Cosmopolis in Eileen Chang's *Love in a Fallen City* and J. G. Ballard's *Empire of the Sun.*" *Journal of Narrative Theory* 39, no. 3: 280–304.

Hansen, Miriam Bratu. 2000. "Fallen Women, Rising Stars, New Horizons: Shanghai Silent Film as Vernacular Modernism." *Film Quarterly* 54, no. 1: 10–22.

Hoskins, Janet, and Viet Thanh Nguyen, eds. 2014. *Transpacific Studies: Framing an Emerging Field.* Honolulu: University of Hawai'i Press.

Huang, Yunte. 2002. *Transpacific Displacement: Ethnography, Translation, and Intertextual Travel in Twentieth-Century American Literature.* Berkeley: University of California Press.

———. 2008. *Transpacific Imaginations: History, Literature, Counterpoetics.* Cambridge, Mass.: Harvard University Press.

Jeon, Joseph Jonghyun. 2012. *Racial Things, Racial Forms: Objecthood in*

Avant-Garde Asian American Poetry. Iowa City: University of Iowa Press.

Knight, Deirdre Sabina. 2003. "Shanghai Cosmopolitan: Class, Gender and Cultural Citizenship in Weihui's *Shanghai Babe*." *Journal of Contemporary China* 12, no. 37: 639–53.

Lee, Leo Ou-fan. 1999. *Shanghai Modern: The Flowering of a New Urban Culture in China, 1930–1945*. Cambridge, Mass.: Harvard University Press.

Leong, Michael. 2014. "Neo-Surrealism's Forked Tongue: Reflections on the Dramatic Monologue, Politics, and Community in the Recent Poetry of Will Alexander and John Yau." *Contemporary Literature* 55, no. 3: 501–33.

Lippit, Seiji M. 2002. *Topographies of Japanese Modernism*. New York: Columbia University Press.

Liu, Lydia H. 1995. *Translingual Practice: Literature, National Culture, and Translated Modernity-China, 1900–1937*. Palo Alto, Calif.: Stanford University Press.

Lowe, Lisa. 2012. "The Trans-Pacific Migrant and Area Studies." In *The Trans-Pacific Imagination: Rethinking Boundary, Culture and Society*, edited by Naoki Sakai and Hyon Joo Yoo, 61–74. Singapore: World Scientific.

Macdonald, Sean. 2004. "The Shanghai Foxtrot (a Fragment) by Mu Shiying." *Modernism/modernity* 11, no. 4: 797–807.

Mu, Shiying. 1932. "Shanghai De Hubuwu (Yige Duanpian)" (Shanghai Foxtrot—a Fragment). *Xiandai (Les Contemporains)* 2, no. 1: 112—20.

Ōmori, Kyoko. 2002. "Merican-Jap and Modernity: Tani Jōji's Popular Negotiation of the Foreign." *Proceedings of the Association for Japanese Literary Studies* 3: 83–96.

———. 2004. "Shinseinen, the Contract, and Vernacular Modernism in Japan." *Proceedings of the Association for Japanese Literary Studies* 5: 153–65.

Park, Josephine Nock-Hee. 2008. *Apparitions of Asia: Modernist Form and Asian American Poetics*. Oxford: Oxford University Press.

Sakai, Naoki, and Hyon Joo Yoo, eds. 2012. Introduction to *The Trans-Pacific Imagination: Rethinking Boundary, Culture and Society*. Singapore: World Scientific.

Shih, Shu-mei. 2001. *The Lure of the Modern: Writing Modernism in Semicolonial China, 1917–1937*. Berkeley: University of California Press.

Stalling, Jonathan. 2010. *Poetics of Emptiness: Transformations of Asian Thought in American Poetry*. New York: Fordham University Press.

Tani, Jōji. 1925. "Shanhai Sareta Otoko." *Shinseinen* 6, no. 5: 100–111.

———. 2005. "The Shanghaied Man" (Shanhai sareta otoko). Translated by Kyoko Ōmori. In *The Columbia Anthology of Modern Japanese Literature*, vol. 1, edited by J. Thomas Rimer and Van C. Gessel, 528–39. New York: Columbia University Press.

Wang, Dorothy J. 2013. *Thinking Its Presence: Form, Race, and Subjectivity in Contemporary Asian American Poetry.* Palo Alto, Calif.: Stanford University Press.

Williams, R. John. 2014. *The Buddha in the Machine: Art, Technology, and the Meeting of East and West.* New Haven: Yale University Press.

Yao, Steven G. 2010. *Foreign Accents: Chinese American Verse from Exclusion to Postethnicity.* Oxford: Oxford University Press.

Yau, John. 1981. *Broken Off by the Music.* Providence, R.I.: Burning Deck.

———. 1989–94. *Radiant Silhouette: New and Selected Work, 1974–1988.* Santa Rosa, Calif.: Black Sparrow Press.

———. 1996. *Forbidden Entries.* Santa Rosa, Calif.: Black Sparrow Press.

———. 2002. *Borrowed Love Poems.* New York: Penguin.

———. 2006. *Paradiso Diaspora.* New York: Penguin.

Yokomitsu, Ri'ichi, and Dennis C. Washburn. 2001. *Shanghai: A Novel.* Ann Arbor: Center for Japanese Studies, University of Michigan.

Yu, Timothy. 2009. *Race and the Avant-Garde: Experimental and Asian American Poetry since 1965.* Palo Alto, Calif.: Stanford University Press.

Zhang, Yingjin. 1999. *Cinema and Urban Culture in Shanghai, 1922–1943.* Palo Alto, Calif.: Stanford University Press.

———. 2006. "Mu Shiying." In *Chinese Fiction Writers, 1900–1949,* edited by Thomas Moran, 178–82. Detroit, Mich.: Thomson Gale.

JERRY WON LEE

Semioscapes, Unbanality, and the Reinvention of Nationness: Global Korea as Nation-Space

Communities are to be distinguished, not by their falsity/genuineness, but by the style in which they are imagined.
  —Benedict Anderson (1936–2015)

I BEGIN THIS ESSAY by asking two different questions: "Where is Korea?" and "Where is Koreanness?" The distinction I draw between "Korea" and "Koreanness," of course, is inspired by the dubious usage of "nationness" found frequently in prominent scholarly writings from a variety of disciplines. Early in Benedict Anderson's (1991, 3) ubiquitous *Imagined Communities,* he writes that "*nation-ness* is the most universally legitimate value in the political life of our time" (emphasis added). Arjun Appadurai (1996, 189) writes, in his equally influential work *Modernity at Large,* that the "nation-state conducts throughout its territories the bizarrely contradictory project of creating a flat, contiguous, and homogeneous space of *nationness*" (emphasis added). Anderson, in a book about "nationalism," uses *nationness* to reflect the appeal of a particular form of collective identification achieved through the political rubric of the nation-state. Appadurai, in a book that confronts the very possibility of the nation-state in an era of globalization, uses *nationness* to emphasize that the political project of nationalism, in trying to establish a collective community identity by consolidating something so nebulous as nationness, was bound to fail from the start. Nationness, in any case, appears not to encapsulate the ontological certainty associated with the "nation" but suggests something otherwise.

To return to the distinction between "Korea" and "Koreanness," the first question is likely to be interpreted as a geographic question, engendering responses indicating that Korea is, obviously, in East Asia.[1] The second question—"Where is Koreanness?"—is perhaps less straightforward. Many respondents would likely draw their attention to the *-ness*, which, as a suffix, evokes a certain degree of proximity; it suggests a feeling, residue, shadow, or approximation of "Korea." Rachel Miyung Joo (2012), for instance, uses the expression "global Koreanness" to describe a constellation of mass-mediated nationalist sentiment resulting from the *segyehwa*, or globalization, of Korean culture.[2] In Joo's work, it is the dispersal of "Korea" into a global space of approximation that compels the usage of "Koreanness." As many may remember, arguably among the most prominent instances of global Koreanness in recent memory occurred during the 2002 FIFA World Cup, cohosted by Korea and Japan. In Los Angeles, home of one of the largest Koreatowns in the world, thousands of fans gathered at odd hours of the morning, owing to the sixteen-hour time difference between Los Angeles and the host countries, to cheer for the Korean football team, which made a historic run to the semifinals, far exceeding even the most idealistic of expectations. Dressed in red, the supporters of the Korean football team, known affectionately as the "Red Devils," swarmed in the streets to the point that it could be said that Los Angeles approached a supersaturation of Koreanness, as it were.

Through phenomena such as this, it has become quite evident that "Koreanness" can be found not only within the Korean peninsula per se but beyond in any number of global spaces. Koreanness is to be found, perhaps most prominently, in the diasporic Korean communities, such as Los Angeles, but that is not to discount the Korean communities in cities such as Osaka, Tokyo, Beijing, Shanghai, Chicago, and New York. But this essay is not merely a report on the different Koreatowns around the world. Furthermore, I am not aiming to reiterate the increasingly evident notion that "Koreans in the world increasingly problematize the distinction between diaspora and homeland" (Park and Lo 2012, 160). The focus of this essay is rather an examination of the possibility that "Koreanness" is not a dilution of Korea insofar as the non-Korean can be, at times, more Korean than Korea itself. This essay aims to account for this possibility by understanding how diasporic communities continually reinvent nationness beyond the nation-state through a specific examination of the deployment and circulation of symbolic resources in the public space of Koreatowns that sustain and re-produce ideological ties to an originary "homeland." I direct us to the possibility that what makes the global Koreatown is not the absence or lack of Koreanness but the

singular conspicuousness, or unbanality, of Koreanness achieved through
material reconfigurations of space in a variety of sites across Asia and
North America.[3] By understanding how the non-Korean is rendered as
simultaneously more and less Korean than Korea itself, this essay considers how national identification occurs not only within the nation-state
but across, as I argue, the nation-space.

■ THEORIZING SEMIOSCAPES

Linguistic landscape, an expression developed by Rodrigue Landry and
Richard Bourhis (1997), refers to the ethnographic study of public language
artifacts found in a particular urban area. Adam Jaworski and Crispin
Thurlow (2010), in contrast, introduce the expression *semiotic landscape*
as an alternative, emphasizing that it is not purely "linguistic" features
but also a wide range of semiotic resources that compose space. Yet the
primary limitation to extant research has been the premise of examining linguistic and semiotic resources *in place,* a geographically designated
region, whether a distinct city or even a distinct country. I am mindful of
Ron Scollon and Suzie Wong Scollon's (2003, 12) notion of geosemiotics,
which offers "an integrative view of . . . multiple semiotic systems which
together form the meanings which we call place." However, the presumed
materiality of place, understood as a social category but ultimately as a
physically bound geographic area, thus becomes a methodological quan-
dary, because one place, it would seem, must be studied in isolation from,
or even in comparison to, another place.

The concept of the *semioscape* is, as I argue, more useful for understanding the nuances and complexities of the co-constitutive materialities of
semiosis and the places to which such semiosis is ostensibly bound.[4] The
usage of *-scape,* of course, draws from Appadurai's (1996) ambitious effort
to think beyond the very notion of territory and the spatial limitations
of territoriality. Appadurai describes five "dimensions of global cultural
flow" to account for the intensified movement of social practice in the
context of globalization: ethnoscapes (flows of people), mediascapes
(flows of information/media), technoscapes (flows of technologies), fi-
nancescapes (flows of money), and ideoscapes (flows of ideologies and
knowledges) (33–36). While the nation-state continues to reign as the
dominant political apparatus for the regulation of peoples across the
globe, because of the movement of peoples, information, technologies,
capital, and ideologies, we bear witness to the reality that aspects of the
nation, such as political allegiances, ideological commitments, traditions, and languages, are migrating rather than operating within fixed
territories of the state.

Implicit in Appadurai's theory of globalization is the role of language in the acceleration of cultural flows across various scapes. Indeed, Appadurai is critiquing the traditional theories of nationalism that point to the importance of ostensibly "natural facts," such as "language, blood, soil, and race," in the maintenance of the nation-form (161). To return to Anderson (1991) once again, it was language, it is argued, particularly in the development of print capitalism, that facilitated the collective imaginations of emergent nation forms. According to Anderson, print discourses (such as newspapers and novels) made it possible for speakers of different dialects within a language to communicate with one another through a relatively stable text in print form. While spoken dialects might have been mutually incomprehensible, print languages enabled a collective consciousness of others who constituted the nation, thus serving as the "embryo of the nationally imagined community" (44). Today, however, the intensified migration of language resources beyond national borders, resulting in dynamic new forms, conventions, and practices, demands a fundamental reconsideration of the very notion of "language" and the derivative assumptions surrounding the territorial boundedness of language. As Monica Heller (2007, 343) writes, "as soon as we start looking closely at real people in real places, we see movement. We see languages turning up in unexpected places, and not turning up where we expect them to be. We also see them taking unexpected forms." And the fact that we still view unexpected encounters with language as such suggests that we still have not come to terms with viewing linguistic mobility as the norm (Pennycook 2012). It additionally suggests an ongoing commitment to an epistemology grounded in the logics of the nation-state. It has been argued repeatedly that language has been crucial to the production of the contemporary nation-state, as acknowledged by not only Anderson but others ranging from Johann Gottfried Herder (1967) to Pierre Bourdieu (1991). But the question that follows is this: what happens to nationness when language resources, as highly mobile units of communication, continue to emerge outside the nation-state, to the extent that encounters with such resources are no longer "unexpected"? And what do we make of the continued insistence on attempting to understand languages *in* place, as is all too common?

I therefore have two distinct but also interrelated objectives in developing the idea of the semioscape. First, the study of linguistic landscapes, or even under the progressive moniker of semiotic landscape, is profoundly limited in that it is bound to the spatiomaterial limitations of physical territory. In attending to the material reconfiguration of space through linguistic and semiotic resources, research continues to treat communities as bound to a particular place. Hence diasporic communities tend to be readily distinguished from their "original" counterparts, such as Koreatown from Korea, reflecting a sheer inability or unwillingness to transcend the epistemic and ontological limitations of the nation-state ideal in any meaningful way. Of course, Appadurai (2001) has famously denounced traditional area studies approaches that treat geographies as fixed and stable, proposing instead the notion of "process geographies." Instead of analyzing "trait" geographies, which assumes that certain areas "rely on some sort of trait list—of values, languages, material practices, ecological adaptations, marriage patterns, and the like," Appadurai argues for area studies "based on process geographies[, which] sees significant areas of human organization as precipitates of various kinds of action, interaction, and motion—trade, travel, pilgrimage, warfare, proselytization, colonization, exile, and the like. These geographies are necessarily large scale and shifting, and their changes highlight variable congeries of language, history, and material life" (7–8). Building on the notion of process geographies, I am proposing that the ways in which everyday actors use language and semiotic resources to reconfigure space disrupt the very boundedness of communities to politically defined territories. Semiosis, in other words, constitutes a cultural scape across which nationness is reproduced and redefined.

The second reason for developing the concept of semioscape is perhaps more symbolic: by merging the "semiotic" and "landscape," I wish to emphasize their necessary inextricability. As Pennycook (2010) argues, developing Michel de Certeau's (1984) notion of "walking in the city" as a means of spatial production, language, somewhat paradoxically, reconstitutes the localities in which it is practiced. Pennycook adds that "local language practice . . . does not simply occur in time and space; time and space are part of the doing, and indeed are produced in the practice" (56). I propose that the very notion of the linguistic production of space has profound implications for how we understand where and how nationness occurs. The feasibility of Pennycook's argument lies in its preoccupation with culture more generally, which is a necessarily fluid concept that, while never homogeneous, and oftentimes bound to geographic regions, is not necessarily bound to territory by its nature. The nation, on the other hand, is a discursive formation that emerges in tandem with, if not subsequent to, rather than anterior to, the political doctrine of nationalism (Calhoun 2007). As such, regardless of whether we are referring to ethnic or civic nationalism, and regardless of whether the distinction between the two is plausible (see Smith 1991), the very discourse of nationalism is necessarily fixated on the occupation of a

predefined territory. In fact, to conceive of a nation-state without a pre-
determined territory would seem paradoxical. It thus would follow that
whatever social practices and cultural phenomena emerge and exist out
of the predefined territory are things only approximately national. Semioscapes thus enable us to consider how and where nationness occurs across
global space in "multiple, simultaneous origins of locality" (Pennycook
2010, 86). Yet the emergence of nationness in semioscapes, constitutive of
simultaneous origins of locality, is not a phenomenon conceivable within
the epistemological metrics of the nation-state, as I will consider in the
following pages.

■ POSTNATIONAL KOREA

There was perhaps a time when the ethnic enclave was a place for migrants
from Korea and others who identify, to varying degrees, as "Korean," to
establish communities, or what John Lie (2008, 8) terms an "enclave
economy," based on a shared national heritage outside the nation-state.
Korean communities around the world have in fact provided a sense of
home for those who had left Korea for various reasons, whether to escape
persecution during Japanese colonial occupation or the turmoil of the
Korean War, because of political oppression during the Park Chung-hee
authoritarian regime, or owing to the precariousness of the financial crisis in the late twentieth century. Today, the global presence of people of
Korean heritage is evident in the establishment of prominent Koreatowns
in major cities around the globe. These communities are necessarily postnational in that they transcend the very paradigm of nationalism, which
as a political doctrine aspires to consolidate a people within a predefined
territory and ideological matrix. Scholars such as Yasemin Soysal (1994)
and Étienne Balibar (2004) have used the expression *postnational* to refer
to forms of political belonging that counteract the ideological expectations of the nation-state. Yet, by invoking the notion of postnational to
describe the emergence of global Koreatowns, I of course do not mean
to suggest that the national is no longer relevant, that it has somehow
been transcended by the macroprocesses of globalization or that official
criteria of state recognition, including documents ranging from passports
to birth certificates, have been rendered obsolete. Indeed, the national
remains central to social belonging in some communities to the extent
that, not only is the national inflected in various everyday social practices,
but also that nationness seems to emerge, in some cases at least, more
prominently than it does in the ostensibly originary point of Korea.

The emergence of Korean nationness in these postnational spaces,
or the nation-space, as I term it, can be attributed to a simultaneous

interplay of both official (state originated) and vernacular (popular, everyday) discourses of social identification. As has been established in the scholarly literature of nationalism, it is scarcely ever the individuals themselves who actively choose to maintain an allegiance to the nation-state. Rather, varying degrees of ideological engineering by state functionaries work to coalesce individuals into identifying with the nation-state ideal. Instructive is Eric Hobsbawm's (1990, 44) oft-referenced anecdote of post-Risorgimento Italy: "In the days of the Mazzini it did not matter that, for the great bulk of Italians, the Risorgimento did not exist so that, as Massimo d'Azeglio admitted in the famous phrase: 'We have made Italy, now we have to make Italians.'"[5] Hobsbawm's point is to trouble the commonsense assumption that the nation-state, as an ostensibly a priori category of political identification, produces the sentiment and desire to belong; rather, the nation-state itself hinges on the sentiment of nationalism itself. That is to say, put as succinctly as possible, "nations do not make states and nationalisms but the other way around" (Hobsbawm 1990, 10). Such a realization, I argue, is crucial to understanding how national sentiment can thrive in diasporic contexts even when unhinged from the ideological groundings of the state. Why, for instance, does an individual with ancestral ties to a national imaginary but no political relation (no citizenship by right of birth within the national territory, otherwise known as the principle of *ius soli*), no linguistic affinity (improficient in the respective language(s), whether the actual official language or a de facto national language), and no physical relation (does not reside in the country and may not have even visited the homeland in question) choose to self-identify with this particular national imaginary? Some may argue that such a phenomenon is especially curious in the diasporic Korean context. Korean national identity, or *minjok*, is derivative of and grounded within a myth of ethnic homogeneity, or *ius sanguinis*, otherwise known as right of blood (Shin 2006). Indeed, because *minjok* can be translated as "nation" but also as "ethnicity" or "race," it might be argued that global identification as Korean is facilitated by an imagined shared bloodline. But the fact remains that diasporic Koreans have varying levels of commitment to their (largely imagined) ethnic ties, ranging from an overzealous conviction of Koreanness to ambivalence or even outright disavowal of ethnic identity, usually with aspirations of assimilating to a host culture.

In diasporic contexts, while there may be no central or "official" locus to disseminate state ideology, it should not be taken to mean that the political does not have a significant impact on shaping national identification, removed from the officially bounded geography of the nation-state.

In fact, to use the example of Koreanness, it may even be said that the sentiment of Koreanness thrives away from the Korean nation-state precisely because of the absence of the state. Indeed, the role of the political was especially influential in heightening national consciousness for Koreans abroad, as made keenly evident in the response, we may perhaps call it a telescopic response, to the Japanese occupation of the Korean peninsula. According to Richard S. Kim (2011), one of the most significant historical events for Koreans abroad occurred in San Francisco at the turn of the twentieth century: the murder of Durham White Stevens, a U.S. counselor to the Residency-General in Korea, by two Korean men. Stevens's controversial public remarks condoning the Japanese annexation of Korea coalesced San Francisco's Korean community that had hitherto been factioned. When the two men, Chun Myung-won and Chang In-whan, were charged with the murder of Stevens, Koreans from across California and other parts of the world, including Korea, Japan, Siberia, Manchuria, Mexico, and Hawai'i, contributed funds to their legal defense. The formation of this diasporic coalition, even if inspired by the advocacy of the justness and expediency of death, or perhaps necropolitical in its nature, to adapt Achille Mbembe's (2003) expression, points to the value of not only nebulous collectivities but the desire to engage in the political beyond and irrespective of the political rubric of the nation-state: to participate in a collectivity, as Koreans, despite a vexed relation to the Korean nation-state, which, to be sure, during Japanese occupation, was nonexistent, at least in a strictly "legal" sense.

The postnational engagement in the political outside of geopolitical territorial limits is evident also in various attempts to achieve official recognition by establishing designated Koreatowns. In Los Angeles, there are several monuments, such as a series of ornamental lampposts and other public signs, that resemiotize the space as a Koreatown (Figure 1). In New York, the Korean district is designated through signs that mark the area as "Korea Way," but this method is comparatively subtler, as such signage, even if clearly produced by the city, and thus officially authorized and placed, closely resembles an ordinary street sign (Figure 2). Like New York's Koreatown, the Koreatown of Chicago is, at least according to official designation, limited to a single street, Lawrence Avenue, accompanied by signage for "Honorary Seoul Drive" (Figure 3). Yet the Koreatowns of New York and Chicago are, of course, not bound to these officially designated streets alone, as one can readily find Korean establishments in neighboring streets. Another reflection of the disconnect between official designation and how individual communities make sense of the corresponding space is to be found in Dallas, where a mural reflects an "Asian Trade District,"

Figure 1. Artifacts in Los Angeles, such as this ornamental lamppost, resemiotize this space as a Koreatown. Photograph by the author.

Figure 2. The "Korea Way" sign in New York resembles an ordinary street sign. Photograph by the author.

Figure 3. Lawrence Avenue of Chicago's Koreatown features signage for an "Honorary Seoul Drive." Photograph by the author.

Figure 4. The Asian Trade District of Dallas is known as a de facto Koreatown. Photograph by the author.

even if it is known by locals to be a de facto Koreatown, corroborated by the presence of *taeguk,* the red and blue symbol found at the center of the South Korean flag on the aforementioned sign (Figure 4).

The Koreatown of Osaka, on the other hand, features a clear "entrance" in the form of two gates in succession that one must traverse, just meters apart from one another (Figure 5). Within the neighborhood itself, the close proximity of the establishments and the narrowness of one of the main streets, Miyuki Street, along with the official landmarks, which encourage the use of two main entrances rather than the side streets and alleys, produce a hermetically sealed space. It is known that Osaka was the site of Japan's earliest ethnic Korean ghetto dating to the early 1900s (Lie 2008), and the compressed space of Miyuki Street is a relic of the Korean community's historical isolation and alienation from the rest of Osaka. The contained space of Osaka's Koreatown is especially evident when juxtaposed with other Koreatowns in East Asia, such as those in Beijing, Shanghai, and even Tokyo, where there are no official designations to be found and the only indication of a Koreatown is the wealth of establishments featuring Korean-language signs. The aforementioned Osaka gates are especially useful for understanding the spatial dynamics of postnational Koreanness. The first gate does feature two *samsaeguitaeguk,* or three-colored *taeguk,* an alternate version of the more common two-colored *taeguk* of the South Korean flag. However, the semiotic Koreanness on both gates is minimalized as well. Significantly, "KOREA TOWN" is repeated on both gates in English rather than in Korean. Additionally, the non-English script that appears on both of these gates, 百済門 and 御幸通中央, alludes to the area's Japanese, not Korean, history. 百済門, or Baekje Gate, is named after the area formerly known as Paekche, where the gate currently stands.[6] 御幸通中央, or Miyuki Street Center, refers simply to the street's Japanese name. As Lie (2008, 85) argues, Japanese–Korean hybridity, unlike categories such as "Korean American" or "Korean Canadian," is not feasible because of the "essentialist mind-set" that prioritizes ethnically homogeneous national imaginaries of both Japan and Korea. Furthermore, as Jackie Jia Lou (2016, 130) notes, drawing on her analysis of Washington, D.C.'s, Chinatown, ethnic enclaves need to be understood as "ritual places," constructed not only through "planning discourse" and "material construction" but also in terms of "celebratory events and tourist spatial practices." Because the gates of Osaka's Koreatown are "official" Japanese discourses (established and endorsed by the city of Osaka), which in turn constitute tourist spatial practices in which readers of Japanese are the primary audience, it becomes difficult to interpret such space as discretely "Korean."

Figure 5. The main entrance to Osaka's Koreatown features two gates just a few meters apart. Photograph by the author.

In other Koreatowns, it could be said that performances of nationness hinge largely on "official" participation in the political. While Osaka's Koreatown suggests the production of a decidedly non-Korean space, an "official" designation of a particular space as "Korean" is nonetheless commonly pursued in Koreatowns globally. For many such Korean communities, the pursuit of an official designation, whether through modest monuments or street signs, is in the interest of establishing symbolic legitimacy within a particular space. If Edward Soja (2014) is correct to argue that the social organization of space is simultaneously causal and consequential, then official signage provides a crucial axis of spatial reconfiguration, simultaneously reflecting the community's heritage and its desire to maintain something of a uniform collective identity. Nonetheless, there can be a nominal distinction between these "official" Koreatowns and the "unofficial" ones, such as Oakland's Korean region. The distinction, of course, is in many senses inconsequential in that it has little bearing on how concentrated the Korean population is and less so on how "authentically" Korean a particular community can be said to be, as I will discuss later. For now, I merely wish to emphasize the point that the establishment and growth of various Korean diasporic communities outside of Korea proper point to the impact of the nation as a metric of social belonging as much as they afford an opportunity to examine how the very notion of nationness is continually performed.

Yet the pursuit of the political is in many ways paradoxical. For one, the pursuit of the political in the form of advocacy for official designations as Koreatowns represents an extension of the nation-state ideal in which one people occupy, and are ostensibly entitled to, a designated territory, but in a manner that is decidedly "unnational" in that the diasporic claiming of space is necessarily a contradiction of the nation-state ideal. But perhaps more interestingly, in these Koreatowns, as zones of difference, it is also the recalculation and recalibration of sovereignty that dislodge the territorial logics of the nation-state. The nation-state is able to reaffirm its sovereignty, and thus be rendered visible, through its ability to both establish and dismiss law, as theorists such as Giorgio Agamben (2005) have suggested. Then, to use the example of the Koreatown in Los Angeles, perhaps it can be said that the very elasticity of U.S. and California law within this space undercuts the possibility of a homogeneous sense of national belonging within a preformed space. Koreanness is enacted and sensed in part through the dubiousness of the enforcement of and compliance with local laws. Smoking is common in many bars, restaurants, and clubs despite California law prohibiting smoking in all enclosed workplaces. Patrons who are under the legal drinking age of twenty-one are able to enter bars and nightclubs with relative ease. Many establishments stay open into the early hours of the morning, contrary to California law, which requires them to close at 2:00 AM, and many serve beer and soju despite lacking a liquor license in the first place. Employees are commonly paid "under the table." There is even an underground network of unlicensed taxis, known colloquially as *bulbeop taeksi,* or "illegal taxi," that will get you home after an evening of drinking for a nominal fee.

In the same way that U.S. laws would not be applicable in Korea, they similarly seem to have minimal impact in Koreatowns. Koreatowns, in other words, are spaces characterized by the negotiability of law and regulation, which constitutes them as spaces of difference within a larger set of regulatory guidelines that construct the state according to criteria of governability. I'm not aiming to make any hasty empirical claims about the loose compliance with rules and regulations, and this is of course not to suggest that the refusal to abide by law is what makes a space decidedly Korean. Put differently, I am not trying to make facile points that Koreatowns are lawless, dystopian spaces, nor am I trying to suggest that there is something inherently Korean about lawlessness. It is rather the point that the atmosphere of Koreanness surfaces through the very unregulatabilty of social practice within an ecological network of other social conventions and behaviors. These behaviors, understood as an assemblage of cultural practices, do not constitute Koreanness per se but produce spaces in which the link between law and territory, and thus nation and state, is diluted or otherwise suspended. Koreatown is therefore not so much an institutionally endorsed exceptional administrative space as it is continually reimagined as such because of the inapplicability, and in many ways unenforceability, of many laws of the nation-state in which the Koreatown ostensibly resides. The momentary disappearance of law constellates into a symbolic suspension of the state, producing a rupture in which difference, in this case, Koreanness, can coexist as a national imaginary within another, so to speak.

To return to Anderson (1991), central to his theory of the nation as sovereign, limited, and imagined community is the ability of peoples to occupy a shared territory without physical contact with or recognition of one another. In Anderson's view, crucial to the collectivity of the nation is not physical acknowledgment of other people of the same nation but the ability to exist in homogeneous empty time, to use Walter Benjamin's (1973) expression. Appadurai (1996) argues that Anderson's concept of "imagined communities" cannot account for the global social imaginaries that people today occupy. "An important fact of the world we live in today," writes Appadurai, "is that many persons on the globe live in such imagined worlds (and not just imagined communities) and thus are able to contest and sometimes even subvert the imagined worlds of the official mind" (33). While both Anderson and Appadurai emphasize the role of the imagination, Anderson's emphasis is on the imagined tie to national territory, a geographically delimited area, while Appadurai's approach is decidedly postnational in its refusal of the very concept of physical territory. It is therefore not so much a rejection of Anderson's theory of national identification as a reimagination, across time but also space, that the postnational becomes a possibility insofar as we proceed with the recognition that the territorial substrate of the nation is secondary to these so-called imagined worlds. What we are seeing, in fact, is not so much social identification around the rubric of the nation-state as a continual reproduction of nationness across an undesignated and continually reconfigured space. This postnational performance of social belonging is achieved in part through a semiosis of space, as I will further develop in the following section.

■ THE REINVENTION OF TRADITION

In Hobsbawm's compelling work on the instrumentalist theory of nationalism, national heritage is viewed as a construct of "invented traditions." An *invented tradition* is defined by Hobsbawm (1983, 1) as "a set of practices, normally governed by overtly or tacitly accepted rules and of a ritual or symbolic nature, which seek to inculcate certain values and norms of behavior by repetition, which automatically implies continuity with the past." The famous example provided by Hobsbawm is the nineteenth-century reconstruction of the British Parliament building in Gothic style; the choice was not simply an anachronistic architectural choice but a deliberate attempt to engineer and manage a temporal link to the distant past. Understanding the nation as constitutive of a series of invented traditions, thereby attributing nationalist sentiment to ideological engineering by political elites, directly confronts primordialist theories that understand the emergence of nationalism as an organic extension of premodern social formations.

Traditions are not merely invented once but continually reinvented, a phenomenon evident in the architecture of "national" monuments around the world. In the case of the British Parliament building, tradition has been blatantly invented; elsewhere, there are instances of a continual reinvention of tradition. Consider the Gwanghwamun, the main gate to the Gyeongbokgung Palace in the heart of Seoul. Originally constructed in 1395, during the Joseon Dynasty, the gate was destroyed during the 1592 Japanese invasion of the Korean peninsula, only to be rebuilt in 1867. In 1926, during the Japanese colonial occupation, the gate was deconstructed and relocated to accommodate the Japanese Governor Building at the center of Seoul. It was destroyed once again during the Korean War (1950–53) and partially rebuilt in 1963. While the 1963 restoration was not faithful to the original design, for instance, having been built with a disproportionate amount of concrete rather than wood, it was again rebuilt and, this time, moved back to its original location in front of Gyeongbokgung Palace; it was unveiled on August 10, 2010, on Gwangbokjeol, a national holiday commemorating Korea's independence from Japan.

Lee Myung Bak (2010), then president of Korea, begins his commemorative Gwangbokjeol speech by drawing his audience's attention to Gwanghwamun: "We can now see Gwanghwamun standing tall here once again, restored to its past glory." He adds the following statement just moments later: "A century ago, we lost our country. Gwanghwamun was blocked and neglected, and the flow of our national spirit was choked off. Though we were deprived of our national sovereignty, we continued to persist as Koreans." On the occasion of Gwangbokjeol, the fact that Gwanghwamun had been, most recently, destroyed as a result of the Korean War is deliberately neglected in favor of emphasizing the role of Japanese colonial officials in the removal of the national monument. In fact, the gate was originally scheduled for destruction by Japanese officials, but it was a Japanese intellectual, Yanagi Muneyoshi, who ensured its preservation (Ch'oe 2008). In 1922, Yanagi wrote an open letter as a plea to the colonial government declaring the following: "Politics must not be insensible to art. One must refrain from infringing on art in the exercise of power" (Ch'oe 2008, 553). The moving letter stirred enough public unrest that the Japanese government decided to deconstruct and relocate the gate to a peripheral location instead of destroying it. As Ch'oe writes, "Yanagi's case is a reminder that in the midst of strong authoritarian, ultra-nationalist, and imperialist trends, there were independent voices among Japanese scholars and writers who spoke for cultural values that should be defended and preserved from both Western and Japanese hegemonism" (552).

In 2010, the choice by Korean officials to have the Gwanghwamun restored and unveiled on the anniversary of Korea's independence from Japanese rule functioned enthymematically, causing most Koreans to infer that it is primarily, if not solely, the Japanese who are responsible for Gwanghwamun's destruction. One is reminded of Ernest Renan's (1990, 11) famous declaration: "Forgetting, I would even go so far as to say historical error, is a crucial factor in the creation of a nation, which is why progress in historical studies often constitutes a danger for [the principle of] nationality."[7] The distinction in the narrative of Gwanghwamun is that the crassness of the historiography is not a result of careless historical inquiry but a deliberate neglect of key details in the historical narrative, which facilitates a reinvention of tradition.

The Gwanghwamun is a conspicuous relic of "tradition" in a city like Seoul, which, like many other affluent Asian cities, comprises many high-rise corporate and residential buildings with features such as cooler tones—silvers, grays, and blues—and mirrored windows that reflect, quite literally, their modernity. Such buildings, which evoke a modern Western architectural aesthetic, produce an unusual temporal and cultural juxtaposition with the Gyeongbokgung Palace, as it is merely a few meters of asphalt that separate the palace from the rest of the city. Gwanghwamun and its semiotic ecology are perhaps best understood as an architectural chronotope, to adopt Mikhail Bakhtin's (1981) expression, as symbols that

Figure 6. Changing of the royal guards in front of Gwanghwamun in Seoul. Photograph by the author.

bridge relations between time (*chronos*) and space (*topos*).[8] Gwanghwamun is the ideal chronotopic centerpiece for Seoul precisely because, in addition to its dubious historical significance, its grandiose presence forcefully demands a recognition to establish a temporal tie to a premodern past. In fact, throughout the day, national history is performed repeatedly in an elaborate spectacle of the changing of the royal guards (Figure 6). On the gate itself, "Gwanghwamun" is presented not in the Korean alphabet (광화문) but in Chinese script known as *hanja* (門化光). The very presence of *hanja*, which predates the modern Korean alphabet, reminds us yet again of Renan's dictum on the importance of "forgetting." The use of *hanja*, in an attempt to conjure a premodern national imaginary, simultaneously asks us to forget that the development of Korea's own alphabet, distinct from *hanja*, borrowed from Chinese, was crucial to the establishment of a uniquely modern "Korean" national identity. In fact, this example also reminds us that the Korean alphabet provides a resource to convey Koreanness in a manner unavailable to other national imaginaries that do not have their own script. It is therefore somewhat curious to encounter uses of *hanja* to mark Koreanness, because contemporary understandings of Koreanness could not have been realized without the development of Korea's own alphabet. Any rendering of traditional Koreanness in the form of *hanja* is a paradoxical indexing of something decidedly non-Korean.

In contrast, the production of nationness in postnational Korean communities has less to do with a remembrance of cultural heritage than it does with reinvention or, to use Renan's expression, "forgetting." I direct our attention toward one such community to illustrate this point. Situated in Oakland, California, along Telegraph Avenue, one finds the Bay Area's Koreatown, an unofficial designation for a concentration of Korean establishments. One is able to find Korean-owned businesses, such as restaurants, banks, real estate offices, and hair salons. Among the most prominent landmarks on Telegraph Avenue is a strip mall called Koryo Village, containing eight businesses, with most of the business names somehow incorporating "Koryo" (Figure 7).

What is immediately apparent is the architectural choice, incorporating tiled roofs, which are, in this particular space, distinctively Korean. Yet, I must emphasize that they are distinctively Korean *in this particular space*. One encounters similar architectural features in San Francisco's Little Tokyo, but in that space, the curvilinear tiled roofs are distinctively *Japanese*. The architecture becomes semiotized as belonging to the architectural conventions of a particular national imaginary (in this case, Korea) in accordance with what the typical viewer expects them to be. The architectural design, in the context of the United States, is obviously not U.S.-American and is understood to be Korean, but only insofar as it occurs within a space in which the objective is the production of Koreanness. Similar, if not identical, architectural choices are to be found elsewhere; they can be found, for instance, in various global Japanese enclaves, and these same buildings, if transplanted to a Chinatown, would become reindexed as Chinese. This not necessarily a problem about ostensibly ignorant consumers who cannot differentiate the particularities of Korean architecture from its similar East Asian counterparts. The reality is that the semiosis of Koreanness need not be discretely or authentically Korean in that that which is pursued, the authentic, is so readily reinvented.

Take, for instance, the very usage of the name of "Koryo" itself. This chronotope evokes the name of the Koryo Dynasty, which ruled the Korean peninsula from AD 936 to 1392. While there is a clear attempt to

Figure 7. In Oakland's Koreatown, Koryo Village is among the most prominent landmarks. Photograph by the author.

signify the timeless and proto-national heritage of Korea, if signifying tradition is the objective in selecting Koryo instead of the more obvious choice of Korea, one wonders why Silla, as in the Silla Dynasty, which predates even the Koryo Dynasty, was not chosen. In fact, the usage of Silla is quite common in diasporic signage, such as in New York's Shilla

Korean Barbeque.[9] One explanation for the preference of one dynastic appellative over the other is the aural proximity of "Koryo" to "Korea," facilitating a causal link for many consumers unfamiliar with the history of the Korean peninsula—it is similar enough that many can infer that there is some cognate relationship between "Koryo" and "Korea." There is, undoubtedly, a degree of uncertainty in its signification, and by being only partially legible as having relationality to "Korea," "Koryo" encapsulates the unknowingness that makes the foreign alluring. At the very least, consumers can infer that "Koryo" is perhaps an alternative spelling of "Korea," which is not altogether inaccurate; the etymological derivative of the Western labels, such as "Korea," "Corea" (Spanish), or "la Corée" (French), is indeed "Koryo." The semiotic versatility of "Koryo" lies not only in its ability to bridge a temporal link to the distant and unknowable past but also in its ability to traverse the very boundaries of language. The case of "Koryo," as an exaggerated and proto-nationalistic symbol of Koreanness, is encountered as an anachronistic index of national authenticity that functions to reinvent authenticity, call attention to the manufacturedness of authenticity, and raise questions about the very possibility of authenticity in the context of our relations to places that can be simultaneously foreign and local.

Yet the Koryo signage should not be taken, in and of itself, as a representation of the global reinvention of Koreanness in the semioscape. To illustrate what I mean, I turn our attention to another encounter with "Koryo," but this time in Dallas, Texas (Figure 8). Here "Koryo" appears on a sign for a restaurant called Koryo Kalbi. The sign, with its brush script stylization, along with the ancient aesthetic of the lamps, creates a mythic timelessness of Koreanness but also calls attention to an anachronistic irony that the Korean BBQ served inside likely did not exist during the days of the Koryo Dynasty. This irony is exacerbated by the production of the sign on a plastic sheet with vinyl decals backlit by fluorescent bulbs, along with the adjacent blue and red neon sign and the notification mandated by the fire marshal: "THIS DOOR REMAINS OPEN DURING BUSINESS HOURS." It serves as a stark reminder that the reproduction of nationness is always contending with the rules and regulatory guidelines of modernity, in this case, literally the rules and regulatory guidelines of local governmental apparatuses.

Elsewhere, in a place like Northern California's Bay Area, comprising demographically diverse cities such as San Francisco, San Jose, and Oakland, it is perhaps by no means unexpected to find a thriving Korean ethnic enclave. Yet it becomes somewhat more unexpected to find such a phenomenon in the heart of the U.S. Southwest. This is, of course,

Figure 8. In Dallas, this sign for Koryo Kalbi achieves an ancient aesthetic through brush script stylization and ornamental lamps. Photograph by the author.

not to suggest that cities such as Dallas are not ethnically diverse. I am simply making the point that cities of the U.S. Southwest, unlike those in coastal regions, have not experienced the same demographic shifts resulting from large-scale transpacific migrations between the United States and Asia. So, upon encountering the sign for Koryo Kalbi in Dallas, one is struck by finding a sign evoking a seven-hundred-year-old Korean heritage. The strangeness of the encounter underscores the very discursive and semiotic climate in which the reinvention of Koreanness needs to occur. The production of Koreanness is at odds with, and thus must contend with, a strong Texan regional identity, which, although by no means homogeneous, is nonetheless characterized by a constellation of symbolic associations with this particular place. When one thinks of Texas, the possibility of a thriving Koreatown is not what one would immediately imagine, because of the immediacy of other stereotypical cultural iconography (such as longhorn cattle and cowboy boots) through which many non-Texans hastily imagine and construct the region. These are, to state the obvious, not representative of how "people in Texas are" but operate as caricatural symbols that accompany imaginations of the region. Thus a restaurant like Koryo Kalbi, in the context of Texas, is a precarious Korean cultural representation in a space generally understood as devoid of an overabundance of Koreanness and at odds with a regional semiosis of Texasness. This very process of caricatural representation is instructive in understanding the semiological mechanics of the global production of nationness, as I will describe in the following section.

■ THE UNBANALITY OF NATIONNESS

Nancy Abelmann and John Lie (1995, 85) are not entirely inaccurate in describing Los Angeles's Koreatown as "a simulacrum of Seoul in Southern California, a Korea away from Korea." "Cultural certitudes crumble," add Abelmann and Lie, "as we wonder whether this is South Korea or the United States" (85). There are no doubt unmistakable sensations of Koreanness within particular establishments, where the interior design choices compel even native Koreans to forget, momentarily, where they are. While it may be commonly assumed that Korean food in the United States is necessarily different from Korean food in Korea, in some eateries in Koreatowns, the taste of the food can deceive even the most experienced connoisseurs of "authentic" Korean cuisine. However, we need to go beyond accounts that are premised on the assumption that Korean diasporic communities represent how peoples migrate to different countries and simply bring their home culture with them with aspirations of producing interstitial and simulacral spaces.

Of course, it is this very assumption that drives people to enclave communities to seek "authentic" ethnic foods and consumer goods that cannot, ostensibly, be acquired outside of these community spaces. In this regard, today, Koreatowns, like other ethnic enclave communities, function increasingly as places for locals to experience an ostensibly authentic excursion attainable by local transit. In today's global economy, one need not take a half-day transpacific commercial flight to arrive in "Korea." Residents of various parts of California's Orange County, for instance, can reach the Korean District in Garden Grove via a fifteen-minute ride in the car; for those residing in San Francisco, Oakland's Telegraph Avenue is but a short half-hour ride via the Bay Area Rapid Transit (BART). The immediacy of access to nationness points to something fascinating about the ways in which we produce the very nationness that we pursue. In a sense, in pursuing nationness, we are producing nationness. To continue with the example of food, as this is one of the most common reasons why one will make a journey to a particular Korean district, it is not the food itself that is authentic. Indeed, as Robert Ku (2014, 35) has argued, the very concept of authentic food, or what he terms "gastronomic authenticity," at least in the context of Asian food, is in and of itself a "discursive strategy for making sense of and coping with the world as it is." As Ku notes, the pursuit of gastronomic authenticity, as opposed to obviously Americanized foods such as California rolls and Chinese take-out, assumes an unadulterated point of origin and is thus by its nature unattainable. I would like to suggest, somewhat alternatively, that in the context of globalization, varying scales of authenticity are attainable through the traversing of space. When I say that the food itself is not authentic, I do not mean to suggest that ethnic foods found in the diaspora are not authentic. Rather, it is the transit to a demarcated space of difference that produces the authenticity, which is not a condition in dialectic opposition to the fake but rather a degree of quality that is merely "more authentic" than that which is readily available. While we want the convenience of the access to nationness, we do not want the extranational to be immediately available in the form of, as Ku has suggested, California rolls and Chinese take-out; once something is readily available in places like chain restaurants or supermarkets, it loses its appeal. In regard to the aforementioned transit to elsewhere, even if the elsewhere is only fifteen minutes away, it is the physical movement to another space that is recognized as a necessary investment to access the authentic. The nonimmediacy of the experience is what gives it value, even if it is, curiously, always the consumer who creates the value.

The question of nonimmediacy and the production of nationness are perhaps better understood through an engagement with Michael Billig's (1995) theory of *banal nationalism*. As Billig writes,

> the citizens of an established nation do not, day by day, consciously decide that their nation should continue. On the other hand, the reproduction of a nation does not occur magically. Banal practices, rather than conscious choice or collective acts of imagination, are required. Just as a language will die rather for want of regular users, so a nation must be put to daily use. (95)

In rejecting Anderson's privileging of the "collective acts of imagination," Billig contends that the performance of national identification, in other words, is not a conscious, conspicuous, or concentrated practice. As Billig argues, "the metonymic image of banal nationalism is not a flag which is being consciously waved with fervent passion; it is the flag hanging unnoticed on the public building" (8). Billig's work is especially useful in that it theorizes not the historical formation of the nation-state but the maintenance of national identification in contemporary democratic societies. Of central importance is the point that, even if nationness is not legible as such, it nonetheless exists, "hanging unnoticed," as it were.

Figure 9. In Itaewon, the Koryo Ceramics store targets tourists seeking "authentic" Korean souvenirs. Photograph by the author.

However, implicit in Billig's theory is the maintenance of national identity *within the nation-state,* so it is fair to ask whether such a theory can be applicable to the global production of nationness.

To address this concern, I first draw attention to the *unbanality* of nationness within the nation-state. I draw our attention to two examples from the semioscape of Itaewon, a neighborhood of Seoul popular among U.S. military personnel, and Insadong, a neighborhood of Seoul that is a popular tourist attraction. In Itaewon, once again, one encounters a Koryo signage (Figure 9). Yet it is not the signage itself that produces the Koreanness here—rather, it is an excess of traditional Korean souvenirs that populate the space. In the space of Itaewon, the heritage of Koreanness produced by the Koryo Ceramics store is compromised by the adjacency of a sign for money exchange, a clear indication that locals do not frequent this region. In Insadong, one also encounters similar instances of the excess of Korean semiosis (Figure 10). The signage for the Korea Traditional Souvenir Center is presented on a distressed wood panel with a notable dominance of Korean alphabetic characters (the English text, although presented in all capitals, is comparatively subtle, as it is featured on the darker portion of the wood panel, enabling a less

Figure 10. In Insadong, the sign for the Korea Traditional Souvenir Center is featured on a distressed wood panel accompanied by a *tal,* a "traditional" Korean mask. Photograph by the author.

dynamic contrast between text and background). The sign is accompanied by a "traditional" Korean mask, or *tal,* which are more likely to be found as decorations outside of Korea than within, in spaces where Koreanness needs to be announced for one reason or another. The conspicuousness, or unbanality, as I have been suggesting, of Koreanness suggests that spaces like Itaewon and Insadong are not so much Korean as they are spaces for visitors to experience and even consume and purchase Koreanness. We are therefore confronted with acknowledging the possibility that the global production of Koreanness perhaps has less to do with a romanticized maintenance of heritage than with commercial considerations. Heller (2010) has argued that a side effect of globalization is the accelerated commodifiability and mobility of cultural resources, increasingly unsutured from their assumed local and authentic points of origin. But the excess, I argue, represents a lack insofar as spaces such as these are spaces not of locality, tradition, and authenticity but of alterity within, so to speak.

There is much to be said of the fact that, when we encounter the unbanality of Koreanness in Korea, it occurs in spaces that are decidedly non-Korean, such as Itaewon and Insadong. And it leaves us to consider where exactly unbanality can exist in the Korean semioscape. Outside of the Korean nation-state, and outside designated tourist traps within the Korean nation-state, there is always already an assumed lack of Koreanness that precipitates the unbanality of Koreanness. In global spaces outside of "Korea," for instance, one will not encounter a restaurant for Korean BBQ that is merely "BBQ" or merely "restaurant." And while the very markedness, of Koreanness or otherwise, represents the semiosis of unbanality, this semiosis need not be reduced to questions of authenticity. As Radhakrishnan (1996) has forcibly argued, the question of whether something is or can or cannot be authentic in the diaspora is to miss the point that such questions are prefigured always on an absoluteness of the point of supposed origin and regard heritage as a credential to be evaluated by an imagined authority of authenticity. I would like to add that the semiosis of unbanality is not so much a charade of authenticity and much less a question of surrogacy. Rather, in absentia of the collectivizing locus of the state, nationness does not necessarily become deontologized through unbanality. The end result of the highly conspicuous reinvention of nationness in global space should not be viewed as an inauthentic, diluted, or alternative form of the nationness of the nation-state, for such an assumption would assume the ontological stability of the former. Semiosis is indeed a conduit for the production of nationness, but the very act producing nationness is premised ultimately on the lack, and semiosis therefore cannot fill such a void. Nationness therefore is continually reinvented in spaces characterized by a void in nationness; the end result, at least from what can be gleaned from the global Korean nation-space, whether in Dallas or Itaewon, is a nationness that is simultaneously more and less real than that which is performed within the space of banal un-alterity of the nation-state.

◼ CONCLUSION: NATION-SPACE

The global diasporic city perpetually attempts that which is impossible: to reinvent the nation outside the nation-state. But this attempt should not be reduced to evaluations of success or failure. Such efforts at reinventing the nation, whether as Little Tokyo, Little Saigon, or, as I have focused on, Koreatown, oftentimes will be confronted by purist and nativist discourses that dismiss the diasporic community as a hybridized counterfeit of the "authenticity" one can ostensibly only encounter and experience in the nation-state itself. But the privileging of the nation-state as the assumed primary site of nationness is to neglect the always already inventedness of the cultural practices, political allegiances, and felt sentiments found within, and preconstitutive of, the nation-state. Therefore, in that nation-ness within the nation-state depends so readily on a practice of continual reinvention, my proposal should not be viewed as a call for a radical epistemic reorientation or a structural reimagination of a ubiquitous political paradigm. Rather, I have attempted to develop criteria other than location and authenticity to understand what, if any, distinctions can be drawn between state and space. A postnational performance of social belonging is achieved through a semiosis of space or a production of the semioscape. Situating this phenomenon of spatial reinvention within a theory of unbanality, I have attempted to foreground how Koreanness, when produced in global space, is simultaneously less *and* more Korean than Korea itself. The spatial production of authenticity is simultaneously local and foreign, and the reinvention of tradition is simultaneously historic and contemporary. By transfiguring the distinction between Koreanness and Korea, as part of a broader project of attempting to understand nationness within and across nation-space, I have attempted to fray the transposability of nation and nationness, unsutured from the territorial and ideological limits of the state.

Jerry Won Lee is assistant professor of English at the University of California, Irvine.

■ NOTES

The field research for this project was generously funded by the UC Irvine Humanities Commons and the Center for Asian Studies. I also owe much gratitude to Verge editor Tina Chen for her invaluable insight, direction, and support, and to Kyung Hyun Kim, José M. Cortez, Eun Young Seong, and the two anonymous reviewers for helping me develop this article into its current form. Remaining oversights are my own.

1. I acknowledge that for some readers the immediate response to the first question would be a counterquestion: "Which Korea?" Much can be said about the frequent unmarkedness of South Korea as Korea alongside the chronic markedness of North Korea as always North Korea. If anything, it points to the hegemonic epistemology of U.S.-based discourses that construct South Korea as an ally of global capitalism and North Korea as a pariah of modernity. It is an important question, but one that I cannot engage with the necessary attention, precision, and depth in the pages of this essay.

2. With the exception of proper nouns, transliterations from Korean

to English are presented according to the conventions of Revised Romanization.

3. This study is based on a thirty-month-long ethnographic investigation of the public language artifacts from fifteen different cities within Korea and global Korean communities across North America (e.g., Los Angeles, Chicago, and New York) and East Asia (e.g., Osaka, Tokyo, Shanghai, Beijing, and Hong Kong).

4. Thurlow and Aiello (2007, 308) also use the expression *semioscape*, imagined as "falling somewhere between" ideoscapes and mediascapes, to "bring into focus the non-mediatized but globalizing circulation of symbols, sign systems and meaning-making practices." My usage, alternatively, focuses more explicitly on the semiotic production of social identification prefigured in relation to the political apparatuses of the nation-state.

5. Il Risorgimento (Resurgence) refers to the political unification of the different states of the Italian peninsula in the nineteenth century.

6. According to the Osaka Convention and Tourism Bureau's (n.d.) English-language website, "it is said that Miyuki-dori is named after Miyuki-no-mori Shrine, which was established around the 5th century on the site where the Emperor Nintoku took a rest when he visited the area to inspect people who had come from Paekche to live there (in the woods formerly located at the west end of where the street now stands)."

7. Renan's lecture, "Qu'est-ce qu'une nation?" (What is a nation?), was originally delivered in 1882.

8. The chronotope, in Bakhtin's (1981) formulation, was originally a concept for literary genre analysis but has since been applied more broadly by scholars across the humanities and social sciences.

9. "Silla" and "Shilla" are alternate transliterations for 신라.

■ WORKS CITED

Abelmann, Nancy, and John Lie. 1995. *Blue Dreams: Korean Americans and the Los Angeles Riots.* Cambridge, Mass.: Harvard University Press.

Agamben, Giorgio. 2005. *State of Exception.* Chicago: University of Chicago Press.

Anderson, Benedict. 1991. *Imagined Communities: Reflections on the Origin and Spread of Nationalism.* 2nd ed. London: Verso.

Appadurai, Arjun. 1996. *Modernity at Large: Cultural Dimensions of Globalization.* Minneapolis: University of Minnesota Press.

———. 2001. "Grassroots Globalization and the Research Imagination." In *Globalization,* edited by Arjun Appadurai, 1–21. Durham, N.C.: Duke University Press.

Bakhtin, M. M. 1981. *The Dialogic Imagination: Four Essays.* Edited by Michael Holquist. Translated by Caryl Emerson and Michael Holquist. Austin: University of Texas Press.

Balibar, Étienne. 2004. *We, the People of Europe? Reflections on Transnational Citizenship.* Princeton, N.J.: Princeton University Press.

Benjamin, Walter. 1973. *Illuminations.* London: Fontana.

Billig, Michael. 1995. *Banal Nationalism.* London: Sage.

Bourdieu, Pierre. 1991. *Language and Symbolic Power.* Cambridge, Mass.: Harvard University Press.

Calhoun, Craig J. 2007. *Nations Matter: Culture, History, and the Cosmopolitan Dream.* London: Routledge.

Ch'oe, Yong-ho. 2008. "Yanagi Muneyoshi and the Kwanghwa Gate in Seoul, Korea." In *Sources of East Asian Tradition,* vol. 2, edited by William Theodore De Bary, 551–53. New York: Columbia University Press.

de Certeau, Michel. 1984. *The Practice of Everyday Life.* Berkeley: University of California Press.

Heller, Monica. 2007. "The Future of 'Bilingualism.'" In *Bilingualism: A Social Approach,* edited by Monica Heller, 340–45. Basingstoke, U.K.: Palgrave Macmillan.

———. 2010. *Paths to Postnationalism: A Critical Ethnography of Language and Identity.* Oxford: Oxford University Press.

Herder, Johann Gottfried. 1967. *Sämtliche Werke.* Vol. 14. Edited by Bernhard Supan. New York: Georg Olms.

Hobsbawm, Eric. 1983. "Introduction: Inventing Tradition," edited by Terence Ranger. In *The Invention of Tradition,* edited by Eric Hobsbawm, 1–14. Cambridge: Cambridge University Press.

———. 1990. *Nations and Nationalism since 1870: Programme, Myth, Reality.* Cambridge: Cambridge University Press.

Jaworski, Adam, and Crispin Thurlow, eds. 2010. *Semiotic Landscape: Language, Image, Space.* London: Continuum.

Joo, Rachael Miyung. 2012. *Transnational Sport: Gender, Media, and Global Korea.* Durham, N.C.: Duke University Press.

Kim, Richard S. 2011. *The Quest for Statehood: Korean Immigrant Nationalism and U.S. Sovereignty, 1905–1945.* Oxford: Oxford University Press.

Ku, Robert Ji-Song. 2014. *Dubious Gastronomy: The Cultural Politics of Eating Asian in the USA.* Honolulu: University of Hawai'i Press.

Landry, Rodrigue, and Richard Y. Bourhis. 1997. "Linguistic Landscape and Ethnolinguistic Vitality: An Empirical Study." *Journal of Language and Social Psychology* 16, no. 1: 23–49.

Lee, Myung Bak. 2010. "Marching Together toward a Greater Republic of

Korea." Address on the sixty-fifth anniversary of National Liberation, August 15, Gyeongbokgung Palace, Seoul.

Lie, John. 2008. *Zainichi (Koreans in Japan): Diasporic Nationalism and Postcolonial Identity.* Berkeley: University of California Press.

Lou, Jackie Jia. 2016. *The Linguistic Landscape of Chinatown: A Sociolinguistic Ethnography.* Bristol, U.K.: Multilingual Matters.

Mbembe, Achille. 2003. "Necropolitics." *Public Culture* 15, no. 1: 11–40.

Osaka Convention and Tourism Bureau. N.d. "Miyuki-dori Shopping Street (Korea Town)." http://www.osaka-info.jp/en/.

Park, Joseph Sung-Yul, and Adrienne Lo. 2012. "Transnational South Korea as a Site for a Sociolinguistics of Globalization: Markets, Timescales, and Neoliberalism." *Journal of Sociolinguistics* 16, no. 2: 147–64.

Pennycook, Alastair. 2010. *Language as a Local Practice.* Abingdon, U.K.: Routledge.

———. 2012. *Unexpected Places: Language and Mobility.* Bristol, U.K.: Multilingual Matters.

Renan, Ernest. 1990. "What Is a Nation?" In *Nation and Narration*, translated by Martin Thom, edited by Homi K. Bhabha, 8–22. New York: Routledge.

Radhakrishnan, R. 1996. *Diasporic Mediations: Between Home and Location.* Minneapolis: University of Minnesota Press.

Scollon, Ron, and Suzie Wong Scollon. 2003. *Discourses in Place: Language in the Material World.* London: Routledge.

Shin, Gi-Wook. 2006. *Ethnic Nationalism in Korea: Genealogy, Politics, and Legacy.* Palo Alto, Calif.: Stanford University Press.

Smith, Anthony D. 1991. *National Identity.* Reno: University of Nevada Press.

Soja, Edward W. 2014. *My Los Angeles: From Urban Restructuring to Regional Urbanization.* Berkeley: University of California Press.

Soysal, Yasemin Nuhoğlu. 1994. *Limits of Citizenship: Migrants and Postnational Membership in Europe.* Chicago: University of Chicago Press.

Thurlow, Crispin, and Giorgia Aiello. 2007. "National Pride, Global Capital: A Social Semiotic Analysis of Transnational Visual Branding in the Airline Industry." *Visual Communication* 6, no. 3: 305–44.

ABIGAIL DE KOSNIK

Perfect Covers: Filipino Musical Mimicry and Transmedia Performance

> I've never noticed so much copying of American culture in any other country outside America.
> —Sanne van Oosten on the Philippines, 2012

> The hair stood up on my arms. I got up off the computer and told my girlfriend, "No way—this guy sounds too good. I don't believe it."
> —Neal Schon of Journey, quoted in *GQ*, 2008

■ A NATION OF MIMICS?

The two epigraphs refer to the same widely observed phenomenon: the proclivity, and apparently common ability, of Filipinos to imitate Americans in cultural performances. The first quotation is an excerpt from a 2012 post by Dutch political blogger Sanne van Oosten during a visit to the Philippine capital city, Manila. Van Oosten notes that Filipinos have staged numerous protests against U.S. foreign policy since the Philippine–U.S. Visiting Forces Agreement (VFA) was ratified by the Philippine Senate in 1999; the VFA allows the U.S. government to retain jurisdiction over U.S. military personnel accused of committing crimes in the Philippines, which many Filipinos say effectively grants immunity to members of the U.S. military for criminal acts against Filipinos. At the same time that anti-American demonstrations frequently take place in the streets of Manila, however, so does Filipinos' "copying of American culture," a seeming paradox that van Oosten names "the intense Filipino love/hate relationship with America." For van Oosten, the most striking evidence of the "love" that Filipinos have for American culture is Filipinos' deep familiarity with, and constant performance of, American popular music.

The blogger's unstated question is, how can Filipinos vehemently protest against the United States, as they did in Manila in November 2011, when sixty anti-VFA activists volleyed red paint at the motorcade of the visiting U.S. secretary of state, while at the same moment, legions of Filipinos sing American songs in near-perfect vocal imitations of the American recording artists who made those songs famous?

The second quotation is from Neal Schon, of the American rock band Journey, which attained global prominence in the 1980s with a series of hits, such as "Any Way You Want It" (1980), "Don't Stop Believin'" (1981), and "Faithfully" (1983). In 2007, Schon wanted to revive Journey without famous lead singer Steve Perry; Perry had left Journey in the late 1990s, and his disinterest in a reunion left the other band members in need of a new front man. In a 2008 *GQ* interview (Pappademas 2008), Schon states that he had searched far and wide for a permanent replacement for Perry but did not find a suitable candidate among the Journey tribute bands in the United States. Turning to the Internet, Schon happened upon a number of videos of a Manila house band called The Zoo, featuring Pineda on the microphone. Schon was so impressed by Pineda's renditions of Journey's canon that he invited the Filipino vocalist to audition for Schon and his bandmates in San Francisco in August 2007. Pineda's performances over a handful of days led the group to offer him a job as Journey's lead singer in December 2007. Since then, Journey, fronted by Pineda, has been touring the world and releasing new albums; the first album the band made with Pineda on lead vocals, *Revelation* (2008), went platinum (Pappademas 2008; Flandez 2008; Liu 2008; Concepcion 2010).

The link between the two quotations is their expressions of doubt about Filipino musical mimicry—doubt concerning this mimicry's pervasiveness, on one hand, and its persuasiveness, on the other. How can it be that copying of American performance styles is so ordinary, so everyday and every*where,* in the Philippines, given the country's history as a former colony of the United States, which has led to Filipinos repeatedly protesting U.S. policies in the Philippines in the twenty-first century? And how can it be that Filipino copies can so thoroughly evoke the American originals that, at least in the case of Journey and Pineda, an "original" American band felt compelled to hire the "copy"(cat)?

This article explores Filipino musical mimicry's roots in the Philippines's complex past with the United States and how the Philippines became a major supplier of performance labor for the United States, with hiring transactions facilitated by old and new media platforms. I will examine Filipinos' efforts to use the Internet to *transmediate themselves,* that is, to transmit a certain brand of Filipino-ness across borders, from the Philippines to both the United States and other nations, and from the margins of U.S. society to the center. I argue that Filipinos are promoting a collective brand via new media: the brand of Filipinos-as-"perfect covers," that is, Filipinos-as-cover-performers-par-excellence—imitators who can potentially become, themselves, stars.

By using Henry Jenkins's (2007; 2011; Jenkins, Ford, and Green 2013) concept of transmedia to frame the actions of the Philippines as a nation and of Filipinos as an ethnic group, I seek to extend the concept's applications beyond the world of corporate marketing and media fan production. Transmediation operates widely today in the realm of transnational labor migrations and also was intrinsic to the operations of colonialism in the nineteenth and twentieth centuries—and these two transmedia moments are causally linked. The imperialist transmediations of more than century ago seeded the transmedia campaigns of former colonized peoples that populate contemporary digital networks.

■ HISTORICAL ORIGINS OF FILIPINO MIMICRY

Much has been written on Filipino people as masters of mimicry, particularly in their performances of American popular music and dance. Pico Iyer's (cited in Perillo 2011, 9) characterization of Filipinos as "master[s] of every American gesture, conversant with every Western song," is taken up by Arjun Appadurai (1990, 1) in his analysis of the "global cultural economy," which, at least in the case of the Philippines, is a "global culture of the 'hyper-real'" (3). Appadurai states,

> Iyer's own account of the uncanny Philippine affinity for American popular music is a rich testimony to the global culture of the "hyper-real," for somehow Philippine renditions of American popular songs are more widespread in the Philippines, and more disturbingly faithful to their originals, than they are in the United States today. An entire nation seems to have learned to mimic Kenny Rogers and the Lennon sisters, like a vast Asian Motown chorus. (3)

John Bowe (2005), writing for *The New York Times,* quotes an executive at a Filipino overseas labor placement company, Jackson Gan, expressing pride in Filipino musicians' mimetic capabilities: "The main talent of Filipino musicians is not originality. [They] have something called the *wido*. It means 'the ear.' By listening to a song once on the radio, they can play it. They can copy anything. This is their real talent. It's inborn." Elaine Chan (2006), in a story for *Asia Sentinel,* states, "Not particularly inventive, Filipino bands and performers nonetheless can and do mimic virtually every singer or singing style in existence." Ethnomusicologist

Lee Watkins (2009, 89) states, "Filipino musicians are renowned for their musicianship, but in many quarters they are criticized for not performing original music. Mention has been made of how musicians imitate the sound and performance styles of models provided by western performers. Many [Filipino] musicians are able to imitate even the grain of the original artist's voice, such that it is difficult to distinguish between the original version and theirs." J. Lorenzo Perillo (2011, 614–15) names the widespread conception of Filipinos as innately and expertly imitative, especially as musical performers, "the 'Filipino mimicry' stereotype": "The stereotype holds that Filipinos are both virtuoso mimics and usually of U.S. culture, and that they are adept singers and dancers. . . . Essentialist cultural accounts like this one persist in everyday discourse, promulgated by non-Filipinos and Filipinos alike."

What might be called "mimicry studies," a subfield of both postcolonial studies and ethnic studies, consists of analyses of how white European and American colonizers, slave owners, employers, and "masters" of all kinds have required nonwhite subjects, slaves, and workers to adopt and imitate white cultures. Many scholars have investigated and described the mandated mimicry by nonwhites of Christianity (Bhabha 1984; Sweet 2003), Western literature and writing (Lamming 1960; Conquergood 2002), the psychology and worldview of racist whites (Fanon 1952), and white cultural norms generally, including styles of self-presentation and social engagement (Braithwaite 1971; Bhabha 1984). Studies of Filipino mimicry, however, concentrate largely on musical imitation. Within mimicry studies, theorizations of Filipino imitation are most closely aligned with theorizations of African American imitation, as both Filipino and African American performers have been widely stereotyped as having innate proclivities for copying the music they hear and the dances they see, and both are subject to what Lee Watkins (2009, 76) calls "social stratification based upon a hierarchy of color," in which African Americans' and Filipinos' darker complexions make them socially inferior to white Euroamericans and Asians with light complexions. Watkins writes, "Labeling [Filipinos] by way of racial color is a continuum with the opinion held by many insiders and outsiders, who compare the musicality of Filipinos with that of black people" (76). A discourse that equates skin color—a trait that is biological and inborn, the definition of a "natural" attribute—with a talent for musical imitation, making mimicry as "natural" as skin tone, is applied to both Filipinos and African Americans:

> Since the Filipino musician's talent is deemed "natural," then it is also indicative of the complex domain of behavior considered imitative. This observa-

tion relates obstinately to the notion that the nonwhite person, following in the paradigm of the noble savage, is more closely attuned to nature than any other assumed racial group. It stands to reason, therefore, that those of a darker hue should naturally be musically superior to others and be more inclined toward imitation as a gesture for survival. (90)

However, as mimicry studies show, when cultural imitation is prevalent among colonized or otherwise subjected peoples, the cause is not "nature" but a specific history of power relations.

It is necessary to consider the pervasiveness of the stereotype of Filipinos as musical mimics in the context of the Philippines's colonization by Spain and the United States and its neocolonial participation in global economic and cultural flows. Lee Watkins (2009, 85) writes, "Ever since his initial contact with the Spanish colonizers [in 1521], the Filipino musician had been disciplined to move from place to place, and to present himself in the public gaze as entertainer and mimic," and Filipino bands, "trained to provide western music at official and social occasions" (79), played in Macau, Shanghai, and Hong Kong starting in the latter half of the nineteenth century, in the last decades of Spanish rule over the Philippines.

But when the United States annexed the Philippine Islands following its victory in the Spanish–American War of 1898, the United States initiated deliberate, archipelago-wide efforts to impose Americanness on its new subjects. As soon as U.S. occupation of the islands began, U.S. president William McKinley (1913, 149) officially proclaimed that "the mission of the United States" with respect to its new colonial possession "is one of benevolent assimilation," indicating that the United States would expect Filipinos to imitate American modes of public and private life. Warwick Anderson (2002) describes the multiplicity of ways that American colonial bureaucrats in the Philippines—including governmental, medical, and educational personnel—mandated Filipinos' mimicry of American civic, hygienic, and schooling practices. "[To] the American regime . . . the copy was becoming as interesting as any typological construction of difference," Anderson argues (688). Filipinos who faithfully adhered to American instruction might "be given limited civic rights, becoming probationary citizen-subjects," whereas Filipinos who failed at mimetic performance were deemed "in need of further surveillance and discipline" (688). Elizabeth L. Enriquez (2006, 124) notes that the United States introduced radio to the Philippines in the 1920s in part to further the colonial project of making Filipinos culturally American: "U.S. entrepreneurs brought in commercial broadcasting in the 1920s both as a business enterprise . . . and as an agent for the 'Americanization' of the Filipino consciousness, the better to make the natives receptive not only to U.S. products but also to U.S. values." Mimicry of American ways of doing, knowing, listening, buying, believing, and being was thus rendered equivalent with personal and collective success for Filipinos for the duration of American colonial rule.

The structural requirement for Filipino mimicry of Americanness did not dissolve with the advent of Philippine independence in 1946. During the Vietnam War, it was the U.S. military that called for Filipino mimicry, as "tens of thousands of American servicemen passed through the [Philippines] wanting live entertainment. Filipinos, already fluent in English, were happy to oblige. By war's end, the country was rich with musicians versed in the latest Western pop," writes Bowe (2005). In 1974, Philippine president (and dictator) Ferdinand Marcos "started exporting manpower . . . when the economy was derelict, and he saw an opportunity" in rapidly developing nations that lacked sufficiently large workforces (Brygo 2011). What began as a program to ship out construction hands swiftly expanded to include many more types of workers, including millions of entertainers. Today, the "hyper-competent reproduction" (Appadurai 1990, 3) of American songs and dances is a valuable export commodity for the Philippines.

Musical performers are just one of many categories of laborers that the Philippines exports. In 2015, remittances from overseas Filipino workers (OFWs) accounted for 8.5 percent of the Philippine gross domestic product (GDP), generated by 1.6 million Filipinos and totaling P1.20 trillion ($26.92 billion). By far, OFWs employed in the United States generated the highest amount of remittances, more than four times the amount generated by OFWs employed in Saudi Arabia, the next highest remittance-generating country (GMANews 2015). Domestic labor, performing, shipbuilding, nursing, hotel staffing, construction, manufacturing, and tech work are the major types of overseas work executed by Filipinos. In 2006, 1 million Filipino overseas workers were categorized as "performing artists" (though human trafficking groups suspect that a large number of Filipino women who labor abroad under this label are sex workers) (Chan 2006). In many cases, the same companies that recruit, train, and place Filipinos in overseas construction, nursing, and manufacturing jobs scout for musical talent and recruit, train, and place Filipino performers. Thus the ubiquity of mimicry of American popular music in the Philippines must be understood as part of a national economic strategy, not as an essential feature of Filipino people nor as just a national pastime.

While Filipino musicians are sought after for their abilities to perform perfect covers of American pop songs, other types of Filipino workers are also required to mimic American modes of public and private performance. Filipino musicians, Filipino nurses and caregivers, and Filipino maids are all part of the same "family" of remittance-generating overseas work, and the family resemblance between these job categories becomes clearer when one considers that all three have to learn how to perfectly imitate their American counterparts (or, at least, the American *ideal* of pop performer, health care worker, and domestic servant). Just as Jackson Gan oversees the musical training of aspiring cover bands, a number of nursing schools in the Philippines specialize in "fast-track" programs to train Filipino physicians to work as nurses in U.S. hospitals—owing to the U.S. shortage of nurses, finding employment as nurses in the United States is far easier than trying to find overseas placements as doctors (Zarembo 2004), and there are "364 registered private training centers for domestic servants" in Manila, where students learn what to expect from their future overseas employers and how to navigate potentially tricky cross-cultural differences (Brygo 2011). Some service jobs located in the Philippines also necessitate mimicry, such as the position of call center worker (there are more than thirteen hundred call center operations in the Philippines [*Call Center Directory*[1]], employing more than 1 million Filipinos and accounting for between 5 and 10 percent of the Philippine GDP [Winn 2014]), which requires Filipinos to perform "hyper-competent reproductions"—in this case, imitations of American accents, idioms, and patterns of speech, so that an American who dials a toll-free number on the back of his credit card doesn't realize that his call has been routed to a cubicle in Quezon City, not Dayton. It is not only Filipino singers who must deliver pitch-perfect renditions of American voices on command, for pay.

■ THE YOUTUBE AUDITION

One can argue that, at least in the entertainment sector, the Philippines is attempting a radical reversal of the colonial dynamic of more than a century ago: Filipinos are *selling back* to Americans the very Americanness that was imposed on Filipinos by colonization.

Having placed millions of its citizens in bars, nightclubs, and cruise ship cabarets all over the world, the Philippines has been striving to place Filipino performers in Western media markets over the past five years. Pineda's hire by Journey is the most successful attempt, but there have been notable others. For example, in July 2007, the Cebu Provincial Detention and Rehabilitation Center (CPDRC) uploaded a video recording of the performance of fifteen hundred inmates dancing to Michael Jackson's "Thriller," imitating the concept and some of the choreography from Jackson's 1983 video. The CPDRC video attracted millions of views in a few weeks and ranked fifth on *Time*'s top ten list of viral videos for 2007 (GMANews 2007). In January 2010, Sony Entertainment sent Jackson's choreographer, Travis Payne, and two American dancers to teach dance routines for several Jackson songs to twelve hundred CPDRC inmates; Sony made a four-minute twenty-seven-second video of Payne, the American dancers, and the CPDRC dancers performing and uploaded the video to YouTube to promote the global release of the official DVD of the Jackson documentary *This Is It* (Napallacan et al. 2010). The CPDRC dance program inspired the creation of a Canadian "12 episode interactive musical webseries," *Prison Dancer,* which launched in spring 2012.[2]

Another Filipino who gained prominence in the United States for her ability to perform American music is pop singer Charice Pempengco (whose stage name is simply "Charice"), who placed third in the Philippine *American Idol*–like TV talent competition, *Little Big Star,* in 2005; her success was attributed to her note-perfect covers of "power ballads" made famous by American soul singers such as Whitney Houston, Jennifer Hudson, and Beyoncé. In 2007, a fan uploaded videos of Charice's performances to YouTube, and the videos received 13 million hits in a short period of time. Charice was then invited to sing on a South Korean TV show, *Star King,* in summer 2007, and U.S. television talk show host Ellen DeGeneres saw a YouTube video of Charice's *Star King* performance. DeGeneres invited Charice to sing on her daytime talk show, *Ellen,* in December 2007, which led to Charice making appearances on a number of U.K. and U.S. television programs and performing concerts all over the world, recording two albums and being cast in the U.S. TV musical sitcom *Glee* as a recurring guest star in 2010–11.

Members of the Filipino diaspora have made similar movements from the ranks of unknown ethnic cover artists into the realm of the white-dominated mainstream Western culture industries: in 2010, a YouTube video of the Filipino-American R&B group Legaci covering Justin Bieber's "Baby" prompted Bieber's manager, Scooter Braun, to hire Legaci as Bieber's world tour backup singers. Legaci has since appeared, with and more often without Bieber, on MTV, top pop radio stations, *Saturday Night Live, The View, Ellen,* and *Today* and has released two original singles.

A specific moment is discernible in these stories of Filipino musical artists traveling from the margins to the centers of Western cultural production. That moment is the "audition": the Filipino performers demonstrate their mimicry skills to the Western world by way of YouTube videos, and if Western media figures like what they hear and see, they give the Filipino artists jobs in their metropoles and media centers and on the road with headliners. Through auditions, performers are discovered and hired. Bowe (2005) describes "the manufacturing process" of Filipino cover bands consisting of the discovery of raw talent in the Philippine provinces, the transfer of recruited aspiring artists to the Philippine capital, the centralized training of those aspirants, and eventually the exportation of them as "finished products" to various wealthier Asian, Middle Eastern, European, and North American live performance venues. But since 2007, this manufacturing process now includes a possible second round of auditions, discovery, physical migration, training, and exportation. The online audition potentially leads to employment in the Western mediascape (Appadurai 1990)—television appearances, recording deals, "official" music videos, and concert bookings offered by major media companies in the West, especially in the United States (as the most influential and largest exporter of English-language media in the world). Rather than auditioning for Filipino overseas worker's agencies, performers audition for American bands, managers, and producers. Instead of moving to Manila upon being discovered, they move to Los Angeles or New York, or wherever a show is taped or a band rehearses and records. Instead of being trained by Filipino choreographers and musicians, they are trained by American publicists and handlers. And rather than being exported to bars and clubs in Dubai or Singapore, they are exported to multiple cities on world tours, or booked for special all-star concerts or guest star spots.

YouTube is currently the primary site of global auditioning for ambitious Filipino cover acts; the CPDRC inmates, Pineda, Charice, and Legaci all were discovered by Western media interests via YouTube videos. Filipino fans participating in social media sites give Filipino performers significant "backup" online, as they post raves of their favorite Filipino singers and dancers on YouTube, Facebook, and Twitter; reblog on Tumblr; create fan sites; make fan videos; and otherwise promote Filipino performers trying to transition to Western media. Fans can play a crucial role in using new media to make Filipino musical artists visible: as mentioned earlier, a Filipino fan's upload of videos of Charice's first appearance on Philippine TV launched her professional career and made possible her crossover to U.S. markets, and it was a fan of Pineda who uploaded videos of The Zoo's performances to YouTube. There is a cadre of Filipino and Filipino-American artists who have built up significant YouTube subscriber numbers and seem to be "waiting in the wings" to join (or replace) Charice, Pineda, and Legaci on the stage of American mainstream media fame (AJ Rafael, Gabe Bondoc, Melissa Polinar, Jr. Aquino, Jennifer Chung, and Melvin Gutierrez are all Filipino and Filipino-American singers mentioned in a 2010 *New York Times* article as rising YouTube stars [Kun 2010]). Filipino performers have transformed YouTube into a virtual theater in which they continually audition; Filipino fans occupy the same virtual theater and fill it (and other social media sites) with their applause and approbation, in the form of praising and encouraging comments.

In this way, Filipino performers are *transmediating* themselves, and their "brand" as expert mimics of American pop music culture, through social media platforms. In a 2007 essay, "Transmedia Storytelling 101," Henry Jenkins uses the term *transmedia storytelling* to describe how media companies use multiple platforms to tell different components of "complex fictional worlds." Transmedia storytelling, states Jenkins, is

> a process where integral elements of a fiction get dispersed systematically across multiple delivery channels for the purpose of creating a unified and coordinated entertainment experience. . . . A media conglomerate has an incentive to spread its brand or expand its franchises across as many different media platforms as possible. . . . Transmedia storytelling practices may expand the potential market for a property by creating different points of entry for different audience segments.

Filipino cover artists are not media conglomerates seeking to market sci-fi and fantasy blockbuster franchises; they are individuals, most of them with minimal financial means, who seek to market only their own cultural labor and whose YouTube videos and Facebook posts generate no revenue for them directly. But these Filipino performers' YouTube videos of their American-style performances are instances of transmedia marketing—they are wagers on future wages. Filipino artists "disperse their performances systematically across multiple media channels" (doing live shows in the Philippines or in their local communities, as most of them must do to earn a living, as well as recording videos for online distribution). They create a "unified and coordinated entertainment experience" across all of their live gigs and videos, demonstrating that they can sing the songs just like Steve Perry or Whitney Houston time and time again, that they can hit the high notes exactly when audiences expect them every time, that they are *reliable products*. Filipino cover performers have just as much "incentive" as any major media corporation to "spread [their] brand[s] across as many different media platforms as possible," for, as argued earlier, each show and each video is potentially an audition for a job in the United States, or Canada, or the United Kingdom, hence their attempts to be constantly "present" on social media sites. And their transmedia practices, like movie studios,' "may expand the potential market for a property"—in this case, the property is themselves and their skill at performing mimicry—"by creating different points of entry for different audience segments." It is highly unlikely that Sony executives, Michael Jackson's choreographer, Schon, DeGeneres, or Justin Bieber's manager would have noticed the Filipino dancers and singers that they did by visiting the restaurants, cruise ship lounges, and karaoke bars (or prisons!) where the Filipinos were regularly performing live. YouTube created a different point of entry, of first contact with these Filipino cover performers, for this different audience of American media decision makers. The Filipino artists had to transmediate themselves to be *seen* by the West.

■ CONTESTING THE COPY

The ostensible logic of the YouTube audition mirrors that of *American Idol* and other television "reality shows" that are talent competitions (including the Philippine and South Korean shows on which Charice appeared and first attracted U.S. media attention): all of these media platforms offer Filipino performers the opportunity to compete—with one another and with performers around the world—to prove that they are among "the best," that their talents make them worthy of fan attention and professional employment. YouTube and television competitions proffer the same promise that global neoliberal capitalism holds out to (presumably) everyone, everywhere, regardless of nationality, class, ethnicity, gender, or sexuality: the promise of merit-based economic success. The assumption that the YouTube audition and the TV singing contest are wide open to all entrants and provide a kind of level playing field is reinforced by the discourse of those who "discover" talent on these media sites. For instance, Schon says, reflecting on his hunt for a front man that led to Pineda's hiring, "I found some good guys, but I didn't feel they had the strength and the power in their pipes to carry themselves over the power of our music. . . . I said [of Pineda], 'This guy is the real deal'" (Harris 2013). In Schon's telling, out of all of the singers whom he screened, Pineda possessed the most vocal "strength" and "power," and on this basis, Schon judged Pineda to be better than an imitator and better than a cover artist—Schon found Pineda worthy of becoming the "real" lead singer for Journey.

But although Pineda won the spot of the "real" front man, many social media users' comments on his hire have highlighted that Pineda is not the "original" lead singer of Journey, Steve Perry, who was not the band's first singer but recorded with the group their most famous, signature songs from the late 1970s through the mid-1980s. There is a distinct contrast in tone between comments posted by Pineda fans and those posted by

Perry fans. One comment posted in 2015 by Kevin McRae in response to *People* magazine's YouTube video on Pineda (reporting how Journey found their new singer via YouTube) reads, "Fuk the Zipper head, Steve Perry will never be replaced! Journey Sucks now with this zipper head"; another 2015 comment on this video, posted by Ellane Jaramillo, states, "Steve is the only VOICE..... Cheap replacements NEED NOT APPLY!" (*People* 2008). A comment posted by geoff101001 in 2015, on a YouTube video of Pineda performing a Journey song with his Manila house band, The Zoo, before he joined Journey, reads, "All he'll ever be is a sing-alike singer. He just copied someone elses style, he isn't his own person he doesnt even have his own style but, its great for journey that he sounds like steve did" (Docnancs 2008). Similarly, a 2015 comment by gc123x on one of Charice's YouTube videos (her performance of the 1975 Eric Carmen ballad "All by Myself," of which Céline Dion recorded a bravura cover in 1996) criticizes Charice for her lack of uniqueness: "there is no doubting she [Charice] is absolutely incredible . . . but it's a shame she didn't put her own spin on it, it was pretty much a carbon copy of celines version" (Luzhaoyong 2012).

These remarks conflate racist views of Asians ("zipperhead" is a derogatory term for Asians originated by American GIs during the Korean War and perpetuated by American soldiers in the Vietnam War), anger at U.S. manufacturing jobs being outsourced to lower-paid workers in developing nations ("Cheap replacements"), and dismissal of cover singers as inherently unoriginal and less skilled than musicians who perform new material ("all he'll ever be is a sing-alike singer"; "carbon copy"). They testify to the unwillingness of some Americans to accept Filipino performers, no matter how "strong" and "powerful" their voices are, and regardless of whether they emerge as the victors from a competitive field of talented amateurs all informally auditioning online or on television for jobs as professional entertainers, adequate substitutes, or what Joseph Roach (1996) would call "surrogates" for American performers.

These critical comments might be read as themselves transmediations—extensions via new media—of the United States's paradoxical attitude toward its colonial subjects in the early twentieth century. Although Americans installed myriad types of infrastructure, beginning in 1898, to instruct Filipinos to resemble their American governors, Americans derided Filipinos for their mimicry at the same time. Lucy Mae San Pablo Burns (2013, 10) cites an American anthropologist who declares in 1905 that the Filipino "lacks inventiveness" and an American literary scholar who, in 1906, derides Filipino literature for being "singularly adulterated by foreign influences." The very imitative capacities that U.S. colonial forces, including schools and hospitals, required Filipinos to routinely employ made Filipinos the target of American charges of unoriginality and noncreativity.

This disdain for Filipino mimicry of American culture, and a lack of awareness or comprehension that American imperialism and neocolonialism have emphatically demanded and incented that mimicry, was apparent in U.S. studies of the Philippines the early 1900s and is visible again in the comment sections of Filipinos' YouTube auditions in the 2010s. The YouTube disparagements are informed by a century of U.S. military interventions in Asia and the diminishment of American manufacturing following the globalization of production, which gave rise to the specific genres of anti-Asian speech used against Pineda (slurs propagated during the Korean and Vietnam Wars and protests against outsourcing). But the 1905–6 and 2015 condemnations of Filipino cultural mimicry are more similar than different. In both, or rather, in *all* eras of Filipino–American relations, contests for American employment and reputation that purport to be pure meritocracies—objective evaluations of how well nonwhite non-Westerners can perform Americanness—are proven to be false promises, for Filipinos can never truly win these contests: they can never be universally accepted as the "real deal."

■ POLICING THE COPY

Some YouTube users post negative comments on the videos of Filipinos' copies of American culture, not to dispute the excellence of their performances, but as attempts to police the entertainers when they deviate from what I call the "Filipino brand." That brand consists of Filipinos delivering perfect covers at every show, without fail and without variation. When a performer veers off brand, fans seek to discipline her.

For example, when the singer Charice rose to fame in the Philippines and the United States between 2007 and 2011, she displayed a highly feminine style, routinely wearing dresses or skirts, makeup, and long hair. Then, in a televised 2014 interview with Oprah Winfrey, Charice wore short hair and masculine clothing and said, "Basically, my soul is . . . male" (Rubenstein 2014). Though Charice did not identify as transgender in the interview (she told Oprah, "I'll cut my hair and wear boy clothes and everything, but that's all" [Rubenstein 2014]), she has maintained a "butch" appearance since then, never reverting to her previous "femme" template. Comments posted in 2015 and 2016 to a 2012 video of Charice performing (Luzhaoyong 2012) lament the star's change, but their ire is focused on what they perceive to be a change in her singing ability: Mylene Socuaje writes, "I MISS THE OLD CHARICE . . . I JUST MISS THE WAY SHE SINGS

A SONG," and in response, DQuizzle K writes, "Same! For some reason she sounds very different. I mean I don't care about the appearance but what did she do to her voice vocally?" August Faelnar writes, "she made her voice lower . . . Idk why she did it but . . . When u hear her sing now, she sounds like a boy," to which DQuizzle K replies, "Ugh now I'm sad, you're voice use to be sooo much more beautiful." Miyuki Brygenwerth comments, "I still like Charice, but I like this [2012] Charice better. Yes I did understand that she's happy for herself and so do I; but some of her recent videos, she seems like she couldn't just hit the high notes she supposed to hit." Chòi báo Phuong Nguyên states, "who is coming back here [to the 2012 video] in May, 2016 because of missing her high notes?" On a 2015 YouTube video titled "Charice Pempengco's New Masculine Look" (Viral and Trending 2015), which is a compilation of numerous clips and still photos of Charice post-2014, lee perez comments, "all I can say she shouldn't have change . . . sayang ang diva voice ["what a waste of a diva voice" or "what a shame about that diva voice" in Tagalog]." Trung Nguyen posts on the same video, "She want to be a transguy. . . . That's the voice she have to sacrifice to be a new 'he,' no more Charice, no more powerful voice."

Though Charice has never publicly stated that she has undergone hormonal treatment or taken any other measures that would alter her voice, she has sung in a lower register since 2014. The commenters cited here unfavorably compare Charice's former voice ("sooo much more beautiful") to her current voice, characterize the change as a kind of self-inflicted damage ("what did she do to her voice?"), blame the singer for being unable to do her job properly ("seems like she couldn't just hit the high notes she supposed to hit"), express their disappointment and dismay at her "new" voice ("sayang [wasted, shame]"; "missing her high notes"; "I MISS THE OLD CHARICE"), and directly attribute the vocal change to what they interpret as Charice's gender shift ("That's the voice she have to sacrifice to be a new 'he'"; "she sounds like a boy"; "she shouldn't have change"). The shared sentiment in these comments is transphobic, to be sure, but compounding that transphobia are sharp criticisms of Charice's job performance. Charice's fans make clear that they dislike that she sings differently now than she did before, that she is not the same performer that they had adored, and that she seems incapable of the same mezzo soprano feats that made her famous in years past. The Filipino brand means consistently singing the expected songs as audiences expect to hear them sung, and by changing her voice, Charice no longer can perform with the precision and repetition promised by the brand. The 2015 and 2016 comments on her YouTube videos declare that Charice fails to meet the brand standard.

Since the Filipino brand follows an industrial logic of identical output that is usually associated with production rather than performance, one can argue that Charice's deviating from that brand constitutes an insistence on her humanity and her artistic creativity. After all, only machines never change (and we might therefore see the Filipino mimicry brand as intertwined with the discourse of techno-orientalism, which views Asian bodies as inherently technological; see Roh, Huang, and Niu 2015). Charice's 2014 revision of her fashion, voice, and possibly gender can be read as a public assertion of an artist's, and person's, right and need to be dynamic rather than static, to periodically launch new phases of her style and perhaps her very being. While self-transformations and stylistic makeovers seem to be an intrinsic part of the "American brand" of popular music (consider the many metamorphoses of U.S. recording artists like Madonna, Miley Cyrus, Prince, or Beyoncé), the Filipino brand of cultural performance is defined by identity and repetition rather than difference: the Filipino cover artist must excel at sounding identical to American singers and at reproducing that identical sound over and over again. The differences between the American brand, which emphasizes creativity, and the Filipino brand, which stresses consistency, mean that Filipino performers like Pineda are subjected to derision for being mere copies, while Filipino performers like Charice risk their fans' rejection when they become unable or unwilling to copy both American artists and their own former performances.

■ TRANSMEDIATING THE FILIPINO MIMICRY BRAND

Earlier, I quoted comments on YouTube criticizing Pineda's hire as the lead singer of Journey; these comments seemed to represent a definitively American perspective, as they included U.S. troops' epithets and the type of anti-outsourcing language common to American public discourse since the late twentieth century. However, the 2015 and 2016 YouTube comments criticizing Charice do not appear to be uniform in national origin. Some of the user names I quoted are common in the Philippines, Japan, and Vietnam, and other user names hint at other nationalities and ethnicities. Although the precise range of different identities and locations represented by these commenters cannot be ascertained, it is clear that it is not only Filipino fans who wish to keep Filipino performers "on brand." There is an international understanding of what the Filipino mimicry brand is: exactitude in copying, technically and aesthetically precise repetition, and giving people what they want and what they expect, every time. It should not be surprising that the fandom of the Filipino mimicry brand, and the need to protect that brand and to discipline Filipinos who threaten or undermine it, transcends national borders and ethnic differences, given that one of the major motivations for Filipinos to post videos of their cover performances on YouTube is to draw other nations' attention to Filipino performance talent, to make that talent go global.

In a 2011 essay, "Transmedia 202: Further Reflections," Jenkins elaborates on his concept of transmedia and states that texts can be transmediated not only through storytelling but through "transmedia performance" as well. Jenkins uses the television show *Glee* (on which Charice occasionally guest starred) as his example of transmedia performance: "*Glee*'s transmedia strategies emphasize transmedia performance, with the songs moving through YouTube, iTunes, live performances, etc., which we read against each other to make sense of the larger *Glee* phenomenon." Jenkins's phrasing allows us to ask what "larger phenomenon" is being transmediated in the YouTube videos of Filipino performers.

The national brand of the Philippines in the twenty-first century is that the Philippines produces great mimics for global markets, especially the United States. Filipino singers and dancers can sing and dance anything and are particularly strong at American performance styles; Filipino call center workers can "speak English fluently with a neutral [read: American] accent" (Winn 2014) and adhere to scripts for American-style customer interactions, and therefore can sonically "pass" as American; Filipino nurses strive to "quickly learn standard nursing practices in the U.S. and integrate into the U.S. healthcare system" (Adeniran et al. 2008); Filipino domestic workers employed by American families "[teach] themselves American-style cooking" (Segre 2012). I interpret the YouTube videos, television appearances, social media participation, live gigs, and other transmedia performances of Filipino cover artists to synecdochally stand for Filipino workers' *collective* hireability, their consistency *as a group*, their competence and desirability as a *national brand of labor products*. By transmediating themselves, Filipino artists are extending the Filipino mimicry brand and helping to ensure that the world becomes increasingly familiar with and accepting of this brand identity. Transmedia thus assists not just individual Filipino artists in being discovered and crossing over from Filipino or Asian markets to Western, especially American, markets. The massive online and live presence of Filipino cover acts, their constant production of performances for virtual and physical spaces, raises the likelihood of employment for all Filipino mimetic laborers by reinforcing the total image of Filipinos as "perfect covers," that is, as performers who can perfectly execute any action that American audiences already know and expect.

Unlike Jenkins's examples of U.S. transmedia franchises, which are owned and controlled by studios, networks, comic publishers, or game companies, and which are "authored" by writers, directors, and producers, transmediations of the Filipino brand are not driven and managed by either corporate divisions or individual "masterminds" who map out product chains and release dates. Transmediations of Filipino entertainers are often carried out by the performers themselves or by their friends, family members, or fans (though some Filipino talent agents, such as Jackson Gan, may pay for the costs of video production and online marketing for their most promising acts). Despite the lack of coordination between Filipino entertainers and other types of Filipino mimetic workers, and although the Philippine government does not order or sponsor transmediations the way that Hollywood studios do, Filipino transmedia performance accomplishes what U.S. media corporations hope to achieve with their transmedia campaigns: global awareness of, and economic success for, a specific brand. Filipino performers' willingness to constantly compete for attention on YouTube, television competition shows, and other media stages contributes to a widespread perception that Filipinos' talent for mimicry is a national, and "natural," trait, one that other countries should find desirable and hireable.

One reason that I emphasize that Filipino transmedia performances *serve to extend* the Filipino national brand is that these performances *do not* serve to bring enduring fame and fortune to the majority of individual performers. Pineda's lasting tenure with Journey has been exceptional among Filipino entertainers who have "auditioned" on YouTube and reality TV competitions; most Filipinos, even when they attract international attention for their videos or when they win or place highly in *American Idol* and other singing competitions, typically attain only what Sue Collins (2008) calls "dispensable celebrity"—they become the foci of media attention and fan consumerism for a few months or a year. As the case of Charice illustrates, even the most popular cover artists can lose their fan followings fairly quickly. Thus, while Hollywood's transmedia strategies are judged successful when each title in a franchise becomes a "hit," and each hit increases the value of the overarching brand of the franchise, Filipinos' transmediations do not often result in individual transmedia performers becoming enduring stars, but they do work to build the worldwide recognizability and popularity of the Filipino mimicry brand.

■ TRANSMEDIA AND IMPERIALISM

But as much as Filipino performers are transmediating a national brand of Filipinos as expert imitators, are they not transmediating American cultural imperialism to an even greater extent? In their 2013 book *Spreadable Media*, Jenkins, Sam Ford, and Joshua Green cite marketing professor

Robert V. Kozinets's statement that "successful branding is successful world-building" (102–3). Kozinets refers here to transmedia texts' contributions to fictional worlds like the "world" of *Star Wars*, but the colonizations launched by the United States in 1898, when it seized control of not only the Philippines but also Hawai'i, Guam, Puerto Rico, and other territories, constituted a more concrete attempt at "world-building," or building up a hegemonic entity that governs large parts of the world and heavily influences the rest—that is, building a world that is politically and culturally *American*. This begs the question of whether, and to what degree, we must consider transmediation as intrinsically imperialist or as inextricably linked to imperialism. Transmedia campaigns always resemble geopolitical expansionism and colonialism. Even when they revolve around fictional texts, they aim at taking over as much "mindshare" (see De Kosnik et al. 2015) and appropriating as great a proportion of the financial resources of as many media consumers in as many nations as they possibly can. And because U.S. companies' transmedia campaigns for fictional texts are typically international in scope, they are not entirely separate from imperialism but must be regarded as key to contemporary American cultural imperialism. I suggest that we consider the manifestation of American cultural imperialism through transmedia campaigns not only as a twenty-first-century phenomenon that arose with the Internet but as having a longer history.

David Morley and Kevin Robins (1995) propose that American cultural imperialism began either in the 1920s (the rise of the U.S. film industry to global dominance) or in 1941 (the publication of Henry Luce's "American Century" essay, in which Luce advocates that the United States "exert upon the world the full impact of our influence" through media exports), but I argue that the start of U.S. cultural imperialism was coeval with the beginning of U.S. overseas imperialism in 1898 (220–21). As I have been arguing, the main cultural product that the United States sought to introduce to its colonial subjects, in the Philippines and elsewhere, was Americanness itself. The United States has been transmediating Americanness—marketing American ways of doing, speaking, singing, being, working, dancing, nursing, and caring to Filipinos via multiple platforms, including books, live performances, films, television shows, educational systems, health protocols, military training, and so on—for more than one hundred years.

In this light, Filipinos' transmediations of their abilities to mimic American cultural performances appear to be merely the present-day results of the United States's long campaign to transmediate cultural Americanness. The transmedia performances that Filipinos might regard as the products of their initiative taking, their ambition, and the many hours of labor they have spent perfecting their mimetic faculties might be regarded as simply a former colony's attempt to sell back to the colonizer what the colonizer sold them in the first place, what it was selling them all along. Perhaps these transmediations mark, not the surprising achievements of Filipinos in the global entertainment marketplace, but rather the full realization of the goals of the American imperial project.

This perspective minimizes the agency and accomplishments of Filipino performers and frames U.S. imperialism as an overwhelming teleological force. But while it has serious flaws, we might use this interpretation of Filipino transmediation to propose an answer to the question, why do Americans buy Filipinos' performances of Americanness? Appadurai (1990) points out that Americans have been in the market for repeated reenactments of their cultural past since the 1980s. Appadurai argues that Americans, reveling in nostalgia for prior eras throughout the postmodern period, enjoy looking to other countries—particularly the Philippines— to deliver that past to them:

> If your present is their future (as in much modernization theory and in many self-satisfied tourist fantasies) and their future is your past (as in the case of the Philippine virtuosos of American popular music), then your own past can be made to appear as simply a normalized modality of your present. (4)

What Americans may appreciate so deeply about Filipinos' transmediating Americanness back to them is that it fulfills their nostalgic yearning for their own colonial past—it makes the "American century," the period when the United States extended its influence worldwide through aggressive military, economic, and media campaigns, "a normalized modality of [Americans'] present." Perhaps Americans are buying the reproductions of American cultural performance that Filipinos are selling because they wish for reassurances that their imperialist project has not yet ended, that it is not the past, and they long for the project to be always made present again, re-presented, in the voices and bodies of people whose very proficiency at sounding and seeming American is proof of the project's success.

■ JUMPING THE GATE

Another view of Filipinos' transmedia performances is possible. Instead of conceiving of Filipinos' transmediations as the inevitable end product of American imperialism, we can think of Filipinos as audiences and consumers of American cultural products who, by uploading their own versions of those products to YouTube, and by expertly performing them on television, seek to correct the imbalance of a global mediascape in which the majority of makers are American and the majority of receivers are non-American. Filipinos transmediate their mimetic talents to enter the mediascape and place their voices alongside those of American performers. Given that their historical circumstances have forced them to develop the capacity to perfectly imitate Americanness, Filipinos do what they can to make their imitations seen and heard.

Jenkins, Ford, and Green (2013) note that, while ethnic minorities in the United States and other nonhegemonic groups produce a great deal of transmedia, their productions often are ignored by mainstream white American society. Referencing S. Craig Watkins's (2009) work, they write, "Social network sites often operate as the digital equivalent of gated communities , protecting participants from online contact with people outside their social circle. . . . Watkins compares this process to the 'big sort,' which has reintroduced segregation in many U.S. cities through residential patterns" (192–93). Therefore, when Filipinos' transmedia performances spread in ways that most minorities' transmedia texts do not—"across ideological and class divides, across language barriers, and especially across the closed minds of many people" (192)—they defy the "systemic bias" (189) of both old and new media platforms, the bias that facilitates the dissemination of white American culture to all people but hinders the dissemination of nonwhite, non-American culture to white Americans. In effect, when Filipinos draw the attention of mainstream white America through their transmediations, they "jump the gate" of online gated communities. They insinuate themselves into the minds and hearts of audiences and occupy (however temporarily) positions of fame and power, when imperialist history and the tendencies of social media users make such a feat highly unlikely.

Pineda no longer covers Journey songs; he is the front man of Journey. The CPDRC inmates performed imitations of Michael Jackson videos and then were choreographed *by Michael Jackson's choreographer* for a video professionally produced by Michael Jackson's record label; for that brief moment, the inmates who were mimics became Jackson's substitute and stand-in. Legaci's YouTube video of their cover of a Justin Bieber song led to them touring *with* Bieber, singing *alongside* him rather than mimicking the songs from a distance and belatedly. Charice's appearances on *Glee* positioned her as a rival and challenger to the preeminence of *Glee*'s female lead: in her first scene on the show, Charice's character engages with the leading female character in an impromptu "sing-off"; their vocal duet/duel, in which they trade verses of a Lady Gaga hit while circling each other in the girls' bathroom, is interrupted by a teacher and so no "winner" is declared. Legaci and Charice have demonstrated that Filipino mimics can achieve parity with the Americans they copy, while the CP-DRC inmates and Pineda have demonstrated that Filipinos can rival or replace American performers. Through their transmedia performances, a handful of Filipinos penetrate, however fleetingly, the gated community of mainstream white American culture.

However, while some Filipino mimetic performers have been able to jump the gate and make themselves visible to the white American mainstream, rarely have these artists *joined* that community and attained a lasting place in the pantheon of American stars. More often than not, Filipinos who successfully transmediate their imitative skills become memes and dispensable celebrities—short-term sensations. Filipinos and Filipino Americans, whose complex history with the United States seems often forgotten or overlooked by U.S. news and fictional media, deeply appreciate even these brief appearances by Filipinos in the American mediascape; as Allan Punzalan Isaac (2006, xix) states, millions of Filipinos and Filipino Americans feel "desire and pleasure [at being] a visible part of the [American] national story *as* a sensation." But Filipinos' efforts to transmediate their mimetic talents as a national Filipino brand have not yet overcome what Isaac calls the "national media blindness [that has] described Filipino presence in the United States" (xxiii) and the "unrecognizability of the Filipino in the American imagination" (xxiv).

"American public memory and vision effectively overlook the Filipino and absentmindedly ask, 'What American empire?'" (xxiii) despite frequent flashes of Filipino mimetic talent across U.S. stages and screens. But the Philippines and its diaspora can never forget the legacy of U.S. imperialism, as its effects on the Philippines's territory, laws, economy, citizenry, and diaspora are still unfolding, as exemplified by the VFA controversy discussed at the start of this essay. Filipinos, forced long ago into a confounding and fraught twinship by and with the United States, may seem to be permanently relegated to the status of mimic by their colonial past. But we can also read Filipinos' multiplatform performances of their mimetic talent as spectacular reenactments and reminders of the United States's twisted kinship with the Philippines—intended to counteract the United States's stubborn amnesia about its (neo)colony—and as constitutive of a transmedia campaign by and for an entire nation and an entire ethnic group. Like all transmedia producers and performers, Filipinos seek to appropriate as much mindshare (in the form of attention and fandom) and resources (in the form of jobs, media visibility, and consumer spending) in as many nations around the world as possible by constantly releasing new iterations and incarnations of the Filipino brand of imitative excellence. Because the transmediation of

Americanness was a key component of the U.S. colonization of the Philippines, twenty-first-century Filipinos transmediate their mastery of
Americanness to simultaneously evoke the colonial past and position
themselves as suitable future rivals to, or replacements for, American
originals.

Abigail De Kosnik is associate professor at the University of California,
Berkeley in the Berkeley Center for New Media and the Department of
Theater, Dance, and Performance Studies. She is the author of *Rogue
Archives: Digital Cultural Memory and Media Fandom* (2016).

■ NOTES

1. http://www.callcenterdirectory.net/call-%20center/Philippines
/directory-2-page-1.html%5D.
2. http://www.prisondancer.com/.

■ WORKS CITED

Adeniran, Rita K., Victoria L. Rich, Elizabeth Gonzalez, Cheryl Peterson,
Sandra Jost, and Melanie Gabriel. 2008. "Transitioning Internationally
Trained Nurses for Success: A Model Program." *The Online Journal of
Issues in Nursing* 3, no. 2. http://www.nursingworld.org/MainMenuCat
egories/ANAMarketplace/ANAPeriodicals/OJIN/TableofContents
/vol132008/No2May08/TIENS.html.

Anderson, Warwick. 2002. "Introduction: Postcolonial Technoscience."
Social Studies of Science 32, no. 5/6: 643–58.

Appadurai, Arjun. 1990. "Disjuncture and Difference in the Global Cultural
Economy." *Public Culture* 2, no. 2: 1–24.

Bhabha, Homi. 1984. "Of Mimicry and Man: The Ambivalence of Cultural
Discourse." *Discipleship,* October 28, 125–33.

Bowe, John. 2005. "How Did House Bands Become a Filipino Export?" *New
York Times,* May 29. http://www.nytimes.com/2005/05/29/magazine
/29FILIPINO.html?pagewanted=all&_r=0.

Braithwaite, Edward Kamau. 1971. *The Development of Creole Society in
Jamaica 1770–1820.* Oxford: Clarendon Press.

Brygo, Julien. 2011. "Filipino Maids for Export." *Le Monde Diplomatique,
English Edition,* October. http://mondediplo.com/2011/10/12maids.

Chan, Elaine. 2006. "Grace Notes: Philippines Musicians on the Road."
Asia Sentinel, July 4. http://www.asiasentinel.com/politics/grace
-notes-philippine-musicians-on-the-road/.

Collins, Sue. 2008. "Making the Most out of 15 Minutes: Reality TV's
Dispensable Celebrity." *Television New Media* 9, no. 2: 87–110.

Concepcion, Pocholo. 2010. "Arnel Pineda Seriously Plans for Life after Journey." *Inquirer,* August 10. http://showbizandstyle.inquirer.net/entertainment/entertainment/view/20100810-286028/Arnel-Pineda-seriously-planning-for life-after-Journey.

Conquergood, Dwight. 2002. "Performance Studies: Interventions and Radical Research." *The Drama Review* 46, no. 2: 145–56.

De Kosnik, Abigail, Laurent El Ghaoui, Vera Cuntz-Leng, Andrew Godbehere, Andrea Horbinski, Adam Hutz, Renée Pastel, and Vu Pham. 2015. "Watching, Creating, and Archiving: Observations on the Quantity and Temporality of Fannish Productivity in Online Fan Fiction Archives." *Convergence* 21, no. 1: 145–64.

Docnancs. 2008. "FAITHFULLY: by Arnel Pineda withe Zoo Band." July 26. https://youtu.be/ragdoUO6s5w.

Enriquez, Elizabeth L. 2006. "Media as the Site of Social Struggle: The Role of Philippine Radio and Television in the EDSA Revolt of 1986." *Plaridel* 3, no. 2: 123–38.

Fanon, Franz. 1952. *Black Skin, White Masks (Peau Noire, Masques Blanc).* Paris: De Seuil.

Flandez, Raymund. 2008. "A Tribute Band Singer Takes a Net Shortcut in Journey Stardom." *Wall Street Journal,* January 24. http://online.wsj.com/article/SB119929495499862495.html.

GMANews. 2007. "Cebu Dancing Inmates Video Makes *Time* List." http://www.gmanetwork.com/news/story/73615/lifestyle/cebu-dancing-inmates-video-makes-time-list.

———. 2015. "INFOGRAPHIC: Where the $26.92B of OFW Remittances Come From." June 9. http://www.gmanetwork.com/news/story/500918/money/infographic-where-26–92b-of-ofw-remittances-come-from.

Harris, Beth. 2013. "Journey Talks Singer Arnel Pineda's Impact, September—Due PBS Doc." *The Billboard,* August 6. http://www.billboard.com/articles/news/5638291/journey-talks-singer-arnel-pinedas-impact-september-due-pbs-doc.

Isaac, Allan Punzalan. 2006. *American Tropics: Articulating Filipino America.* Minneapolis: University of Minnesota Press.

Jenkins, Henry. 2007. "Transmedia Storytelling 101." *Confessions of an Aca-Fan: The Official Weblog of Henry Jenkins* (blog), March 22. http://henryjenkins.org/2007/03/transmedia_storytelling_101.html.

———. 2011. "Transmedia 202: Further Reflections." *Confessions of an Aca-Fan: The Official Weblog of Henry Jenkins* (blog), August 1. http://henryjenkins.org/2011/08/defining_transmedia_further_re.html.

Jenkins, Henry, Sam Ford, and Joshua Green. 2013. *Spreadable Media: Creating Value and Meaning in a Networked Culture.* New York: NYU Press.

Kun, Josh. 2010. "Unexpected Harmony." *New York Times,* June 18. http://www.nytimes.com/2010/06/20/arts/music/20legaci.html?pagewanted=all.

Lamming, George. 1960. *The Pleasures of Exile.* Ann Arbor: University of Michigan Press.

Liu, Ling Woo. 2008. "Journey's YouTube Lead Singer." *Time,* June 17. http://content.time.com/time/arts/article/0,8599,1815257,00.html.

Luzhaoyong 陸昭勇. 2012. "Charice Pempengo~All by Myself." https://youtu.be/IiroHFtwlpU.

McKinley, William. 1913. "The Benevolent Assimilation Proclamation." In *The American Occupation of the Philippines, 1898–1912,* edited by James H. Blount, 147–50. New York: G. P. Putnam's Sons.

Morley, David, and Kevin Robins. 1995. *Spaces of Identity: Global Media, Electronic Landscapes, and Cultural Boundaries.* New York: Routledge.

Pappademas, Alex. 2008. "He Didn't Stop Believin.'" *GQ,* April 30. http://www.gq.com/entertainment/music/200805/arnel-pineda-journey-lead-singer.

People. 2008. "Meet Journey's New Singer—Found on YouTube!" https://youtu.be/VccPl_uLpWA.

Perillo, J. Lorenzo. 2011. "'If I Was Not in Prison, I Would Not Be famous': Discipline, Choreography, and Mimicry in the Philippines." *Theatre Journal* 63, no. 4: 607–21.

Roach, Joseph. 1996. *Cities of the Dead.* New York: Columbia University Press.

Roh, David S., Betsy Huang, and Greta A. Niu. 2015. *Techno-orientalism: Imagining Asia in Speculative, History, and Media.* New Brunswick, N.J.: Rutgers University Press.

Rubenstein, Janine Rayford. 2014. "Charice Pempengco: My Soul Is Male." *People,* October 17. http://www.people.com/article/charice-pempengco-gender-sexuality-oprah-winfrey-own.

San Pablo Burns, Lucy Mae. 2012. *Puro Arte: Filipinos on the Stages of Empire.* New York: NYU Press.

Segre, Francesca. 2012. "The Heartache of the Migrant Nanny." *New York Times,* August 13. http://parenting.blogs.nytimes.com/2012/08/13/the-heartache-of-the-migrant-nanny/?_r=1.

Sweet, John Wood. 2003. *Bodies Politic: Negotiating Race in the American North.* Baltimore: Johns Hopkins University Press.

van Oosten, Sanne. 2012. "The Intense Filipino Love/Hate Relationship with America." *Bloggers without Borders* (blog), March 12. https://blog

gerswithoutbordersdotcom.wordpress.com/2012/03/12/the-intense
-filipino-lovehate-relationship-with-america/.

Viral and Trending. 2015. "Charice Pempenco's New Masculine Look."
https://www.youtube.com/watch?v=caZcYaxFu9Q&feature=youtu.be.

Watkins, Lee. 2009. "Minstrelsy and Mimesis in the South China Sea:
Filipino Migrant Musicians, Chinese Hosts, and the Disciplining of
Relations in Hong Kong." *Asian Music* 40, no. 2: 72–99.

Watkins, S. Craig. 2009. *The Young and the Digital: What the Migration to
Social Network Sites, Games, and Anytime, Anywhere Media Means for
Our Future*. Boston: Beacon Press.

Winn, Patrick. 2014. "How the Philippines Is Crushing the Indian Call Center Business." *The Week,* May 12. http://theweek.com/articles/447063
/how-philippines-crushing-indian-call-center-business.

Zarembo, Alan. 2004. "Physician, Remake Thyself." *Los Angeles Times,* January 10. http://articles.latimes.com/2004/jan/10/local/me-nurse10.

JENNIFER HUBBERT

The Biopolitics of Gratitude and Equivalence: Debt, Exchange, and Disaster Politics at the Shanghai World's Fair

ON MONDAY AFTERNOON, May 12, 2008, a massive earthquake struck Sichuan Province in southwest China. The earthquake, which measured 8.0 magnitude on the Richter scale, killed nearly ninety thousand people, left more than 14 million residents homeless, and destroyed nearly 80 percent of the region's buildings. Included in this devastation were 7,444 schools, 34,000 kilometers of highway, and 11,028 hospitals and clinics (UNISDR 2009; World Bank 2012).[1] By some estimates, the losses resulting from the earthquake totaled between $86 and $112 billion, and poverty levels in the region rose to more than one-third of the population (Hoyer 2009; Zhi and Ivy 2008). Even before the earthquake, the average annual per capita income in the ethnically diverse rural regions of the county hovered around five hundred dollars, one-twentieth of that in Shanghai (Lan 2010), reflecting the income differentials between China's ethnic minorities and its Han majority.

Within just two years of the earthquake, much of the region had been rebuilt as the result of a massive influx of humanitarian financial aid and a volunteer force that numbered in the hundreds of thousands. According to a variety of governmental publications, per capita income grew by 35 percent (Lan 2010); cultural heritage buildings were restored; and most homes, schools, and clinics were rebuilt. Describing the reconstruction process, China.org, the "authorized governmental portal site to China," notes that the "once picturesque town of Shuimo," which was devastated by the Sichuan earthquake, "is sporting a brand new look. It [has become] a livable tourist and cultural spot featuring ecological construction with

162

ethnic minority influences, attracting thousands of tourists from home and abroad" (China.org 2011). This narrative was echoed by a resident of Shanghai who told me in 2010, "The new homes for the earthquake victims are so much better. They are in a new style and have their own bathrooms and kitchens. The recipients are all minorities. Now they have three-story buildings and jobs. The government created new employment opportunities and built new schools. This will help them to get better educated." One reporter visiting the reconstructed area described the rebuilt residences as simply "too beautiful" and quoted a seventy-year-old recipient as saying, "If it were not for the help of the government, I would not even be able to cover a thatched-roof dwelling, much less live in this kind of home" (Lin 2009). In case the point should be missed, the article also reported, "Old people, speaking in plain dialect, explained the source of their good fortune to the reporter as, 'good government, good government.'"[2]

A regime's construction of a national narrative involves paying homage not only to a nation's glories but also to how it addresses its calamities. The two-year anniversary of the earthquake in May 2010 coincided with the opening of the Shanghai World Exposition, which utilized a portion of its stage to tell the story of the disaster and the reconstruction process in venues ranging from the Sichuan provincial pavilion to the Broad Air Conditioning Pavilion and in exhibits that included earthquake simulators, movies, remembrance walls, and live performances. Such world's fairs offer prime venues for examining narratives of the nation-state. Typically state and corporate funded, they construct ideal-type and hegemonic representations of state practices that highlight official visions of national modernity.[3] This was particularly true at the Shanghai Expo, which was directed and authorized by the Chinese state.[4] The Shanghai Expo, visited by 73 million people and costing twice as much as the Beijing 2008 Olympics, was the biggest and most lavish world's fair ever constructed, offering an immense platform upon which to communicate the state's vision of the nation's modernity to domestic and international audiences alike. As we shall see, the Expo offered what I am calling a "disaster politics" narrative about earthquake reconstruction—that, according to one reporter, had been accomplished with an "amazing speed" that was "seldom seen in the world" (Li 2009). This narrative was intended to recount not only China's humanitarian intentions toward its citizens but also its contemporary modernity. Disaster thus emerged as a politicized site through which the state attempted to augment its power.

This analysis of the Shanghai Expo's chronicle of the postearthquake reconstruction process explores how a disaster illuminates the politics of citizenship and belonging. Building on recent scholarship in anthropology that links humanitarianism to biopolitical processes (Bornstein and Redfield 2011; Fassin 2005; 2007; Redfield 2005; Ticktin 2006), it considers how these Expo representations functioned discursively as a technology of power employed to manage life and regulate the population by achieving what Foucault (1998, 140) has termed the "subjugations of bodies."[5] But unlike much of that literature, which often appears to take the triumph of biopolitics for granted, this article examines the structural prerequisites necessary for the state to accomplish its sovereignty project within the framework of humanitarian praxis. Thus it diverges from earlier studies of the biopolitics of humanitarianism by focusing not on what a biopolitics of humanitarianism *does* but on what a biopolitics of humanitarianism theoretically *needs* to accomplish its goals.

As the following examination of Expo earthquake representations will show, the forms of remembrance at the Expo constructed two distinct subject-citizens and situated them hierarchically in relationship to the earthquake—as either victims who needed to be brought into the modernity project or as volunteers who were representative of it. Through what I am terming a *biopolitics of gratitude* and a *biopolitics of equivalence,* the impoverished minority victims of the natural disaster were constructed as thankful for their earthquake-enabled participation in China's commodity modernization practices and the earthquake volunteers as equivalent to the state in their role as civic-minded models of modern benevolence, in the process underscoring how inequality is structured through exchange.

As others have demonstrated, humanitarian efforts in contemporary neoliberal and postsocialist states often are not only complicit with state biopower but, as Makley (2014) argues, also serve as a central component of the construction of sovereign power.[6] As we shall see, the biopolitics of gratitude and equivalence at the Expo constructed ideals for both the citizen-subject and the state, memorializing earthquake victims and volunteers to validate the state's modernization schemes and legitimize its sovereignty. Through such practices, the state both speaks to or solicits certain kinds of citizens and communicates a sovereign self to the nation and the global community.[7] Unlike other investigations of Expo representations that legitimize the state (e.g., Schneider and Hwang 2014), however, this analysis suggests that the process can never be automatic; sometimes interpellation misses its mark.[8] Given that the interpellative process of biopolitics involves both a call and a response, it argues, we must understand biopolitics as a form of *exchange* in which the hailed subjects incur a *debt* as recipients of state humanitarian endeavors that must be repaid if the state is to maintain its sovereign power. By bringing the insights of gift theory to bear on this issue, the following analysis demonstrates that to be effective, the technologies of biopolitics require a form of exchange in the classic anthropological sense in which Mauss and Boas understood the potlatch and other such gifting processes: as acts of giving and reciprocation that mobilize social and moral categories of belonging.[9] The biopolitical management of life, in other words, requires the managed body to reciprocate in particular ways for the supervisory biopolitical project to succeed in its quest for sovereignty.[10] Ultimately, this article asks, if the state sovereignty project mandates that biopolitical interventions of humanitarian aid stipulate an involuntary debt, should such interventions be viewed as indicators of the success or the limits of state power?

This investigation is based on ten eleven- to twelve-hour visits to the Shanghai Expo during summer 2010 and on conversations and interviews with exhibition attendees and Shanghai residents during and following the mega-event. At first glance, it is surprising that representations of the earthquake figured so prominently at the Shanghai Expo, given that world's fairs are typically designed to impress the world with the host nation's technological achievements and cultural expressions.[11] The organizers' reasoning may be clearer, however, when we consider that more than 95 percent of the Expo's visitors hailed from within the nation's borders, which, along with the obscurity of many of the cultural references and general lack of foreign-language explanations throughout its exhibits, suggests that the Chinese-language-speaking audience was a significant pedagogical target for the event's messaging. Furthermore, China's specific history of disaster relief presented a quite different context and set of expectations for a domestic audience than for an international one. Thus, whereas the Expo's exhibits on the wonders of green technology were intended to signal China's position as a leader of the sustainability movement to foreign visitors, those on earthquake reconstruction would have spoken to a domestic audience about the will of the modern state and the reconstruction as a triumphal public display of state power. The following analysis first examines the empirical construction of victims and volunteers in Expo representations and then discusses how they and the sovereign power of the state were maintained by the notion of a debt to the state. Last, the article briefly considers the potential instability of the biopolitical project, should subjects refuse to acknowledge that debt.

■ CATEGORIES OF BELONGING

The China Pavilion, centrally located and three times higher than any other pavilion, loomed large over the Expo. So popular was the pavilion that it required time-specific entrance tickets that were usually gone within an hour of the park's opening, and even then it took visitors hours of queuing to enter the building. One of the pavilion's central highlights was an eight-minute film by acclaimed director Lu Chuan that played on a massive tripartite screen. Titled *Licheng (Process)*, the film's English subtitle reads *The Road to Our Beautiful Life*, reflecting the tribute to the rapid development of the post-Mao nation that was a central theme of both the pavilion and the larger Expo.[12]

Process traces a multigenerational tale of a wizened patriarch of humble rural origins whose sons and grandsons embody the last thirty years of China's development and progress. The first minutes of the film establish an evolutionary narrative of progress that opens with images of lush rural landscapes and a majestic musical backdrop against which the patriarch's son rushes to join a host of migrant laborers who are shown building the infrastructure of the nation on bare ground. The images and dates on the screen locate the action in time; the construction process begins in the late 1970s, erasing the Maoist years of high socialism from the film's saga of development and advancement. As the patriarch's son ages, he is shown traveling through the increasingly urban landscapes of the 1980s in the center screen, while the side screens document technological innovations and cultural celebrations of the period. As the film progresses into the 1990s, the next generation is represented in the person of the patriarch's grandson, who spins dizzyingly through a revolving door while dates flash by on the side screens, moving through the 1990s and into the 2000s, accompanied by an increasingly modern array of urban infrastructure, sophisticated fashion, and technological wizardry. As the child emerges from this revolving door into the year 2008, he has become an adult who gazes with apparent amazement at a futuristic urban landscape of avant-garde skyscrapers and personal automobiles whizzing by on a vast array of intricately laced freeways.

At that point in the film, the music turns ominous, the passage of time slows to a near standstill, and the young man gazes at a ticking clock that stops at 14:28, the moment of the Sichuan earthquake. The faces of the urban citizens surrounding him register fear and dismay as they stare at a large screen projecting images of the earthquake's devastation. Scenes of rescue workers are interspersed with those of military helicopters delivering aid and retrieving bodies from the rubble as subtitles and voice-overs narrate the action: "The volunteer teams from Beijing are here, running the risks of aftershocks and landslides. The volunteer teams from Shanghai are here. They said good-bye to their family and friends. More than two hundred thousand volunteers from all over the country are here. They gather here because of a deep sense of love." The grandson appears on the screen as one of the volunteers, grasping the hand of a young woman reaching out from the depths of the debris and then looking on as army personnel carry her away on a stretcher. As the images progress to the following year, the narration announces, "One year later, new towns rise up one after another in the earthquake-stricken areas. China is shocking the world with the quick pace of the reconstruction."

Process, central to the Expo's representations of the Sichuan earthquake, thus established two crucial categories of belonging: the victims of the earthquake and their volunteer benefactors. The film intimated that the earthquake victims had been brought into the fold of the nation and its modernity project through the humanitarian efforts of the state in the form of funding, state rescue personnel, and a civilian volunteer force. In this depiction, the victims are not simply pulled from the rubble of the disaster but figuratively reborn as citizens of a modern nation by being granted access to commodity products in the form of new houses. This rebirthing process is suggested again toward the end of the film, when the camera shows the grandson and the rescued woman now dressed in wedding clothing and celebrating their nuptials; as the passage of time is signaled by newscasters announcing additional milestones in China's modernization, the camera focuses on the young wife's pregnant abdomen and then, turning from representational live-action to animation, zooms to a future of bucolic green urban spaces, thereby implying that the earthquake had given birth to a utopian future China. The year 2008, which appears midway in the film, thus also marks a watershed moment in the film's depiction of past and future: the year not only of the earthquake but also of China's symbolic global "emergence" as a site of the modern through the Beijing Olympics.

■ THE BIOPOLITICS OF GRATITUDE: THE VICTIM

As previous scholarship on the biopolitics of humanitarianism has established, the recipient of humanitarian aid—the "victim"—serves as a key figure in the construction of the humanitarian state.[13] Through this essentializing process, Fassin (2007, 512) argues, humanitarianism constructs an ontological principle of inequality by positioning the victim as the beneficiary of aid: "They are those for whom the gift cannot imply a counter-gift, since it is assumed that they can only receive. They are the indebted of the world." In contrast to Fassin's argument that victims' ostensible inequality inheres in their inability to repay their indebtedness for the humanitarian gift, this analysis argues that, from the perspective of state sovereignty, the process of the victim's publicly recognizing and paying back the humanitarian gift is precisely what renders the biopoliticization of the victim possible. As we shall see, the form and content of Shanghai Expo earthquake remembrance practices both implicitly and explicitly communicated that the recipients of the humanitarian aid owed a debt of gratitude to the state for its humanitarian efforts.

Many of the earthquake exhibits and performances I visited at the Expo featured residents from the affected region. These Sichuan participants—predominantly women—were inevitably clad in the intricately patterned clothing that is recognizable in China as a marker of ethnic minority status. Some of the earthquake victims at the Expo passed out samples of their hometown culinary specialties or handcrafted products, while others offered embroidery exhibitions or performed folk dances in public squares. One particularly expressive performance featured seven dancers of the Qiang ethnicity wearing elaborately embroidered traditional clothing in an outdoor musical performance that, in the words of one of the dancers, was meant "to express our gratitude" for the state and volunteer reconstruction efforts. The performance, *The Soul of Qiang*, was, according to one reporter, intended to "capture the essence of the ethnic group that lost over 30,000 people [in the earthquake], 10 percent of the minority's total population" (*People's Daily* 2009). In an article in the *China Daily*, one of the dancers, Yang Jiali, was quoted as saying, "Today we want to sing, we want to dance, and most of all we want to say thanks. . . . We have moved to our new homes. Today . . . we also brought our special product, red cherries. We hand-picked them before we came here, we want to give them to the people who helped us" (*China Daily* 2010). Similarly, the deputy director of the Sichuan Pavilion, where the performance took place, stated, "We are having this event to mourn for the people we have lost, to show you what we have achieved, and to say thank you to the people who have been there supporting us" (*China Daily* 2010).

This performance and the attendant media coverage succinctly encapsulate how Expo representations both empirically constructed the earthquake victim and structured the form of debt owed to the state. The victim was most frequently posed as a member of a minority group (typically female) through visual and recognizable markers of ethnicity and difference, which located her on a domestically recognizable evolutionary scale relative to the Han modern as living reminders of a distant past. This practice mirrored wider representations of minorities in China that typically portray them as female and traditional others whose elaborate, colorful clothing (understood as "costumes") differs from the subdued, practical apparel of modern Chinese women and whose gender locates them lower in a social hierarchy that favors male subjects and equates minority subjectivity with being female (Gladney 2004).

The earthquake victims featured in this performance presented traditional ethnic songs and dances and passed out what a reporter called "special product[s]" (i.e., natural resources) that also reinforced stereotypes of the political periphery as a geographically and temporally confined space of encounter in which "locals" trade primary resources and "traditions" for modern commodity products.[14] Like the representations of Acehnese objects at the Indonesian Taman Mini theme park described by Siegel (1997, 4), this was a "story of another place and another time" structured by an evolutionary scale of practice and essence. The reporter underlined this distance by mentioning that before the Expo the victims had "never stepped out of their village." The forms of these presentations thus communicated both the victims' authenticity as minorities and their difference from modern Chinese citizens, locating the victims ethnically, socially, and economically at a distance from the unmarked norm. These representations thereby established the victim as needing what the state has labeled "civilizing."[15] Through being granted the possibility of participation in a modernity defined by material commodities and thereby being made ostensibly commensurable to nonvictims, the victims' identity as victims was reproduced because of their presumed lack and hence need for such modernity.

But more importantly for this argument, these various depictions of the earthquake posed their subjects not simply as distanced minority victims but also as grateful victims, and it was through this offering of gratitude for humanitarian assistance that the state's sovereignty project became visible and was legitimated. The Sichuan Pavilion hosted numerous displays of such gratitude. One particularly popular section of the pavilion, "Grateful Sichuan," featured a wall on which visitors could leave a digital imprint of their hands; upon contact, the wall responded with the words "gratefulness" and "blessing." After the first three weeks, more than fifteen thousand handprints had already been recorded. Precisely to whom the victims were presumably grateful was made explicit in text adjacent the thanksgiving wall:

> During the Wenchuan earthquake of 12 May 2008, the Qiang villages of Beichuan and Wenchuan suffered massive destruction. With the assistance of all local governments and their provincial and municipal counterparts, a brand new Qiang village was erected. The Qiang people have their own beautiful new homeland after the disaster.[16]

Near the thanksgiving handprint wall, one of the red Chinese banners hanging on a reproduction of a postearthquake reconstructed house read "A beautiful new home," replicating *Process*'s focus on the reconstruction of modern residential dwellings, while another banner read "Endless thanks to the hands of love," referencing both the hands of the earthquake volunteers and those of the visitors imprinted on the nearby digital wall. Such displays of thanksgiving were not limited to the Sichuan Pavilion. As one earthquake survivor volunteering at the China Pavilion reportedly explained, "I think of this is as a 'thanksgiving trip.' The Wenchuan earthquake linked Shanghai and Dujiangyan, which if you were to visit today you would not recognize.... Having witnessed new buildings appear on the ground, one after another, we the people of Dujiangyan were touched by the selfless dedication of our Shanghai friends" (Women of China 2010).

These representations of gratitude were also disseminated beyond the Expo site. The official Expo website, for example, featured vibrant photos of the Sichuan survivors' performances with laudatory captions explaining that the "victims" had offered their exciting performances to "express their thankfulness to the nation for its support" (Liu and Xu 2010). Similarly, Xinhua News, the state press agency, reported that one of the afflicted townships had renamed itself "Thanksgiving Village" after being rebuilt as a hamlet of "villas" (Liu and Xue 2009). These rituals of gratitude also continued after the close of the Expo, traveling, for instance, to Beijing in the form of a museum exhibit at the Military Museum of the Chinese People's Revolution. There, reported an article titled "Lovely People, Grateful Hearts" (*Xinhua* 2011), visitors waited in long lines to view exhibits of the "great feat of scientific reconstruction" that had been accomplished in Sichuan under the "scientific leadership" of the central government. The exhibits were described as featuring "neat rows of beautiful houses" and "the most beautiful of residential areas," again defining modernity through a material product, the house, and identifying its provision as the reason for gratitude. Similarly, at the earthquake reconstruction site, local party members and nongovernmental organizations (NGOs) ran "gratitude education campaigns" that instructed citizens on how to repay the Communist Party for its efforts (Sorace 2014).

This notion of gratitude differs from that of the classic anthropological tale in which an unsuccessful Inuit hunter's expression of gratitude for a fellow hunter's gift of walrus meat prompted the benefactor to protest, "Up in our country we are human! ... And since we are human we help each other. We don't like to hear anybody say thanks for that" (Graeber 2011, 79). In that conception of the moral endeavor of humanitarianism, being human implies *not* perceiving the gift as necessitating repayment in the form of gratitude. In the Expo narrative, in contrast, being human meant expressing thanks, specifically to the state, for helping the victim participate in the modernity project by providing those "neat rows of beautiful homes" that reveal "good government, good government." Thus the structural potential for the success of a biopolitics of humanitarianism at the Expo and the gifting of gratitude necessarily entailed a mutual exchange, as the state might not be perceived as benevolent without public gratitude to demonstrate and praise its humanitarian acts. Otherwise, the state's humanitarian efforts would be merely a "free gift" that constructs all Chinese citizens as inherently entitled to the gift of walrus meat. In this formulation, the "gift" of state humanitarianism is ultimately an assertion of power of the giver over the recipient, producing what Povinelli (2011) terms a "perpetual war of debt" in which the recipient becomes the grateful object.[17]

The Shanghai Expo thus suggests that the power to construct the nature of the debt and appropriate forms of repayment also confers the authority to define the boundaries of state sovereignty and legitimacy.[18] Indeed, as Lee and LiPuma (2002) argue about cultures of circulation, the exchange becomes a constitutive act in and of itself in which its performance both presupposes and re-creates the hierarchies of power it communicates. Within this framework, the state's biopolitical project offers a disaster politics narrative through a display of humanitarianism that constructs the earthquake victim as an essentialized victim and the state as the source of modernity. This projection allows the state both to consolidate its domestic power and to suggest its global commensurability as a liberal humanitarian state that cares about its citizens.[19] As Chu (2010) posits in a different context, the notion of debt thus reflects and orders the sociality of exchange.

■ THE BIOPOLITICS OF EQUIVALENCE: THE VOLUNTEER

The Expo earthquake-related performances and exhibits also constructed a second subject—that of the volunteer. Whereas Expo representations depicted the victim as minority, distant, rural, and in need of modernizing, they depicted the volunteer as urban, cosmopolitan, youthful, and benevolent—in short, the embodiment of China's "new era" and the "new model citizen."[20] In what I am calling a biopolitics of equivalence, Expo representations and the attendant media coverage described this citizen-subject variously as building a harmonious society, representing a burgeoning civil society, and embodying liberal humanism, all of which the state has claimed as central to its modernity project. Through these accounts and ubiquitous visual images showing the volunteers standing alongside government officials and soldiers at the scene of the earthquake, the volunteers were posed as the equivalent of the state in that they held the same relationship to the victims as their "saviors." At the same time, however, these representations posed the volunteer as separate from the state by depicting volunteer participation as a symbol of a more cosmopolitan "structure of feeling" of wanting to give—of humanitarianism—rather than as a political compulsion to act.[21] Like the biopolitics of gratitude, a biopolitics of equivalence required an exchange to lay the foundation for the state sovereignty project to succeed, one that conferred a debt to the state on the volunteer despite being positioned as equivalent to the state.

Within a week of the 2008 Sichuan earthquake, more than two hundred thousand civilian volunteers had descended upon the disaster-struck region, working alongside an estimated one hundred thousand troops and countless Communist Party members to collect and distribute resources (Huang 2013; Shieh and Deng 2011).[22] Some 3 million citizens from outside the region also volunteered blood, financial resources, and material goods for disaster relief (Teets 2009; Zhang 2012). Commentary on the official Expo website, while noting that the disaster had been a "sorrowful moment" and a "test for the nation" in which the volunteers had faced "grief" and "tears," also represented the volunteers as a source of national strength and cohesion. In the face of such power, the Expo website asked, "What kind of difficulty can beat us?"

In the film *Process*, the volunteer is depicted as central to the earthquake relief efforts and subsequent rebuilding: the grandson grasps the hand of the young women buried in the rubble, saves her life, weds her, and procreates, metaphorically giving birth to a modern nation. As mentioned earlier, the volunteers and state workers are shown toiling side by side to save the victims and rebuild the towns, while the voice-over stresses the sacrifices of the volunteers, their abiding love for the nation, and the rapid reconstruction of the stricken villages. In an interview with China's main state-run news agency, *Process* director Lu Chuan reported that this scene of rescue and reconstruction by volunteers and state representatives was meant to "exemplify the greatness of the Chinese people in their tenacity in the face of disaster."[23] Another such example at the Expo was the film *Home of Hopes: 2076*, which was shown in the Hebei provincial pavilion and recounted, in animated form, the fictional story of a young hero, Phoenix One, who had perished in the massive 1976 Tangshan earthquake in Hebei province that had resulted in more than 250,000 casualties. In this phantasmagorical romp, Phoenix One is cloned and brought back to life in 2076 to witness a *Jetsons*-like city filled with mind-boggling technologies such as free-floating motor vehicles that drive themselves and park suspended in the air. Against the realist backdrop of black-and-white images of the 1976 Tangshan earthquake, *Home of Hopes* begins with a cartoon reporter from 2076 announcing that Phoenix One has gone missing from the scientific lab where he was cloned. The film then shows Phoenix One visiting a local museum whose representations of the Tangshan earthquake are so realistic that he assumes it is the actual event and speedily proceeds to dig through the rubble to save the victims. At that point, the film shifts back to the devastation of the Tangshan earthquake in 1979 and then depicts the following century of progress in China, juxtaposing images of miraculous futuristic cities with those of China's natural wonders and historical landmarks, including the Great Wall and Tibet's Potola Palace. At the film's conclusion in 2079, fireworks flash in the sky over Phoenix One's head as a narrator announces that the new space-age city on the screen is the "beautiful city of Tangshan" resurrected from the ashes, while a golden phoenix, a traditional Chinese auspicious omen, is shown flying overhead. Phoenix One, like the volunteer in *Process,* is thus depicted as personifying the rebirth of the city and the nation, signified here in the form of iconic markers of tradition.

Expo depictions such as *Process* and *Home of Hopes* thereby establish the volunteer as central to earthquake rescue and reconstruction and set the stage for the construction of the volunteer as a particular kind of subject. The structural composition of the rescue scene in *Process,* for example, implies that volunteers are equivalent to the state through their parallel position as saviors to the victims. Gestalt theories of visual perception that reveal how proximity is visually read as similarity explain how the film sets up an equivalence between volunteer and state that was typical of many of the earthquake memorials at the Expo, including volunteer appreciation ceremonies, photo exhibits, and media coverage, that posed volunteers next to representatives of the state, whether members of the army or local and national politicians, and lauded both for their humanitarian efforts.[24] One noticeable example was found in a wing of the Sichuan Pavilion that was divided into three sections located in chronological order as "disaster," "rescue," and "reconstruction." Among the photographs featured in the rescue section was one of then-premier Wen Jiabao at the disaster scene that was surrounded and compositionally mirrored by a series of pictures of government cadres and volunteers helping at the disaster sites. This particular image of Wen was repeatedly shown on media coverage of the earthquake, and by the time of the Expo, its significance was instantly recognizable in China (Makley 2014; Xu 2009). In the televised version of the scene, Wen could be heard reassuring a crying girl orphaned by the earthquake, "Don't cry . . . it'll be all right. The government will take care of you all. The government cares about your life."[25] These visual arrangements merged state and volunteer as equivalent moral subjects through the practice of humanitarian compassion from their parallel relationship to the victim as rescuers.[26]

While these films and displays suggested equivalence, they and other representations projected more specific ideas about the constitution of the volunteer as subject. One common theme was that of youthfulness, in which young volunteers represent the modernity of the nation-state as humanitarian actors.[27] In the aforementioned interview, for example, *Process* director Lu Chuan remarked that he had "wanted to show how the younger generation, especially the post-80s generation, has the ability to shoulder the revitalization of the nation, to go through disaster and assume the task of rebuilding the city" (*Xinhua* 2010).[28] *Process* presented youth in general as representatives of the modern nation throughout the multigenerational saga of the film as the grandson's maturation mirrors China's rapid urban development and through specific images that exalt youth. One celebratory scene of people dancing in the streets, for instance, features a red banner proclaiming, "The glory belongs to the new generation of the 80s" and is set to a popular 1984 song, "On the Fields of Hope" by singer Li Guyi, that praises the changes and outlook of the nation after the post-Mao reforms. Similarly, reporter Cao Lingjuan of the *People's Daily* noted that the earthquake gave the post-80s generation a chance to "show themselves" and labeled them the "treasure" generation for their spirit and dedication that "touches the world" (Cao 2010).[29] Another reporter argued that although this generation was often criticized for its "extreme individualism," its volunteer efforts following the earthquake should be regarded as a "national monument" to China's humanity (A 2011).

Through such messaging, young volunteers were posed as representing a new humanitarian China, invoking a new kind of politics that deemphasized state imperative in favor of an individualism or personal agency that emerged as civic-mindedness rather than selfishness. While volunteering per se is nothing new in China, and in fact was an important part of political subject formation during the Maoist era (Oksenberg 1968), here it was invoked and lauded as done in the interests of the people rather than of socialist politics. These renderings called on the volunteer to act on behalf of the nation, not the state, and in turn allowed the state to distance itself rhetorically from global accusations of totalitarian control by presenting an agentive subject whose volunteer activities are not motivated by state demands for participation.

Even as Expo representations depicted volunteers as equivalent to the state, this rhetorical move hints at a kind of distance from the state essential to the construction of the volunteer subject. As previous scholars have noted, a nation-state is often defined as modern and cosmopolitan because of the presence of a civil society (Lee and LiPuma 2002; Taylor 2002), and volunteerism in China has frequently been cited as evidence of the growth of civil society (Shieh and Deng 2011; Teets 2009; Yang 2008). Such claims during the earthquake reconstruction period often accompanied depictions of and references to earthquake volunteers. One newspaper report, for example, called the volunteers an important "measure of civil society responsibility" and an "indicator of the integrity of civil society" (Zhu 2012), whereas an article on the official Communist Party news website claimed that the massive number of earthquake volunteers offered an opportunity to improve the quality of civil society and to show the world China's spirit of volunteerism (Tan 2008).[30] Similarly, an article from the *Journal of Democracy and Law* reprinted on the popular sina.com website refers to volunteers as the "backbone of civil society" (A 2011), while the *Guangming Daily* likens the volunteers to the "beautiful scenery of civil society" (*Guangming Ribao* 2008).[31] Such representations suggested that philanthropy itself was a constituent part of modern subjectivity and of a new China.

As commonly used in Western academic discourse, the term *civil society* suggests a particular form of modernity in which citizens are emancipated by the state to participate as socially responsible individuals, thereby implying a distance between the citizen and the state and a concomitant space in which citizens could reflect—often critically—upon the activities of the state.[32] While the Expo and attendant media representations constituted the volunteers as the instantiation of civil society and hence as an enunciation of the modern, they nonetheless gave no indication that civil society constituted anything more than the civic-mindedness that volunteering implies, and certainly not the possibility of critique. Although the debt that volunteers owe the state in this narrow construction of civil society does not entail the expressions of gratitude expected of victims, the representations of the disaster at the Expo clearly modeled that equivalence with the state also implied refraining from criticism of the state—civil society defined and lauded as volunteerism in the interests of the nation's people, not as critical engagement with the nation's political representation. Indeed, as Sorace (2014, 408) notes, the role of NGOs in the reconstruction process was "transformed from augering [*sic*] a new era of civil society" into managing and suppressing citizen critiques of either the process of reconstruction or the earthquake damage itself.

This restraint from critique is perhaps most evident regarding the Expo's absence of discussion of the kinds of earthquake deaths in China, particularly those of children attending schools that collapsed into rubble because of shoddy construction techniques. These building practices are known in China as "tofu dregs construction" and result, many argue, from corrupt practices in which state officials pocket funds intended to build public works and construct structurally substandard buildings incapable of withstanding geological catastrophes. This problem continued during the reconstruction process; even official accounts have revealed that hundreds of thousands of reconstruction dollars have been embezzled (Lim 2013). That there is no critique of this failure of the state at the Expo is unsurprising given its function as a celebration of Chinese culture and progress. Thus we must look outside the Expo to find more explicit examples of citizens' obligation to pay their debt to the state by relinquishing the right to dissent and of what happens when subjects refuse to pay a debt of silence.

The Chinese state has made attempts to excise from the public record discussions and representations of child deaths in the earthquake and of the continued victimization of those whose homes and livelihoods were also destroyed by the earthquake. For instance, for parents who lost children in the disaster to receive compensation, the state has forced them to sign documents stating they will cease from public questioning about the substandard construction of their children's school buildings (Wong 2008). Similarly, filmmaker Qi Zhao's documentary *Fallen City,* which follows three families who lost members in the earthquake, has yet to receive a permit for public viewing in China. Quite unlike the messages at the Expo, *Fallen City* expresses residents' skepticism about the value of the new housing provided by the state (which they see as alienating and shoddily built) and reveals that local government cadres unlawfully appropriated donations intended for the victims. International independent media have also reported that rights activists have been jailed for investigating the massive collapse of school buildings during the earthquake and that parents of children who died have been harassed by local officials while holding memorials.

Perhaps the most internationally known example of a subject's refusal to accept complicity with the state regarding these unnecessary deaths and what may happen as a result was a 2009–10 installation by artist Ai Weiwei. To make a public statement regarding the unnaturalness of this supposedly natural disaster,[33] Ai positioned nine thousand children's backpacks (representing the estimated number of schoolchildren's deaths) on the façade of the Haus der Kunst art museum in Germany to spell out "She lived happily for seven years in this world," quoting the words of a mother whose child perished in the earthquake.[34] But rather than being saluted as a representative of national modernity, Ai was beaten by state police and imprisoned for his reflections. In a later exhibit (2012–13) at the Hirshorn Museum in Washington, D.C., Ai listed the names of all the children who died in the earthquake and included an MRI image of the brain hemorrhage he had suffered from the 2009 beating that was the state response to his investigations into their deaths. Ai's productions offer an alternative form of citizenship that rejects the Expo's narratives of citizen belonging constructed through a refusal to speak.

As Martin (2012, 482) observes regarding his Papua New Guinean informants, "the power to define the nature and extent of debt is often simultaneously the power to define the nature and boundaries of those that hold it or might benefit from it." The problem faced by the Chinese state in constructing the earthquake volunteer in its likeness is precisely the problem of defining those boundaries—in this case, boundaries regarding what constitutes civil society and its role in the construction of a national modernity. As others have noted, the growth of a civil society in China has not been seamless or uncontentious, and the state, which has as much reason to fear as to laud its development, has embraced it only ambivalently (Hoffman 2013; Huang 2013; Zi 2009). A fundamental question of strategy for the state is how to contain the potential threat to authority when the boundaries of civil society are both inconstant and permeable. The Chinese state therefore faces the dilemma of how to remain "modern" when the modern exceeds the bounds of permissibility. Although the Expo lauded the volunteer as the instantiation of the modernity of the nation-state, this relationship always has the potential for instability if the citizens who constitute civil society choose to question the biopolitical project—if, in effect, like Ai Weiwei and Qi Zhao, they turn the Expo *narrative* of civil society into the *practice* of civil society in the form of a critique of the state.

Thus, it might be concluded from the Expo example, the potential success of the biopolitical project of equivalence requires that civil society remain understood as civic-mindedness rather than as distance and critique. It follows, therefore, that in this case, the biopolitics of equivalence requires an assenting subject, one whose "awakening of citizenship" (Zi 2009, 88) takes the form of volunteering rather than speaking up about political and economic systems and practices that create and perpetuate classes of victims and saviors. As the state increasingly devolves itself of financial commitments to provide for social support systems and depends on private institutions and volunteers to compensate, the volunteer is "provided" an opportunity to be modern as a member of a class with the financial and social wherewithal to volunteer (Hoffman 2013). The resulting equivalence with the state in the earthquake representations creates a particular salvational relationship to the victim through mechanisms that hide how such class-based relationships are based on continuing forms of inequality. For earthquake volunteers to represent the state's potency as an embodiment of its modernity and thus to reinforce its sovereignty, they are also implicitly asked to repay the debt by remaining publicly mute to both the state's shortcomings and the structural mechanisms that offer different possibilities for obtaining subjectivity.[35]

■ WHO OWES WHAT TO WHOM?

The earthquake remembrances at the Shanghai Expo, this article has argued, served not simply as memorials for the dead but as a form of disaster politics that worked to construct state sovereignty through offering modernity to victims and volunteers, but as differently situated citizen-subjects. Through a variety of exhibits and performances at the Expo and the attendant media commentary, the discursive construction of a sovereign state was represented in this analysis as a precondition for enunciating the specific and limited forms of citizenship available to particular subject-citizens through humanitarianism. What is more, humanitarianism—as a biopolitical project—was shown to necessitate an exchange that incurs a debt owed to the state to be paid with thankfulness by victims and with assent and silence by volunteers.

But if giving is humanitarian, we might ask, why must the participants—whether victims or volunteers—respond with a sense of obligation? What if the participants do not accept the terms of the debt through which they are marked as modern? What if, like artist Ai Weiwei and filmmaker Qi Zhao, citizens choose to pay their debt in a form that draws attention to a state's failures to protect and provide for its citizens rather than in a form that overlooks them?

When we begin to question the assumptions on which the biopolitical project is based—its exchange of modernity for a debt-laden subjectivity—we might also begin to see how the Expo narrative contains an additional and less obvious implication, one in which the expectation or need for gratitude and silence represent a diminution rather than a heightening of state power to set the terms of exchange. It is important to note, too, that while the Expo narratives solicit the volunteers as model citizens and representatives of a new modern China, much of the volunteer presence at the earthquake was not state organized but a spontaneous expression of citizen involvement, and the massive presence of the volunteers was sometimes met with resistance by the state.[36] If in fact gratitude and silence regarding the state's flaws and failures are necessary for the biopolitical project, this article would argue, a refusal to render them has the potential to defetishize the new house and all it represents as a form of value for the state, unsettling the state as the sole progenitor of good or enabler of cosmopolitan global belonging. This possibility suggests that these forms of humanitarian biopolitics are not necessarily marks of sovereignty and power but potentially of failure of the biopolitical project when the state's debt to its citizens cannot be repaid with a house.

Jennifer Hubbert is associate professor of anthropology at Lewis & Clark College.

■ NOTES

1. This mortality rate includes 18,500 people still listed as missing.

2. Unless otherwise noted, all translations from Chinese are my own.

3. For a more detailed discussion of hegemonic representation at expos, see Harvey (1996) and Ley and Olds (1988) in general and Nordin (2012b) and Winter (2013) specifically on the Shanghai Expo. This article examines the discursive purposes and operations of the state at the Expo, not its effects. Although this article does not address the reception of Shanghai Expo discourses, I have done so elsewhere through an examination of the narratives surrounding ecological sustainability (Hubbert 2015).

4. The "state" in this article refers explicitly to the Chinese Communist Party (CCP)-run national state, which (unlike in many other expos that receive extensive private funding) determined and authorized the Expo's goals and messages (Brady 2008; Nordin 2012c; Schneider and Hwang 2014). This is not to argue that the Expo's messages were entirely consistent with state guidelines (see Callahan 2012; Nordin 2012a), that the CCP itself does not experience internal polarizations (see Cheng Li 2009), or that the Chinese state is a unified object (see Hubbert 2014). Recognizing the factional nature of the Chinese state is important for understanding Chinese domestic and international politics, although an extended discussion is outside the scope of this article.

5. Bennett (1988) also explores the exhibitionary complex by considering how expositions express state power through constructing certain citizen-subjects.

6. The literature on the construction of sovereign power through humanitarianism is fairly extensive. See, e.g., Agamben (1998), Clough and Willse (2011), Bornstein and Redfield (2011), and Farmer (2004).

7. In referring to the sovereignty project and state sovereignty in relation to disaster politics, I draw on other scholars of humanitarianism who examine states' responses to disasters as a form of sovereign power

over the lives of citizens. See, e.g., Agamben (1998), Parisi and Goodman (2011), Piotukh (2015), and the edited volume by Clough and Willse (2011).

8. Such investigations include Butler (1997) and Pace (2009).

9. For contemporary applications of the concept of exchange in the context of disaster politics, see Bornstein and Redfield (2011) and Hattori (2003).

10. As discussed earlier, the "success" of the biopolitical project understood through a discursive analysis is always necessarily one of potential and depends on the effective acceptance of the terms of exchange.

11. For more on world's fairs' typical focus on culture and high technology, see Benedict (1983), Bolin (2006), and Harvey (1996).

12. The title of the film has also been translated as *Beautiful Progress*.

13. Rather than assume that the effects of humanitarian interventions are inevitably benevolent, these examinations have focused on the regulatory, often disempowering, and stratifying manner in which humanitarianism is constituted. See, e.g., Clough and Willse (2011), Korf (2007), McKay (2012), and Redfield (2005).

14. The idea that minority tradition is a sign of backwardness differing greatly from a dominant Expo narrative about tradition in which Han Chinese tradition is linked to future national glory (Hubbert, 2017).

15. For discussions on discourses surrounding Chinese minorities and the civilizing process, see Gladney (2004), Litzinger (2000), and Schein (2000).

16. The translation is from Schneider and Hwang (2014, 648).

17. As explored later in the article, Expo representations often constructed the volunteer as the equivalent of the state. In that sense, we can think about this gratitude as directed also toward the volunteer, even though much of the language was explicitly directed toward the government.

18. Martin (2012) offers a similar argument.

19. This point regarding the importance of gratitude and the construction of the modern state is supported by Emily Yeh's (2013) book on development in Tibet. Korf (2007) also looks at the staging of gratitude and its importance for donors in a different context.

20. This language of new era and new model citizens appears in several studies, such as Chong (2011), Hoffman (2013), and Zhang (2012). Anthropologist Ning Zhang goes so far as to suggest that the image of the earthquake volunteer may replace the Tank Man of 1989 as the new icon of the Chinese nation and its state–society relations.

21. Zheng Yuanchang (2009, 255), then director of disaster relief

donations of the Earthquake Relief Headquarters of the Chinese Ministry of Civil Affairs, called this structure of feeling "a social responsibility to engage in charitable activities as a way of life."

22. Ultimately, more than 1.5 million volunteers visited the area (Zhi-yuanzhe Pingtai 2008).

23. Interview excerpts are available at *Xinhua* (2010).

24. For an art historical perspective on these visual theories, see Bal and Bryson (1991).

25. Makley (2014) also describes this scene and its implications for the state. See Schneider and Hwang (2014) for another discussion about discursive constructions of state power at the Expo.

26. The frequent juxtaposition of the state and the volunteer in the Expo's disaster narrative established what Thompson (2005, 8) in a different context calls an "ontological choreography": a process through which "what might appear to be an undifferentiated hybrid mess is actually a deftly balanced coming together of things that are generally considered parts of different ontological orders." As in Marx's analysis of the commodity fetish, the process of establishing equivalence creates the asset, the object's ontological presence (Johnson 2013).

27. The Expo's links between youth, modernity, and the future have an established precedent, as discussed in a different context in Cole and Durham (2008).

28. The phrase "post-80s" refers to the generation that was born after 1980 and grew up entirely in the post-Mao reform era.

29. Chinese media reports on youth participation in earthquake relief were extensive; see, e.g., Min (2009) and Yu (2008).

30. Continuing this theme in a published newspaper interview, the lead singer of one of the Expo volunteer theme songs (evocatively titled "The World") explained that volunteers "are gradually moving toward the world, and winning international recognition with their efforts," thereby showing "the aspiring side of the Chinese people to the world" (*Nanhai* 2010).

31. The difficulty of translating the English term *civil society* into Chinese has been well noted (Ma 2006), and these articles use a variety of Chinese terms usually translated into English as civil society.

32. A growing literature on volunteerism and civil society in China has focused on whether a "true" civil society exists and on the significance of volunteering and civil society to new subject formations. See, e.g., Hoffman (2013), Huang (2013), Teets (2009), and Yang (2009).

33. The reference here is to Neil Smith's (2006) contention that there is no such thing as a natural disaster.

34. Estimates of child deaths in the disaster have since reached more than 10,000, although the official count released by Chinese state media is 5,335 (Bristow 2009).

35. This is not to suggest that the only manner of having a "voice" in China is through critique of the state but that in this instance, the debt is constructed as such. I would like to thank an anonymous reviewer for pushing me on that point and point to my earlier work on the spectacle of the Olympics for a further discussion (Hubbert 2010).

36. The Expo representations thus reveal how the Chinese government used this global mega-event to co-opt an outpouring of humanitarian civic-mindedness as a mandate for its own sovereignty.

■ WORKS CITED

A, Ji. 2011. "Wenchuan Dizhen Zhongguo Zhiyuanzhe Yuannian" (The year of the China earthquake volunteer). *Minzhu yu Fazhi Zazhi* (Journal of democracy and law), February 24. http://blog.sina.com.cn/s/blog_764f6dfso100q3e1.html.

Agamben, Giorgio. 1998. *Homo Sacer: Sovereign Power and Bare Life.* Palo Alto, Calif.: Stanford University Press.

Bal, Mieke, and Norman Bryson. 1991. "Semiotics and Art History." *The Art Bulletin* 73, no. 2: 174–298.

Benedict, Burton. 1983. *The Anthropology of World's Fairs: San Francisco's Panama Pacific International Exposition of 1915.* Berkeley, Calif.: Scolar Press.

Bennett, Tony. 1988. "The Exhibitionary Complex." *New Formations* 4: 73–102.

Bolin, Goran. 2006. "Visions of Europe: Cultural Technologies of Nation-States." *International Journal of Cultural Studies* 9, no. 2: 189–206.

Bornstein, Erica, and Peter Redfield. 2011. *Forces of Compassion: Humanitarianism between Ethics and Politics.* Santa Fe, N.M.: School for Advanced Research Press.

Brady, Anne-Marie. 2008. *Marketing Dictatorship: Propaganda and Thought Work in Contemporary China.* Plymouth, U.K.: Rowman and Littlefield.

Bristow, Michael. 2009. "No Blame in China School Collapse." BBC News, May 8. http://news.bbc.co.uk/2/mobile/asia-pacific/8039376.stm.

Butler, Judith. 1997. *Excitable Speech: A Politics of the Performative.* New York: Routledge.

Callahan, William. 2012. "Shanghai's Alternative Futures: The World Expo, Citizen Intellectuals, and China's New Civil Society." *China Information* 26, no. 2: 251–73.

Cao Lingjuan. 2010. "Haibao Yidai Zhanfang Shibo" (Treasure generation blossoms at Expo). *Renmin Ribao* (People's daily), August 12. http://politics.people.com.cn/GB/1026/12414822.html.

China.org. 2011. "Shuimo Town Sports a Brand New Look." May 17. http://www.china.org.cn/china/earthquake_reconstruction/2011–05/17/content_22582507.htm.

China Daily. 2010. "Sichuan Holds Show of Gratitude." May 13. http://www.chinadaily.com.cn/video/2010-05/13/content_9845396.htm.

Chong, Gladys Pak Lei. 2011. "Volunteers as the 'New' Model Citizens: Governing Citizens through Soft Power." *China Information* 25, no. 1: 33–59.

Chu, Julie. 2010. *Cosmologies of Credit: Transnational Mobility and the Politics of Destination.* Durham, N.C.: Duke University Press.

Clough, Patricia Ticineto, and Craig Willse, eds. 2011. *Beyond Biopolitics: Essays on the Governance of Life and Death.* Durham, N.C.: Duke University Press.

Cole, Jennifer, and Deborah Durham, eds. 2008. *Figuring the Future: Globalization and the Temporalities of Children and Youth.* Santa Fe, N.M.: School for Advanced Research Press.

Farmer, Paul. 2004. *Pathologies of Power: Health, Human Rights, and the New War on the Poor.* Berkeley: University of California Press.

Fassin, Didier. 2005. "Compassion and Repression: The Moral Economy of Immigration Policies in France." *Cultural Anthropology* 20, no. 3: 362–87.

———. 2007. "Humanitarianism as a Politics of Life." *Public Culture* 19, no. 3: 499–520.

Foucault, Michel. 1998. *The History of Sexuality: The Will to Knowledge.* London: Penguin.

Gladney, Dru. 2004. *Dislocating China: Muslims, Minorities, and Other Subaltern Subjects.* Chicago: University of Chicago Press.

Graeber, David. 2011. *Debt: The First 5,000 Years.* Brooklyn, N.Y.: Melville House.

Guangming Ribao (Guangming daily). 2008. "Zhiyuan Fuwu: Wenming Shehui de Liangli Fengjing" (Volunteering: The beautiful landscape of civil society). October 10. http://www.gmw.cn/01gmrb/2008-10/10/content_846537.htm.

Harvey, Penelope. 1996. *Hybrids of Modernity: Anthropology, the Nation State, and the Universal Exhibition.* New York: Routledge.

Hattori, Tomohisa. 2003. "The Moral Politics of Foreign Aid." *Review of International Studies* 29, no. 2: 229–47.

Hoffman, Lisa. 2013. "Decentralization as a Mode of Governing the Urban in China: Reforms in Welfare Provisioning and the Rise of Volunteerism." *Pacific Affairs* 86, no. 4: 835–55.

Hoyer, Brian. 2009. "Lessons from the Sichuan Earthquake." *Humanitarian Exchange Magazine* 43: 14–17.

Huang, Shu-min. 2013. "Building China's Nascent Civil Society: The Roles of Nongovernmental Organizations." *American Anthropologist* 115, no. 3: 499–501.

Hubbert, Jennifer. 2010. "Spectacular Productions: Community and Commodity in the Beijing Olympics." *City and Society* 22, no. 1: 119–42.

———. 2014. "Ambiguous States: Confucius Institutes and Chinese Soft Power in the American Classroom." *PoLAR: Political and Legal Anthropology Review* 37, no. 2: 329–49.

———. 2015. "'We're Not THAT Kind of Developing Country': Environmental Awareness in Contemporary China." In *Sustainability as Myth and Practice,* edited by Gary McConogh, Melissa Checker, and Cindy Isenhour, 29–53. New York: Cambridge University Press.

———. 2017. "Back to the Future: The Politics of Culture at the Shanghai Expo." *International Journal of Cultural Studies* 20, no. 1: 48–64.

Johnson, Leigh. 2013. "Catastrophe Bonds and Financial Risk: Securing Capital and Rule through Contingency." *Geoforum* 45: 30–40.

Korf, Benedikt. 2007. "Antinomies of Generosity: Moral Geographies and Post-tsunami Aid in Southeast Asia." *Geoforum* 38, no. 2: 366–78.

Lan, Tian. 2010. "Quake-Ravaged Wenchuan Incomes Exceed Levels before the Disaster." *China Daily,* May 12. http://www.chinadaily.com.cn/cndy/2010-05/12/content_9837361.htm.

Lee, Benjamin, and Edward LiPuma. 2002. "Cultures of Circulation: The Imaginations of Modernity." *Public Culture* 14, no. 1: 191–213.

Ley, David, and Kris Olds. 1988. "Landscape as Spectacle: World's Fairs and the Culture of Heroic Consumption." *Environment and Planning D: Society and Space* 6, no. 2: 191–212.

Li, Cheng. 2009. "China's Political Trajectory: Internal Contradictions and Inner-Party Democracy." In *Global Giants: Is China Changing the Rules of the Game?,* edited by Eva Paul, Jon Western, and Penelope Prime, 51–71. New York: Palgrave Macmillan.

Li, Junping. 2009. "Wei Yingying: Guangyuan Chongjian Sudu Quanqui Dou Shaojian" (Wei Yingying: The pace of Guangyuan reconstruction is rarely seen globally). *Guangyuan Xinyan* (Guanyuan news), November 13. http://www.gyxww.cn/gy/ZWZT/200911/42412.html.

Lim, Louisa. 2013. "Five Years after a Quake, Chinese Cite Shoddy Reconstruction." NPR, May 13. http://www.npr.org/blogs/parallels/2013/05/14/183635289/Five-Years-After-A-Quake-Chinese-Cite-Shoddy-Reconstruction.

Lin, Yongchuan. 2009 "Wenchuan Dizhen Zhounian Qianxi Jianwen: Zaimin Zhushang Huayuan Xiao 'Yang' Fang" (Knowledge on the eve of the earthquake anniversary: The victims live in "foreign" garden homes). *Xinhua*, August 8. http://news.xinhuanet.com/politics /2009-04/08/content_11146021.htm.

Litzinger, Ralph. 2000. *Other Chinas: The Yao and the Politics of National Belonging.* Durham, N.C.: Duke University Press.

Liu, Mei, and Xue Wenjuan. 2009. "Wenchuan Dadizhen Zhounian Jinian: Haopingcun • Ganencun • Beishucun" (Wenchuan Anniversary Memorial: Artimesia Village • Thanksgiving Village • Villa Village). *Xinhua*, May 4. http://news.xinhuanet.com/society/2009-05/04/con tent_11306671.htm.

Liu, Xue, and Xu Xiaoqing. 2010. "'Qiduo Qianghua' Liangxiang Shibohui Biaoda Wenchuan Ganen Zhiqing" ("Seven Qiang Flowers" appearance expresses Wenchuan feelings of gratitude at the Expo). Shanghai Shibohui 2010 (Shanghai World Expo 2010). http://www.expo2010 .cn/a/20100512/000023.htm.

Ma, Qiusha. 2006. *Non-governmental Organizations in Contemporary China: Paving the Way to Civil Society?* New York: Routledge.

Makley, Charlene. 2014. "Spectacular Compassion: 'Natural' Disasters and National Mourning in China's Tibet." *Critical Asian Studies* 46, no. 3: 371–404.

Martin, Keir. 2012. "Big Men and Business: Morality, Debt and the Corporation." *Social Anthropology* 20, no. 4: 482–85.

McKay, Ramah. 2012. "Afterlives: Humanitarian Histories and Critical Subjects in Mozambique." *Cultural Anthropology* 27, no. 2: 286–309.

Min, Daiying. 2009. "Fudan Daxuesheng Diaocha Wenchuan Dizhen Zhong Zhiyuanzhe Faxian Wu Dawenti" (Fudan University students investigate the Wenchuan earthquake, find five key issues). *Xinmin Wanbao* (Xinmin evening news), March 23. http://sh.xinmin.cn/shms /2009/03/23/1722588.html.

Nanhai. 2010. "Shanghai Shibohui Zhiyuanzhe Gequ 'Shijie' Zaihu Fabu" (Shanghai Expo volunteer song "World" published in Shanghai). January 20. http://www.hinews.cn/news/system/2010/01/20/010714313.shtml.

Nordin, Astrid. 2012a. "How Soft Is 'Soft Power'? Unstable Dichotomies at Expo 2010." *Asian Perspective* 36, no. 4: 591–613.

———. 2012b. "Space for the Future: Exhibiting China in the World at the Shanghai Expo." *China Information* 26, no. 2: 235–49.

———. 2012c. "Taking Baudrillard to the Fair: Exhibiting China in the World at the Shanghai Expo." *Alternatives: Global, Local, Political* 37, no. 2: 106–20.

Oksenberg, Michel. 1968. "The Institutionalisation of the Chinese Communist Revolution: The Ladder of Success on the Eve of the Cultural Revolution." *The China Quarterly* 36: 61–92.

Pace, Richard. 2009. "Television's Interpellation: Heeding, Missing, Ignoring, and Resisting the Call for Pan-National Identity in the Brazilian Amazon." *American Anthropologist* 111, no. 4: 407–19.

Parisi, Luciana, and Steve Goodman. 2011. "Mnemonic Control." In *Beyond Biopolitics: Essays on the Governance of Life and Death,* edited by Patricia Ticineto Clough and Craig Willse, 163–76. Durham, N.C.: Duke University Press.

People's Daily. 2009. "Exploring the Soul of Qiang." August 7. http://english .people.com.cn/90001/90782/90873/6721673.html.

Piotukh, Volha. 2015. *Biopolitics, Governmentality, and Humanitarianism: "Caring" for the Population in Afghanistan and Belarus.* New York: Routledge.

Povinelli, Elizabeth. 2011. "Routes/World." *E-Flux* 27, no. 9. http://www.e -flux.com/journal/routesworlds/.

Redfield, Peter. 2005. "Doctors, Borders, and Life in Crisis." *Cultural Anthropology* 20, no. 3: 328–61.

Schein, Louisa. 2000. *Minorities Rules: The Miao and the Feminine in China's Cultural Politics.* Durham, N.C.: Duke University Press.

Schneider, Florian, and Yih-Jye Hwang. 2014. "The Sichuan Earthquake and the Heavenly Mandate: Legitimizing Chinese Rule through Disaster Discourse." *Journal of Contemporary China* 23, no. 88: 636–56.

Shieh, Shawn, and Guosheng Deng. 2011. "An Emerging Civil Society: The Impact of the 2008 Sichuan Earthquake on Grass-Roots Associations in China." *The China Journal* 65: 181–94.

Siegel, James. 1997. *Fetish, Recognition, Revolution.* Princeton, N.J.: Princeton University Press.

Smith, Neil. 2006. "There's No Such Thing as a Natural Disaster." June 11. http://understandingkatrina.ssrc.org/Smith/.

Sorace, Christian. 2014. "China's Vision for Developing Sichuan's Post-earthquake Countryside: Turning Unruly Peasants into Grateful Urban Citizens." *China Quarterly* 218: 404–27.

Tan, Jianguang. 2008. "Wenchuan Dadizhen Zaiqu Zhiyuan Fuwu Diaocha Fenxi" (Wenchuan Earthquake Volunteer Service Survey). *Zhongguo Dangzheng Ganbu Lun* (Chinese cadres tribune), September 18. http:// theory.people.com.cn/GB/49154/49156/8071481.html.

Taylor, Charles. 2002. "Modern Social Imaginaries." *Public Culture* 14, no. 1: 91–124.

Teets, Jessica. 2009. "Post-earthquake Relief and Reconstruction Efforts:

The Emergence of Civil Society in China?" *The China Quarterly* 198: 330–47.

Thompson, Charis. 2005. *Making Parents: The Ontological Choreography of Reproductive Technologies.* Cambridge, Mass.: MIT Press.

Ticktin, Miriam. 2006. "Where Ethics and Politics Meet." *American Ethnologist* 33, no. 1: 33–49.

UNISDR. 2009. "CRED Disaster Figures: Deaths and Economic Losses Jump in 2008." January 22. http://www.preventionweb.net/english /professional/news/v.php?id=7798.

Winter, Tim, ed. 2013. *Shanghai Expo: An International Forum on the Future of Cities.* New York: Routledge.

Women of China. 2010. "Chen Qiaoqiao, Expo Volunteer, and Wenchuan Earthquake Survivor." http://www.womenofchina.cn/html /node/101903-1.htm.

Wong, Edward. 2008. "China Presses Hush Money on Grieving Parents." *New York Times,* July 24. http://www.nytimes.com/2008/07/24/world /asia/24quake.html?_r=0.

World Bank. 2012. "Supporting Post-earthquake Recovery in China." December 4. http://www.worldbank.org/en/news/feature/2012/12/04 /supporting-post-earthquake-recovery-in-china.

Xinhua. 2010. "Zai Zhongguoguan Ganwu Wenchuan Chengzhang" (China Pavilion expresses Wenchuan growth). May 12. http://news.xinhuanet .com/world/2010-05/11/c_1290353.htm.

———. 2011. "Keaideren Ganende Xin-Wenchuan Zaihou Huifu Chongjian Zhanlan Ceji" (Lovely people, grateful hearts: Wenchuan disaster reconstruction exhibition highlights). May 11. http://www.gov.cn/jrzg /2011-05/11/content_1862231.htm.

Xu, Bin. 2009. "Durkheim in Sichuan: The Earthquake, National Solidarity, and the Politics of Small Things." *Social Psychology Quarterly* 72, no. 1: 5–8.

Yang, Guobin. 2008. "A Civil Society Emerges from the Earthquake Ruble." *New Perspectives Quarterly* 25, no. 3: 39–42.

———. 2009. *The Power of the Internet in China: Citizen Activism Online.* New York: Columbia University Press.

Yeh, Emily. 2013. *Taming Tibet: Landscape Transformation and the Gift of Chinese Development.* Ithaca, N.Y.: Cornell University Press.

Yu Tai. 2008. "Yongbao 80 Hou—Xian Gei Wenchuan Dizhen Zhiyuanzhe Zhuli Jun" (Embrace the post-80s generation—the main force of the earthquake volunteers). *Sina* (blog), May 23. http://blog.sina.com .cn/s/blog_48d0278c010090dk.html.

Zhang, Ning. 2012. "The Wenchuan Earthquake, Social Organization, and the Chinese State." *Urban Anthropology* 41, no. 2–4: 211–45.

Zheng Yuanchang. 2009. "Wenchuan Earthquake Civic Donation and the Inspiration of Modern Philanthropy within China." *The China Nonprofit Review* 1, no. 2: 247–62.

Zhi, Wenjun, and Robert Ivy. 2008. "Sichuan Earthquake and the Chinese Response." *Architectural Record,* July. http://archrecord.construction.com/community/editorial/archives/0807.asp.

Zhiyuanzhe Pingtai (Volunteers platform). 2008. "5.12 Wenchuan Dizhen" (5.12 Wenchuan earthquake). http://news.sohu.com/s2008/zhiyuan zhepingtai/.

Zhu, Lei. 2012. "Zhiyuan Fuxu Shiye Jiankang Fazhan Huhuan Lifa Zhu-tui" (Call for legislation to encourage the healthy development of volunteer service). *Wangyi Xinwen* (NetEast News), May 12. http://news.163.com/12/1205/06/8HUM85H600014AED.html.

Zi, Zhongyun. 2009. "Civil Society, from Afar." In *China 2009: Forecasts and Strategies,* edited by Hu Shuli, 88–90. http://english.caijing.com.cn/upload/english%20annual2009.pdf.

FAN YANG

Temporality and Shenzhen Urbanism in the Era of "China Dreams"

ON SEPTEMBER 30, 2014, twenty-four-year-old Xu Lizhi, a Foxconn worker in Shenzhen, China, jumped from the seventeenth floor of the Meili AAA Plaza in Longhua District. The next day, October 1, or the National Day of Celebration (*guoqing jie*, the equivalent of July 4 in the United States), Xu's Weibo account sent out a preset message, "A New Day" *(xinde yitian)*, which became his last and thousandth post on the popular, homegrown social media platform. Prior to ending his life, Xu had been composing poems while working long hours at Foxconn Technology Group, the Taiwanese-owned Fortune 500 manufacturer known to assemble 40 percent of the world's electronics and the biggest share of Apple products. Since 2010, more than a dozen worker suicides have taken place in Foxconn's gigantic compounds, only a handful of which were reported in global media. The haunting imagery of these premature deaths is invoked in one of Xu's poems, "A Screw Fell to the Ground" ("Yike luosi diaozai dishang"):

> A screw fell to the ground
> In this evening of overtime
> A vertical plunge, a gentle sound
> Attracting no one's attention
> Just like some time ago
> On a night like this
> When a person plunged to the ground (Xu 2014, translation mine)

Xu's self-chosen form of death, which embraces the same downward verticality referenced in the poem, becomes a distinct way of "occupying" the city. Jumping from a high-rise not only enables an acceleration

189

of bodily movement, at a speed comparable to that of a motor vehicle traveling on a highway; it also allowed Xu to obtain a view of the city from above, albeit for only a few minutes, as captured on security camera (Zhang and Li 2014). This is a view perhaps quite different from the one that he was accustomed to, living in a "village in the city" (*chengzhongcun*) that is nonetheless quite far from the city center.[1] Feeling perpetually outside to this urban space, Xu seemingly turned to a different mode of "belonging to time" (Grossberg 2000, 157), both by way of speeding up his movement in space and by ending his life *before* welcoming "a new day" on Weibo. This posthumous pronouncement, synchronized with the birthday of the "new China," thereby establishes an uncanny connection between the rebirth of the nation and the death of the poet.

Time, or more precisely temporality—a complex and uneven relation to time—is central, I will argue, to grasping urbanism in Shenzhen, the first Special Economic Zone (SEZ) set up by Deng Xiaoping in 1979 at the onset of China's Reform and Opening Up. As a city whose life trajectory more or less coincides with post-Mao China's integration into the global economy, Shenzhen stands as a privileged locale through which to discern some of the nation's most glaring contradictions. While cities like Shanghai have been subject to rigorous examination from the perspective of temporality (e.g., Lagerkvist 2013), it is curious that Shenzhen, a frontier city that pioneered, among other things, China's "first stock issuance" and "first electric taxis" (Liauw 2012, 206), has not garnered nearly as much attention from cultural critics.[2] Nonetheless, two extant accounts of Shenzhen are worth noting. One comes from journalist Martin Jacques (2009), the author of the best-selling *When China Rules the World*. For Jacques, Shenzhen (along with Shanghai) exemplifies that "the past and the future are combined in East Asian modernity in a way that is quite distinct from Western modernity"—that is, "the present is layered with both the past and the future" (109). In a different but related vein, sociologist Manuel Castells (2009, 407–10) envisions Shenzhen as part of "a megacity in the making" that links several locales in the Pearl River Delta, along with Guangdong and Hong Kong; deeply embedded in global connectivity, it is marked as much by its "economic, technological, and social dynamism" as by its capacity for "cultural and political innovation." While Jacques points to the hybrid temporality that characterizes Shenzhen as an East Asian metropolis, Castells reminds us of the city's status as an experimental zone for a nation that remains mired in the struggle for an alternative modernity. These perspectives combined seem to suggest that the place that gave birth to such labels as "Shenzhen Speed" is well positioned to tell a vivid story about the tensions that underlie China's recent "rise" within Asia and the world.

This essay, primarily based on fieldwork I conducted in January 2014, sets out to explore how a Shenzhen-specific urbanism might present rich openings for connection and comparison with other megacities in Asia. Key to this comparative perspective, I argue, is a sense of time that is far from "homogeneous and empty" but is rather heterogeneous and multiple. This temporality-based approach is of particular value at a time when the "China Dream" (Zhongguo Meng)[3] discourse propagated by the Xi Jinping administration was gaining visibility both nationally and globally. If historically the city has primarily figured in a nationalist narrative of development and progress, especially in terms of the speed in economic growth, today it also appears to be offering a stage for carrying out new kinds of experiments, ones that acknowledge the various kinds of contributions from its diverse urban populations. It was this invigorating energy that motivated me, as someone who had inhabited Shenzhen as a teenager between 1986 and 1996, to see the city anew in the assemblage of cultural artifacts that I encountered, from numerous exhibitions staged around the city to street scenes in the Dafen Oil Painting Village. Captured in the slice of time that is 2014, Shenzhen appears to be a prime site for examining the possibilities and limits of "China Dreams" and, indeed, for carving out new visions for the nation and the world in what many perceive to be the beginnings of an "Asian century."

■ SHENZHEN SPEED

"Time Is Money, Efficiency Is Life." Perhaps no other Reform-era slogans that originated in Shenzhen speak to the city's relation to time better than this one. Back in 1981, the construction of the then tallest building on mainland China, the International Trade Building (Guomao), brought the famous "Shenzhen Speed" into the national spotlight. As Shenzhen-based anthropologist Mary Ann O'Donnell (2008, 11) recounts, the architects of this landmark construction were among the first in the nation's history to tackle such challenges as "stabilizing a fifty-three-story building with a revolving restaurant" and "installing exposed glass elevators." Each floor at Guomao from the thirtieth floor up was built within three days, a rate that surpassed that of Hong Kong and America, where each floor took five and four days, respectively. This record was refreshed in the 1990s, when the building time per floor in Shun Hing Square was further shortened by a half-day. Completed in 1996, Shun Hing also outshined Guomao to become not only the tallest building in China but also in Asia, even the fourth tallest in the world, hence earning it a new name: Earth King (Diwang) (Wang 2008).[4] Between 1979 and 1997, the SEZ maintained an economic growth rate of 33 percent, doubling every other year. Thanks to the coverage of national media outlets, such as China Central Television (CCTV), Shenzhen became an "overnight metropolis" even before everyone knew for certain how to pronounce the rather obscure character *zhen* (Hai 2011, 90), which literally refers to "a drainage in the field."

While those celebratory of "Shenzhen Speed" might like to proclaim that "no other place or time has experienced the transformations that have characterised this city" (Cartier 2002, 1520), Shenzhen's rate of development has not gone unchallenged. After all, its aura is predated by "Daqing Speed"—referring to the productivity in the 1960s at the biggest oil field in northeast China (a symbolic site of the Great Leap Forward)—and is increasingly eclipsed by "Pudong Speed," prompted by the central government's shift in stimulus focus to Shanghai in the 1990s. After China's 2001 accession to the World Trade Organization (WTO), the "special" policies from which Shenzhen has benefited were extended to many other cities and regions (Hai 2011, 93), whose rapid economic growth has become just as impressive. However, the logic of speed has arguably permeated so many aspects of urban life in Shenzhen that it has remained the city's most defining self-image. In the eyes of Hai Mo (2011), the author of the book *Reading City—A 360-Degree Critique of Chinese Cities* serialized in *Ningxia Pictorial,* the pedestrians in Shenzhen walk at a faster pace than those in any other mainland city; this walking speed has presumably even accelerated the rate of shoe consumption, thus contributing to the city's famously prosperous shoe industry (91).

From a remote fishing village of twenty thousand to today's metropolis of more than 18 million residents—only one-sixth of whom are officially registered—Shenzhen's growth also coincided with the rise of China as the world's biggest market for cars. Six thousand to seven thousand vehicles pass through the main street, Shennan Avenue, every hour, and the road is centrally featured in a poem from 1996 called none other than "Shenzhen Speed." There author Li Li describes the "running cars" as "flying bullets," allowing the poet to "hear the speedy wind" and "the dizziness," even "feel the wheels of Shenzhen rotating desperately" (quoted in Lin 2001, 181). When interviewed in 2014, middle-class car owners who grew up riding bicycles to school on designated bike lanes routinely lamented the fact that their kids are deprived of the "freedom" they once had to roam the city streets of Shenzhen.

One of the most distinct spatial manifestations of "Shenzhen Speed" is, predictably, the compression of space. As Jonathan Bach (2010, 423) points out, the so-called rural urbanization movement, which legally transformed 241 rural villages into urban areas between 1991 and 2004, gave rise to the spatial formation known as "villages in the city," exactly the kind inhabited by Xu after he decided to move out of the factory dormitory. Within these urban villages, the original villagers performed their own version of "Shenzhen Speed" by building up multistory, closely adjacent "handshake" buildings (429). This buildup was in part driven by the migration from the inland countryside to Shenzhen, which created a high demand for housing with which neither the socialist work unit–based construction of dormitories in the early days of Shenzhen nor the commercialized real estate development since 1999 could keep up (O'Donnell 2008, 14).

The making of these urban villages, of course, had to do with the conjoined forces of nationalist modernization and the relocation of the subcontracting global production chains from other Asian locales (such as Japan, Taiwan, and Hong Kong) to Shenzhen. The spatial compression that resulted from these forces was even more fantastically expressed in the Overseas Chinese Town (OCT) along the Shenzhen Bay. As a site reserved for "returned overseas Chinese," often those likely to bring in capital from Southeast Asia, the OCT was "imagined as a manifesto of the 'Asian metropolis'" and built by a collaborative team from Singapore and Hong Kong (Cracium 2001, 133). It became the location for some of the nation's first "miniature" theme parks, most notably Splendid China and Window of the World—the former featuring historic landmarks and natural landscapes from within the country and the latter highlighting those from outside. The building of these theme parks began as early as 1986 and was motivated by interests in the tourist industry as well as in real estate speculation, because views of the parks from the apartment buildings erected in the surrounding area were "their most expensive asset"; the parks, indeed, "scatter signs of the city even before the 'city' was present" (Cracium 2001, 133–35).

The OCT and its theme parks were therefore emblematic of the ways in which Shenzhen figured in the Dengist imagination of the SEZ as "a window to technology, management, knowledge, and foreign policies"—in other words, a window "open to previously forbidden realities" (Lin 2001, 87–89). The decision to move the area "One Step Ahead" was largely driven by the perception that this tabula rasa could not only provide "an incentive for exposure to Western influences and a catalyst for modernization" but also offer "a sudden enhancement of the cultural desert" (Cracium 2001, 111–13). After all, the Pearl River Delta from which the SEZ was carved out, despite the transnational trade routes long established by merchants from the region, never held much of a "high cultural" reputation. Yet, for authors like Hai Mo, theme parks like this have also come to manifest the "opportunist" ethos of "Shenzhen Speed," whose condensed artificiality bespeaks the city's "anxiety and hunger for culture and history" (Hai 2011, 92). For anthropologist Ann Anagnost (1997, 162–63), the building of Splendid China is also intricately tied to the construction of the nation as a "bounded entity" that is "retrospectively" construed, with "the economic miracle of Shenzhen as the most recent element in a historical series emerging out of the mists of the past."

In this way, the built environment of the OCT, part of the state project to "[open] up a narrow path between reality and representation" (Cracium 2001, 89), became an architectural sign deployed to showcase the nation's high-speed development. It was therefore no surprise that award-winning filmmaker Jia Zhangke would choose one of its theme parks, Window of the World, as a main location for shooting his 2004 film *The World (Shijie)*. In interviews, Jia often speaks of his first trip to the park—the place where his longtime collaborator and muse Zhao Tao once worked as a dancer—as a source of inspiration for the film. Some of the most memorable scenes in *The World* include tourists posing for pictures in front of replicas of the Eiffel Tower and the Leaning Tower of Pisa, among other historical landmarks, the result of which is often no different from posing in front of the real sites. As Jia recalls, Window of the World struck him as a reflection of "the impact of high-speed economic development on the human psyche," as people's distance to the world has become "so close" and "so far at the same time" (Cheung 2005). What Jia has sought to question in *The World* is none other than the "cost" of such "sped-up urbanization," which invariably falls on "the peasant workers who have floated from the countryside to the city" and who reside in low-rent urban villages (Cheung 2005). Whether performers, security guards, or construction workers, the film's main characters are "all living in a world that is speeding up." Yet this is also a world that denies them the opportunity to accumulate "experience" *(Erfahrung)* over time. Left with a constant sense of floating "uncertainty," they are henceforth "enslaved by (Shenzhen) speed" (Cheung 2005).

The theme of enslavement is the focus of another poem by Xu Lizhi, "Terracotta Warriors on the Assembly Line" ("Liushuixian shang de Bing-mayong"):

> Standing along the assembly line
> Xia Qiu
> Zhang Zifeng

Xiao Peng
Li Xiaoding
Tang Xiumeng
Lei Lanjiao
Xu Lizhi
Zhu Zhengwu
Pan Xia
Ran Xuemei
These migrant workers who labor day and night
Donning the uniform
Anti-static clothes
Anti-static hats
Anti-static shoes
Anti-static gloves
Anti-static wrist bands
Fully equipped at attention
Awaiting military orders
At the bell
All return to the Qin dynasty (Xu 2013, translation mine)

By inserting his own name in a list of workers-turned-warriors ready to report to the first emperor of China (221 BC), Xu poignantly reminds us that the "Golden Businesscard" that is "Shenzhen Speed" comes from the "blood, tears, and sweat of the Shenzhen people" (Hai 2011). For Qin Xiaoyu, a literary editor who started a crowd-funding site to publish Xu's poems posthumously, the description of the workers as Terracotta Warriors brings into sharper focus the "alienation" of the migrant workers, whose bodies are now turned into "sacrificial burial objects" within an "industrial empire" (Qin 2014). This is an observation echoed by O'Donnell, for whom the trope of "Shenzhen Speed," once "a sign of patriotism and national commitment," has today "come to refer to the speed at which people burn out" (O'Donnell 2014).

Underlying these cultural narratives, one may argue, is an attempt to nuance what speed theorists like Paul Virilio would call the "yielding of space to time," which "not only dissolves the grounding of politics but also gives rise to a way of being in time that is adverse to a political public sphere" (referenced in Sharma 2014, 6). To be sure, in a place defined by a constant pursuit of "the future" itself, the temporality of "Shenzhen Speed" has overdetermined a "culture of the new" that threatens to erase any attempts at accumulating historical consciousness (O'Donnell 2009). Both Jia and Xu, however, by probing the uneven "power relations" that "play out in time," have turned their attention to "the complexity of lived time" even as they grapple with the hegemonic discourse of "Shenzhen Speed" (Sharma 2014, 4–6). This is the kind of perspective, more in line with Henri Lefebvre's (2004) "rhythmanalysis" than Paul Virilio's speed theory, that I wish to bring to bear on Shenzhen's urbanism in 2014.

■ THE POLYRHYTHMIC SPACE

One of the ways to complicate the rhetoric of "Shenzhen Speed" is to turn to the incongruent, multiple temporalities that converge in shaping Shenzhen's urban sensibilities. Indeed, a closer scrutiny of temporal *disjuncture*, referring to "a polyphonous and polyrhythmic social order but one lacking harmony," which Murphy and Hogan (2012) have taken up in the context of Manila, can be productively deployed to examine Shenzhen's urban experience. This focus on discordance has the benefit of rescuing our analysis from the "logics of globalization arguments" that reduce these cities to mere "variations" of their Euro-American counterparts (Murphy and Hogan 2012, 10). In cultural studies of contemporary Asia, such as David Goh's (2014) work on the politics of "walking" in Singapore, Raka Shome's (2006) account of the "hybrid" encounters of time among call center workers in India, and Allan Isaac's (2015) research of "offshore" workers' engagement with multiple time zones in the Philippines, one can discern a shared attentiveness toward the manner in which diverse urban dwellers engage in a negotiation of coexisting but oftentimes incongruent temporal frameworks.

Several urban spaces that I visited in 2014 Shenzhen enact this kind of temporal negotiation quite vividly. Among them is the Shenzhen-Hong Kong Bi-city Biennial of Urbanism/Architecture (UABB), which prides itself as "the one and only biennial of urbanism/architecture in the world." Celebrating its tenth anniversary, UABB chose Shekou, a harbor at the southern end of the Nantou Peninsula in southwest Shenzhen, as the location for the latest biennial (2013–15). Two remnants of Shekou's industrial history, the former Guangdong Float Glass Factory and the old warehouse at Shekou Ferry Terminal, were transformed into exhibition venues and renamed as Value Factory and Border Warehouse, respectively. A $100 million joint venture between China, America, and Thailand that began its operation in 1987, the Glass Factory was once an award-winning structure with "an annual output of 2,730,000 loaded vans" (Ole Bouman Team 2013). When the production at the factory was terminated in 2009, the buildings remained despite the disassembling of the machinery, and they became the basis for installing one of the biennial's key spaces for exhibition. The naming of the venue as Value Factory is directly tied to the biennial's professed goal "to ask itself, which new value can be found there.

And if not found, how can it be created?" As its artistic team (headed by Dutch curator Ole Bouman) explains, this is not an event "to only please an audience" but one that "dares to take a risk." That is, it seeks to "shift its venues from background into foreground" at the precise moment when the "production of the known, such as industrialized commodity, is no longer enough and Shenzhen is on the cusp of exploring the unknowns" (Ole Bouman Team 2013).

At first sight, the message of the Value Factory is much in line with the state-promoted policy discourse "From Made in China to Created in China," which came into circulation after China's 2001 entry into the WTO. Such a developmental trajectory, which begins with "Made in Shenzhen" and "Processed in Shenzhen" but moves toward "Invented in Shenzhen" (with "invented" and "created" both translated from *chuangzao*), is clearly mapped out in a permanent exhibition at the Shenzhen Industrial Museum. Located on the ninth floor of the Civic Center (itself newly constructed in 2004), the exhibition, titled *Shenzhen's Path of Industrial Development*, features a giant, digitized portrait of Deng Xiaoping alongside one of his famous quotations: "Shenzhen's growth and experience have proven the correctness of our policy to set up SEZs."[5] Central to the "Created in China" discourse is the desire to transform the nation from the "world's factory" into an inventor of its own brands whose values will largely derive from proper recognition by the globalizing intellectual property rights regime. This narrative of economic upgrade has no doubt informed UABB's conception of the biennial as one that seeks to simultaneously draw on and "contribute to the energy of a new historical cycle in the modernization of the city" (Ole Bouman Team 2013).

However, while the exhibition at the Civic Center deploys Shenzhen's "success" as the first SEZ to emphasize the "correctness" of state policy, UABB has taken a much less deterministic stance. "This time," announces the curating team, "there is no need to pioneer on tabula rasa or to push to another frontier"; instead, "we can start with existing qualities, identifying them, highlighting them, dramatizing them and, by doing so, begin a new practice of social and urban renewal" (Ole Bouman Team 2013). In other words, rather than presupposing a developmental path that promises to upgrade Shenzhen's position in the global "value chain," what UABB proposes is an approach that "doesn't glorify" but "experiments" by way of exploring "alternative histories and a new future" (Ole Bouman Team 2013).

One of the exhibitions that embodies this attempted experimentation can be found at the pavilion of the Victoria and Albert Museum (V&A). Titled *Rapid Response Collecting*, the show makes an explicit effort to challenge the long-standing practice of museums to collect "objects that they feel are valuable and representative of the past," which often institutionalizes "a value system that they are invested in maintaining." Labeling itself as a "laboratory" to "road-test a new approach to collecting," V&A invited "designers, architects, curators and others engaged with Shenzhen to collect objects" in order to "represent the moment at which Shenzhen finds itself at present state: between industry and post-industry, between production and culture and between business and public life" (Victoria and Albert Museum 2013). The objects thus gathered include an old plaque displaying the Shenzhen-born slogan "Time Is Money, Efficiency Is Life," a currency counter bearing a reverse sign of Apple's brand logo, a fake iPhone that accommodates dual SIM cards, and items typically found in migrant workers' daily lives, such as plastic stools, hygiene products, wash towels, and underwear.

This collection of objects, all chosen to represent Shenzhen's "present state," brings into view the city's dynamic and uneven relation to time. While the rusty "Time Is Money" sign hints at the rate of deterioration propelled by "Shenzhen Speed," its inclusion also points to the speed at which Shenzhen's present objects can transform into museum collectables, on a par with those items conventionally deemed "valuable and representative of the past." This explicit reference to Shenzhen's rapid urbanization is juxtaposed with everyday objects of the migrant workers, including two bras without underwire. As the curator Corinna Gardner explained, the female workers who make up the majority of the labor force in this "electronic manufacturing hub of the world" prefer these bras because they do not set off the metal detector during "security checks on the way in and out of the factory," hence allowing them to evade the resulting physical searches. For Gardner, who is aware of the frequent violations that take place during these searches, "the idea that a non-underwired bra is a valued currency is a design narrative that tells you about the sexual politics of manufacturing in that city" (Etherington and Long 2013). The bras, along with the other everyday objects that represent the city's "informal urbanism"—among them the secondhand SIM cards popular among migrants who use mobile phones to call distant homes—offer an uncompromising glimpse into the "lived time" of the "floating population" that made "Shenzhen Speed" possible (Victoria and Albert Museum 2013).

Perhaps the most attention grabbing among the objects selected, however, are not these indices of "made in China" but rather those that bespeak the more troubling label "faked in China." Next to the self-branded

"Apple" money counter (nicknamed "iCash" by the collector)—which ironically proclaims to be a detector of counterfeit currencies—is a hybrid of iPhone 4, 5, and 5s models that uses Android's operating system. Phones like these are known to be of the *shanzhai* brand in the Chinese media, with *shanzhai* literally translatable into "mountain fortress" but connoting Robin Hood–style rebelliousness toward global brand ownership and state regulations alike. These Shenzhen-manufactured mobile phones often have features that cater to the needs of the working class, such as long-lasting batteries and "extra-strong signals" (L. Qiu 2009), and therefore have quickly expanded into markets in the Global South, from sub-Saharan Africa to the Middle East, thus indexing a sort of globalization from below.

Similarly displaying "the rapidity of response of *shanzhai* manufacture" (Victoria and Albert Museum 2013) in a global context is a reproduction of Vincent van Gogh's *Café Scene by Night,* standing next to the iPhone–Android hybrid. This is the work of an artist based in Dafen Oil Painting Village, a small urban village in Shenzhen. As Winnie Wong (2013, 5) shows in her in-depth investigation of Dafen, the village has grown in the past three decades into "the world's largest production center for handpainted art, China's model art industry, and the Western retailer's best source for oil reproductions of Western masterpieces." Described as "a part of Shenzhen that is reaching international popular cultural status" (Victoria and Albert Museum 2013), Dafen has arisen as a sought-after site for conceptual art making frequented by numerous established artists from China and abroad, including the designer Hao Zhenhan, who suggested the van Gogh painting here. Hao's original proposal was to display a Dafen painter's business card that illustrates not only the wide-ranging services that his workshop offers but also "the methods of contacting them: email and websites are out, the QQ social network or a direct phone contact is the only way to keep in touch" (Victoria and Albert Museum 2013). QQ, a homegrown online messaging program, much like the *shanzhai* iPhone that "arguably improves on the original design" (Victoria and Albert Museum 2013), is of course among the low-cost information technologies that contribute to the Pearl River Delta as an exemplary "working-class network society" (J. L. Qiu 2009). The presence of these artifacts, therefore, drives a wedge into the "From Made in Shenzhen to Created in Shenzhen" narrative highlighted at the Civic Center. Indeed, they may be usefully seen as manifesting what Ackbar Abbas (2000, 786) calls "arbitrage with a difference"—that is, "everyday strategies for negotiating disequilibria and dislocations," taken up by "at

Figure 1. Street scenes, Dafen Oil Painting Village, January 2014. Photograph by the author.

least some of the less privileged men and women placed or displaced in the transnational space of the city and who are trying to make sense of its spatial and temporal contradictions."

On a day after the Chinese New Year (also known as the Spring Festival) in 2014, the coexistent signs of contradiction and negotiation in Dafen Village were everywhere to be found. For instance, Spring Festival couplets in bright gold and red—traditionally symbolic of good fortune—were seen in storefronts alongside postmodern artifacts painted in multiple colors. The contact information underneath the name of the shops invariably included both numbers for cell phone and QQ (see Figure 1). Not unlike the V&A collection at UABB, which seeks to represent Shenzhen urbanism in all its temporal multiplicities rather than within the "teleology" of "Shenzhen Speed," Dafen Village may be seen as a polyrhythmic space that congeals "the collective production of a contradictory, even cacophonous, identity" (Bach 2010, 425). A village no larger than 0.4 square kilometers located in the Buji subdistrict of the Longgang district in Northeast Shenzhen, Dafen had only roughly three hundred farming residents prior to the Reform. Like other urban villages that "provide the cheapest rentals in the city" (O'Donnell 2008, 15), Dafen quickly attracted large numbers of migrant workers from the Chinese interior, creating an environment that ultimately motivated the relocation of art reproduction business from Hong Kong to Shenzhen (Wong 2013, 48). As its gross revenue grew to RMB 300 million in 2006, it has also become home to more than ten thousand painters (Fang 2010).

If the growth of Dafen appears to fit into a national trajectory of urbanization, the linearity of this process is also complicated by the mobility of global capital, on one hand, and the resilience of local village practices, on the other. Since the 1990s, "the unprecedented rise in global residential property markets" has generated tremendous demand for paintings from Dafen, creating "an art bubble that ended with the financial crisis of 2008" (Wong 2013, 96). Despite large orders from such American retailers as K-Mart and Walmart, however, the mode of production at Dafen is hardly reminiscent of the temporal structure characteristic of a modern factory. As Winnie Wong describes, drawing on her participant observation,

> freed of distractions from shop visitors, the late evenings are the most productive time. Giant rolls of canvas are unfurled on the pavement and cut in the street. Amid the naked bulbs, fans whir away as painters work in their open studios into the night, stopping to smoke, chat, and drink with each other. (182)

To be sure, the painting trade, unlike the "academic practice" of art making, values the skill of speed over "thinking"; "paint faster, earn money" is unsurprisingly a common saying within the trade. But the evening "work" of Dafen painters strikes one as uncommonly leisurely. Perhaps this is why, to many artists from the outside, the place often appears as "either exhilaratingly active and community oriented or totally disillusioning in its matter-of-fact productivity" (182). Yet it is precisely the coexistence of these seemingly contradictory practices that works to destabilize dominant Western conceptions that separate art from craft, original from copy, work from life.

When observed during the Chinese New Year of 2014—that is, after the busy Christmas season driven by large orders from Euro-America— the village appeared to be enjoying a period of peaceful "downtime." Children were seen playing with their peers in the streets, inside the gallery hallways, and in the open square outside the Dafen Museum, constructed in 2007 amid a number of high-rise residential buildings and local district offices to create a "three-tier layer" that connects work in the street (i.e., oil painting) with life in the community (Fang 2010, 116) (see Figure 2). Far from replicating a discrete, orderly, and disciplined social

Figures 2a and 2b (above and right). Children playing in Dafen Oil Painting Village, January 2014. Photographs by the author.

space prototypical of Western industrialization, Dafen has arguably retained the disorderly and chaotic daily rhythms of a premodern village, despite its formal "integration" into the hypermodernizing city of Shenzhen. This is why Bach (2010, 428), adopting the Barthesian analytics of urban semiotics, argues that "Shenzhen's villages"—of which Dafen is part—"define Shenzhen yet resist signification." While its "*shanzhai* art" trade may well distinguish Dafen from other urban villages, the manner in which its dwellers have come to disrupt the city's official narrative of "progress" (as staged at the Civic Center) is by no means unique. As Bach's ethnographic account shows, instead of being the "vestige of a feudal past" (425), villages like Dafen have in fact pioneered numerous aspects of the city's industrialization, in part because they were able to "embed themselves in translocal and transnational circuits" (432), often through exploiting the villagers' global diasporic ties, especially via bordering Hong Kong. In this sense, the polyrhythmic space that is Dafen, much like the V&A exhibition at UABB, has presented an illuminating counternarrative to the (nationalist) trope of "Shenzhen Speed."

■ DREAMING A MULTIFUTURE

In November 2012, two weeks after his election into office, China's new president Xi Jinping publicly introduced the hallmark of his administration, the "China Dream," or what he defined as "the grand rejuvenation of the Chinese nation."[6] The slogan quickly took the Chinese media by storm, showing up in wide-ranging cultural productions, from street posters and television documentaries to singing and speech contests.[7] When wandering around Shenzhen's Book City (where Xu Zhili had once submitted an unsolicited and fruitless job application) in 2014, I came upon *Shenzhen Dreams: The Development Trajectory of 100 Shenzheners*. On the book jacket was the following proclamation: "Shenzhen Dream is the [most] vibrant chapter of the China Dream, (and) Shenzheners are the pioneering force of this 'Dream Team'" (Wang 2013).

While the publication of this collection of essays written by Shenzheners from all walks of life may easily be deemed opportunistic, it is not exactly an exaggeration to say that Shenzhen had served as a precursor for the discursive formation of "China Dreams." Two years before Xi's "Dream" speech, the Shenzhen case pavilion of the 2010 Shanghai Expo, co-organized by the city government and the local architectural start-up

Urbanus, had already claimed the title "Shenzhen, Frontier for China Dreams" (*Zhongguo mengxiang shiyanchang,* alternatively translatable as "Experimental Zone for China Dreams"). A giant reproduction of the *Mona Lisa*—or, as the curators have come to call it, "Dafen Lisa," with "Dafen" serving as a pun for "da Vinci"—decorated the pavilion's facade. The painting was the work of five hundred artists from Dafen Village, but none of the contributors was identified by name. This "evacuation" of individual authorship, as Wong (2013, 214) points out, reinforced the idea that "the omnipresent author of the exhibition was 'China,' whose anonymized 'people's' dreams were being brought to the surface." Such a "narrative strategy" was no doubt part of the official efforts to "open up Dafen village as a metonym for a new imagined frontier" (211), a zone of "creative" experiments at the forefront of the expanding state project, "From Made in China to Created in China."

This rebranding of Dafen, much like the emphasis on "development" in the subtitle of the book *Shenzhen Dreams,* has relied on a subsumption of the heterogeneous temporalities of the polyrhythmic city into a more linear trajectory of national upgrade. For instance, in the last room of the Shenzhen pavilion, a documentary called *Shenzhen Faces* features a range of "working people" in Shenzhen "who keep this city running" (Mou Sen, quoted in Wong 2013, 215), be it middle-class doctors or migrant factory workers. Recounting his archival research on Shenzhen history in preparation for this "spatial theater," Mou Sen, the Beijing-based theater director who designed the video projection and took pains to convince city officials to accept his proposal, said the "calamitous price of Shenzhen's thirty years of urbanization is no less than that of wars" (Zhu 2010). It was perhaps his intent to make visible the numerous behind-the-scenes stories of "Shenzhen Speed" that led Mou to produce his documentary, as well as filling other sections of the pavilion "with the faces and voices of Dafen workers announcing their 'truest dreams'" (Wong 2013, 214). The irony, however, is that for many Dafen artists who participated in the exhibit without being granted name recognition, such dreams were often expressed as none other than the desire to become genuine "authorial" artists (Wong 2013, 218). As such, Mou's attempt to glorify the working people by way of displaying their presence in the city becomes no more than a simulacrum of presence, or "the present that gives itself as presence" (Lefebvre 2004, 23). As "an endeavor infused with the sense of permanent transition that buttresses the Chinese reform era" (Wong 2013, 218), the pavilion has in effect erased the multiplicity of experiences in Dafen/Shenzhen, whose temporal hetereogeneity in many ways defies such Western-centric notions as "progress" and "originality."

Yet the naming of Shenzhen as an "experimental zone" for "China Dreams" is worth pondering. After all, as William Callahan (2013, 58) suggests, despite its proliferation within the party-state's sloganeering machinery, the "China Dream" discourse is foremost "a raucous debate of the direction of China's future." While Xi and numerous state officials have aimed to align the dreams of the "people" with the nation's march toward a political, economic, and even military "revival," the "futures" that emerged in spaces like UABB are far more polyphonic than what state discourse suggests. The curators of the biennial have in fact stated this goal quite clearly (Ole Bouman Team 2013):

> We also will use our intuition, sensitivity, romantic inclination, and all our cultural subjectivities, to explore the potentials of the future and guide our visitors along a repertoire of hope, towards new futures.
>
> A future that perhaps makes Shenzhen into a place that gives people a reason to stay and grow old.
>
> A future that perhaps gives amnesty to history and heritage.
>
> A future that is contrary to the self-perpetuating regime of GDP.
>
> A place that creates value by preserving it.

Unlike the one-dimensional pursuit of "progress" exhibited at the Shenzhen Pavilion of the Shanghai Expo and at the Civic Center, the futurity presented at UABB is decidedly plural. This effort in pluralizing the vision for Shenzhen can also be discerned at a multimedia show called *Multifuture*, which was on view in January 2014 during my visit to the OCT. There the early spatial rendition of "Shenzhen Speed," whose simulated theme parks had seemingly failed to compensate for the city's cultural "lack," has now become the hosting site for OCT-LOFT, a newly built and fast-growing creative and cultural park, also designed by Urbanus. As show curators Wang Wei and Shen Boliang explain, "We are not concerned with 'future' in terms of material technology so much as with changes in thought and consciousness which are happening or will happen due to influences from current reality." The documentaries and texts on diverse Chinese locales they have gathered to put on display thus serve as a Gramscian "starting point of critical elaboration," which Wang and Shen reference as "the consciousness of what one really is . . . a product of the historical process to date which has deposited in you an infinity of traces, without leaving an inventory." What cultural producers like Wang and Shen hope to achieve is the creation of an "inventory" within which visitors "can look up an ongoing history of how people relate to their possibilities" (Wang and Shen 2012).

As Shenzhen, along with the nation itself, encountered the (lagged) economic slowdown initiated by the global financial crisis of 2008, the pressure to conform to the globally dominant mode of "cultural" development had become all the more apparent. Yet it was within this context that the construction of OCT-LOFT came to infuse "Shenzhen Speed" with new meanings. When redesigning this former manufacturing complex, Urbanus opted "to maintain the spatial qualities and aesthetics of the industrial texture" while embellishing the decaying production facilities with small architectural details so as to transform them into bookstores, cafés, galleries, and studios (O'Connor and Liu 2014, 135). Within four years of its official opening on January 28, 2007, the space had already attracted 150 firms and 2,000 employees (O'Connor and Liu 2014, 135). This booming new spot on Shenzhen's cultural map, which now provides venues for exhibits like *Multi-future* and numerous UABB events, has led optimists to suggest that Shenzhen has the potential to become yet again an "exportable" example for postindustrial urban regeneration (e.g., Liauw 2012, 217).

To be sure, the sped-up formation of a perhaps yuppie-fied culture of consumption and leisure could just as well be contributing to the much-mystified "creative class" as a preferred subject of neoliberal globalization. But the simultaneous imaginings of multiple futures that have taken place at UABB's Value Factory, OCT-LOFT, and Dafen are suggestive of a new opening for rethinking the city's and its dwellers' relations to time. In her reading of Shanghai, Anna Greenspan (2014) has discerned "a type of deep and far-reaching urban creativity" (8) that would allow Shanghai/China to redefine modernity by way of reinventing "what the future might mean" (xv). It is worth noting that Greenspan attributes China's first "hacker space" of innovative design, located in Shanghai, to the "bottom-up culture of *shanzhai*," which can be traced to Shenzhen (204–5). The fact that *shanzhai* mobile phones, popular among Shenzhen's working migrants, appeared at the V&A collection in UABB *prior to* the official launching of the *Rapid Response Collecting* show in London offers quite a powerful challenge to the Eurocentric narrative that routinely pits the developing world in a temporal lag *behind* the West. *Shanzhai* phones, as an embodiment of Shenzhen's informal urbanism, much like Xu Zhili's posthumous Weibo[8] post, are therefore better grasped as catalysts to "name a different temporality" (Morris 1998, xxii) for the nation in the era of "China Dreams." Indeed, they serve to remind us of "the socialist tenet that in making history, human beings create their future" (O'Donnell 2008, 12). Rather than reproducing an obsession with speed meant for "catching up with the West," the temporally disjuncted urbanism of Shenzhen has demonstrated the city's potential to reorient the "dreaming nation" toward a recognition of simultaneity and copresence, not only between China/ Asia and the West but also among the city's diverse constituents. This is the kind of potential that a rhythmanalysis of the various exhibitionary spaces and spatial practices in 2014 Shenzhen has allowed us to discern.

■ CONCLUSION: TEMPORALITY AND ASIAN URBANISM

I have argued for a temporality-based approach to the study of Shenzhen urbanism, an approach that I believe also presents broader heuristic implications for examining the multiply connected urban spaces and spatial practices in Asia. For one thing, this approach helps to contest the dominant modes in which Asian cities are represented in Western media and scholarship; the former, in its Hollywood version, almost exclusively takes the dystopian form of "techno- orientalism" (Morley and Robins 1995), while the latter often lapses into essentialist explanatory frameworks like "Asian values." What a temporality-based approach offers instead is a more critical lens through which to comparatively analyze the many Asian locales that, despite their vast differences, share the experience of fast-paced urbanization, high population density, blurred urban–village boundaries, and a diffused informal economy, whether it is East Asia (Rowe 2005), Southeast Asia (Murphy and Hogan 2012), or South Asia (Sundaram 2010).

A rhythmanalysis, as I have brought to bear on Shenzhen in the era of "China Dreams," may also help to remap a geopolitical imagination of China/Asia that resituates these spaces and practices in the third world or Global South, as advocated by the Taiwan-based cultural studies scholar Kuan-Hsing Chen. Key to this move to "return" Asian locales to their "third-world structural location," as Chen (2010, 63–64) suggests, is the need to challenge the "imperialist paradigm that maps an abstract and universal theoretical framework onto the earth" and instead engage "the phenomena and problems of lived reality." In this sense, paying analytical attention to the heterogeneous and oftentimes interlinked temporalities of Asian cities not only opens up the possibility to defy Eurocentric perspectives on modernity and urbanism but also offers critical resources for generating alternative visions for global (and Asian) futures.

Fan Yang is assistant professor in the Department of Media and Communication Studies at the University of Maryland, Baltimore County (UMBC). She is the author of *Faked in China: Nation Branding, Counterfeit Culture, and Globalization* (2016). Yang's work on cultural studies, globalization, and Chinese media has appeared in *Theory, Culture, and Society, New Media and Society, Quarterly Review of Film and Video,* and *Critical*

Studies in Media Communication, among other journals. She is currently working on a project that examines the imaginary fusion of China and America in a growing number of transnational media artifacts.

■ NOTES

1. One of Xu's poems, "In This City," contains the following line: "In this city / urban villages are a hundred thousand and ten *li* from the city center." Elsewhere (in various microblog posts and a letter), Xu also mentions the crowded buses and subway lines he has to take to get to his beloved Book City downtown from his one-room apartment in Longhua. For a picture of a typical view from within the village, see Zhang and Li (2014).

2. The recently released edited volume *Learning from Shenzhen* will stand to make a great contribution in this regard; see O'Donnell, Wong, and Bach (2017).

3. While both translations, "China Dream" and "Chinese Dream," exist in English-language publications on the subject, I will adopt "China Dream" in this article to emphasize the dreaming subject of the nation as opposed to the "people." For a discussion of the disjuncture between the nation and the people in the "Dream" rhetoric, see Yang (2015).

4. In 2011, however, "Earth King" had to again cede this "top building in Shenzhen" status to the hundred-floor Kingkey Financial Center, also known as KK100.

5. For 3-D panoramic views of this exhibition, see http://www.szind .net/3d/3Dquanjingzhan/.

6. Xi brought up the "China Dream" rhetoric during an unscripted speech on November 29, 2012, after a visit to a *Road to Revival* exhibition at the National Museum in Beijing. The phrase is also translatable as "the Chinese Dream," though here I will retain the usage of "China Dreams," as adopted in Wong (2013), for consistency.

7. For a closer analysis of a number of these "Dream-themed" cultural artifacts, see Yang (2015).

8. Weibo's popularity is increasingly superseded by Wechat, a mobile phone app developed by Tencent, a tech company based in the Nanshan Science and Technology Park in Shenzhen.

■ WORKS CITED

Abbas, M. A. (M. Ackbar). 2000. "Cosmopolitan De-scriptions: Shanghai and Hong Kong." *Public Culture* 12, no. 3: 769–86.

Anagnost, Ann. 1997. *National Past-Times: Narrative, Representation, and Power in Modern China—Body, Commodity, Text.* Durham, N.C.: Duke University Press.

Bach, Jonathan. 2010. "'THEY COME IN PEASANTS AND LEAVE CITIZENS':
    Urban Villages and the Making of Shenzhen, China." *Cultural Anthro-
    pology* 25, no. 3: 421–58.
Callahan, William A. 2013. *China Dreams: 20 Visions of the Future.* Oxford:
    Oxford University Press.
Cartier, Carolyn. 2002. "Transnational Urbanism in the Reform-Era Chi-
    nese City: Landscapes from Shenzhen." *Urban Studies* 39, no. 9: 1513–32.
Castells, Manuel. 2009. *The Rise of the Network Society.* Hoboken, N.J.:
    John Wiley.
Chen, Kuan-Hsing. 2010. *Asia as Method: Toward Deimperialization.* Dur-
    ham, N.C.: Duke University Press.
Cheung, Lik Kwan. 2005. "Sudu yu jingguan de tielong-lun Jia Zhangke
    de Shijie" (The iron cage of speed and spectacle: On Jia Zhangke's *The
    World*). Research Centre for Foreign Sinology (Chinese Literature) of
    Suzhou University. http://www.zwwhgx.com/content.asp?id=2714.
Cracium, Mihai. 2001. "Ideology: Shenzhen." In *Great Leap Forward,* edited
    by Chuihua Judy Chung, Jeffrey Inaba, Rem Koolhaas, and Sze Tsung
    Leong, 44–155. Cambridge, Mass.: Harvard Design School.
Etherington, Rose, and Kieran Long. 2013. "Interview with Kieran Long on
    Rapid Response Collecting at the V&A." *Dezeen,* December 13. http://
    www.dezeen.com/2013/12/18/rapid-response-collecting-victoria- and
    -albert-museum-kieran-long/.
Fang, Hua. 2010. "Shenzhen Dafen guoji bihua yaoqingzhan yu 'Shen-
    zhen Gaizao'" (Shenzhen Dafen International Mural Exibition and
    "Shenzhen renewal"). *Rong Bao Zhai* 12: 110–17.
Goh, Daniel P. S. 2014. "Walking the Global City: The Politics of Rhythm
    and Memory in Singapore." *Space and Culture* 17, no. 1: 16–28.
    doi:10.1177/1206331212451686.
Greenspan, Anna. 2014. *Shanghai Future: Modernity Remade.* New York:
    Oxford University Press.
Grossberg, Lawrence. 2000. "History, Imagination, and the Politics of
    Belonging: Between the Death and the Fear of History." In *Without
    Guarantees: In Honour of Stuart Hall,* edited by Paul Gilroy, Lawrence
    Grossberg, and Angela McRobbie, 148–64. New York: Verso.
Hai, Mo. 2011. *Wen cheng—360 du pipan Zhongguo chengshi* (Reading
    city—a 360-degree critique of Chinese cities). *Ningxia Huabao* (Ningxia
    pictorial) 1: 88–95.
Isaac, Allan. 2015. "Creating Offshore Identities in 300 Seconds for the
    21st Century." Paper presented at Trans/National Imaginary: Global
    Cities and Racial Borderlands, April 23, Evanston, IL.
Jacques, Martin. 2009. *When China Rules the World: The End of the Western*

World and the Birth of a New Global Order. New York: Penguin Press.
Lagerkvist, Amanda. 2013. *Media and Memory in New Shanghai: Western Performances of Futures Past.* New York: Palgrave Macmillan.
Lefebvre, Henri. 2004. *Rhythmanalysis: Space, Time, and Everyday Life.* New York: Continuum.
Liauw, L. W. W. 2012. "Shenzhen's Evolution from Tabula Rasa Laboratory of New Chinese Urbanism to Post-industrial UNESCO Creative City of Design." In *New Economic Spaces in Asian Cities: From Industrial Restructuring to the Cultural Turn,* edited by P. W. Daniels, Kong-Chong Ho, and T. A. Hutton, 202–19. New York: Routledge.
Lin, Nancy. 2001. "Architecture: Shenzhen." In *Great Leap Forward,* edited by Chuihua Judy Chung, Jeffrey Inaba, Rem Koolhaas, and Sze Tsung Leong, 156–263. Cambridge, Mass.: Harvard Design School.
Morley, David, and Kevin Robins. 1995. "Techno-orientalism: Japan Panic." In *Spaces of Identity: Global Media, Electronic Landscapes, and Cultural Boundaries,* 147–73. New York: Routledge.
Morris, Meaghan. 1998. *Too Soon Too Late: History in Popular Culture.* Bloomington: Indiana University Press.
Murphy, Peter, and Trevor Hogan. 2012. "Discordant Order: Manila's Neo-patrimonial Urbanism." *Thesis Eleven* 112: 10–34.
O'Connor, Justin, and Lie Liu. 2014. "Shenzhen's OCT-LOFT: Creative Space in the City of Design." *City, Culture, and Society* 5: 131–38.
O'Donnell, Mary Ann. 2008. "Vexed Foundations: An Ethnographic Interpretation of the Shenzhen Built Environment." Paper presented at Vexed Urbanism: A Symposium on Design and the Social, February 13, New York.
———. 2009. "Temporal Dislocations." *Shenzhen Noted* (blog), May 9. http://shenzhennoted.com/2009/05/08/temporal-dislocations-2/.
———. 2014. "Theorizing Shenzhen Speed." *Shenzhen Noted* (blog), January 10. http://shenzhennoted.com/2014/01/10/theorizing-shenzhen-speed/.
O'Donnell, M. A., W. Wong, and J. Bach, eds. 2017. *Learning from Shenzhen.* Chicago: University of Chicago Press.
Ole Bouman Team. 2013. "Ole Bouman Team: Biennale as Risk." Shenzhen–Hong Kong Bi-city Biennale of Urbanism/Architecture, September 27. http://en.szhkbiennale.org/Explaning/default.aspx?id=2.
Qin, Xiaoyu. 2014. "Yige diceng dagong shiren de yizhu: Xu Lizhi shiji Xinde Yitian" (The posthumous writings by an underclass worker poet: A New Day poetry collection by Xu Lizhi). http://www.zhongchou.cn/deal-show/id-37669.

Qiu, Jack Linchuan. 2009. *Working-Class Network Society: Communication Technology and the Information Have-Less in Urban China*. Cambridge, Mass.: MIT Press.

Qiu, Linchuan. 2009. "Wangluo shidai de 'Shanzhai wenhua'" (Shanzhai culture in the network age). *Ershiyi shiji* (Twenty-first century) 112: 121–29.

Rowe, Peter G. 2005. *East Asia Modern: Shaping the Contemporary City*. London: Reaktion.

Sharma, Sarah. 2014. *In the Meantime: Temporality and Cultural Politics*. Durham, N.C.: Duke University Press.

Shome, Raka. 2006. "Thinking through the Diaspora: Call Centers, India, and a New Politics of Hybridity." *International Journal of Cultural Studies* 9, no. 1: 105–24. doi:10.1177/1367877906061167.

Sundaram, Ravi. 2010. *Pirate Modernity: Delhi's Media Urbanism*. New York: Routledge.

Victoria and Albert Museum. 2013. *V7 Rapid Response Collecting*. Shenzhen-Hong Kong Bi-city Biennale of Urbanism/Architecture. http://en.szhk biennale.org/Exhibits/exhibitsDe.aspx?id=10000361.

Wang, Gang. 2008. "Santian yiceng de 'Shenzhen sudu'" (Shenzhen speed: Three days per floor). *Gongchandangyuan* (Chinese Communist Party) 21: 54.

Wang, Jingsheng, ed. 2013. *Shenzhen Meng: 100 Ge Shenzhenren de Chengzhang Shi* (Shenzhen dreams: The development trajectory of 100 Shenzheners). Shenzhen: Shenzhen Press Group.

Wang, Wei, and Boliang Shen. 2012. "OCAT Exhibitions—New Works #1—Multi-future." OCT Contemporary Art Terminal. http://www .ocat.org.cn/index.php/Exhibition/?aid=281&lang=en.

Wong, Winnie. 2013. *Van Gogh on Demand: China and the Readymade*. Chicago: University of Chicago Press.

Xu, Lizhi. 2013. "Liushuixianshang de Bingmayong" (Terra Cotta Warriors on the assembly line). *Xinlang Boke* (Sina blogs), December 7. http:// blog.sina.com.cn/s/blog_69463e160101kbg4.html.

———. 2014. "Yike luosi diaozai dishang" (A screw fell to the ground). *Xinlang Boke* (Sina blogs), January 19. http://blog.sina.com.cn/s /blog_69463e160101l645.html.

Yang, Fan. 2015. "The Chinese Dream: A Global-National Ideological Formation." In *Commercial Nationalism: Selling the Nation and Nationalizing the Sell*, edited by Zala Volcic and Mark Andrejevic, 65–85. New York: Palgrave Macmillan.

Zhang, Rui, and Xiaojin Li. 2014. "Liushuixian Shang de Bingmayong:

Dagongzhe Xu Lizhi de xiezuo shi" (Terracotta Warriors on the assembly line: The writing history of worker Xu Lizhi). *Nanfang zhoumo* (South weekend), November 27. http://www.infzm.com/content/105911.

Zhu, Youke. 2010. "Dafen Lisha: guole he hai mo shitou" (Dafen Lisa: Still feeling the stones after crossing the rivier). *Nanfang zhoumo* (South weekend), May 13. http://www.infzm.com/content/44853.

JOSEPHINE NOCK-HEE PARK

"A Strange Form of Love": The Global Asian American Subject in Richard E. Kim's *The Martyred*

RICHARD E. KIM'S ([1964] 2011) first novel, *The Martyred,* an existential account of the Korean War told through the eyes of a South Korean officer, was met with rave reviews and a surge of critical acclaim that propelled it up to number five on the *New York Times* best-seller list. Celebrated as a triumph "written in the great moral and psychological tradition of Job, Dostoevsky, and Albert Camus,"[1] *The Martyred* was nominated for the National Book Award, and Kim was prominently featured on the cover of the *New York Times* book review section as well as in the pages of *Life* magazine (*Life* 1964).[2] From its sensational reception, however, the novel fell into obscurity and out of print until 2011, when it reappeared as a Penguin Classic.

Novelist Susan Choi's (2011) foreword to the Penguin edition recounts her discovery of Kim's forgotten work: though she was presented with a first edition of *The Martyred* in 1998, it remained unopened on her bookshelf for the next twelve years. Choi explains her reluctance to read Kim's novel:

> All these years walking around with a Korean last name, scribbling and publishing stories—and now just as success is in reach, this grandfather whom no one has mentioned turns out to have done it all first, and is crashing the party? Richard E. Kim had never been discussed at the Asian American reading group, he had never appeared on the syllabus. (xiii–xiv)

The Martyred was published before the ethnic nationalist movements of the late 1960s, when the term *Asian American* was born. The literary end of the Asian American movement unearthed and claimed a series of texts written before the movement, but Kim's novel was not—and remains—an uneasy candidate for the canon fashioned out of such acts of recovery. *The Martyred,* for one, is not set in the United States, and furthermore, its cast of characters is entirely Korean—but the novel itself is entirely American.

In a recent survey of Korean War literature, Steven Belletto (2015, 54) presents two phases: the first "written in the 1950s and early 1960s generally by white, male Americans who fought in the war, reported on the war, or had some other ties to the US military," and the second written by Korean Americans, which "posits an important disjunction between what the United States claimed about the war to Koreans and what these writers imagined the war actually meant to the Koreans who experienced it" (61). Belletto cites *The Martyred* as the inaugural work of this second phase, which does "not gain traction until the 1980s and 1990s" (54) with the appearance of novels like Susan Choi's (1998) *The Foreign Student.* In the lag between Kim and his successors, of course, lies the rise of ethnic nationalism, a critical turn that, as Choi noted, played a greater part in Korean American imaginations of the war than "this grandfather whom no one has mentioned." Indeed, *The Martyred* is better suited to Belletto's first phase: not only because its protagonist, a South Korean Army officer, operates as a proxy for the U.S. military but because it ultimately does not challenge superpower designs—instead, Kim's novel presents an apotheosis of Cold War logic.

The Martyred is a strange and elegant book. It uses a philosophical register to tell a tale of military intrigue, and the writing is at once spare and tormented. The plaudits it garnered upon its publication catapulted the novel beyond the swath of middlebrow publications in the early Cold War era that, as Christina Klein (2003, 7) writes, "tried to educate Americans about their evolving relationship with Asia, and how they created opportunities—real and symbolic—for their audiences to participate in the forging of these relationships." Klein's reading of the middlebrow imagination elaborates a new mapping of Asia that aimed "to replace a national imaginary based on separation from a global imaginary based on connection" (13), and in Richard E. Kim's curious fiction, we discover a highbrow aspiration derived from the modes of Cold War integration Klein significantly revealed as the other side of the coin of Manichean division. Kim's Korean War novel is rigorously purified of what Klein terms the "pervasive sentimentalism" (15) of the mainstream, however. *The Martyred* strikingly reverses the formula of "Masscult and Midcult" that Dwight Macdonald (1962, 29) established in the early 1960s, in which he decried a debased culture that, for the spectator, "does his feeling for him." Macdonald marked the "special threat" of Midcult: "it exploits the discoveries of the avant-garde" (50) and so can "pass itself off as the real thing" (38). Though *The Martyred*'s lavish reception in the pages of *Life* is a telltale sign of Midcult exploitation of the grand literary tradition to which such critics claimed it belonged, the novel is most compelling for refusing middlebrow dictates of feeling. Instead, it elevates the middlebrow mapping elaborated by Klein into highbrow fable.

Long unread by Asian America, its middlebrow dictates fastened to existential designs: this is the puzzle of *The Martyred,* and this article reads the singularity of this novel, which ultimately crafts a proto-American subject in the hinterlands of the Cold War. Richard E. Kim captivated an American readership by weaving political alignment into philosophical terms. The first part of the article explores the novel's central mystery of Christian martyrdom, which I consider in the context of a modern history of religious revivals in Korea. The second part turns to the skeptical figure of the protagonist, who paradoxically sustains his detachment from the politics of the local scene by subscribing to global Cold War alignment. Between these two parts, I trace a particular structure of sacrifice deeply informed by Korean Protestant practice into secular and ultimately neocolonial attachment. My conclusion reads the pervasive influence of Albert Camus in *The Martyred,* through which I situate Richard E. Kim's literary ambitions and political allegiances. Kim's novel showcases a transcendent Cold War enlistment that is in fact evident in works like Susan Choi's *The Foreign Student*—despite her too-late reading of it—and this article ultimately reads Richard E. Kim's Cold War universalism as a significant and continuing mode of securing an American audience without the comforts of sentiment—and indeed vouchsafed by a highbrow readership via disenabling such feeling. *The Martyred* transports middling interests into the upper reaches, and in so doing, it reveals an ongoing process by which Asians become Americans.

■ "SACRIFICE, MARTYRDOM"

The Martyred presents a brief and extraordinary period of the Korean War: the three-month occupation of Pyongyang by South Korean, U.S., and United Nations (UN) forces. The war began on June 25, 1950, with North Korea's strike across the thirty-eighth parallel, the line hastily etched by the United States to divide Japan's former holdings between the superpowers. Northern soldiers captured Seoul three days later, and they drove rapidly southward—but their advance was checked by a dramatic reversal: on September 15, 1950, MacArthur famously landed in Inchon and pushed northward, and by October, Southern forces had captured Pyongyang and MacArthur set his sights ever northward, all the way to the Yalu River—until Mao entered the fight and forced a headlong retreat. By early December, Chinese and North Korean forces recaptured Pyongyang, and Christmas Eve 1950 marked the near-complete evacuation of Southern forces from North Korea. The occupation of Pyongyang from October to December 1950 stands as "the only instance throughout the cold war period of 'rollback' in action, that is, the military occupation of communist territory by anticommunist forces led by the United States" (Armstrong 2003, 74). This single instance of rollback was a failure, and in its wake a policy of containment—which respected agreed-upon lines between friend and foe[3]—came to define the Cold War.

Delving into this brief, unsettled period, *The Martyred* constructs a literary frame for understanding a doomed occupation.[4] The novel's protagonist is a young South Korean military officer, Captain Lee, who is assigned to "Army Political Intelligence" (1). His detachment has arrived in Pyongyang in the wake of its capture, and he describes their reception in the city: "for the first few weeks I was in a state of buoyancy, partly because of the exciting novelty of finding myself in an enemy city that our victorious Army occupied, and partly because of the irresistible enthusiasm and affection with which the people of the city greeted us, their liberators" (2). Lee is both occupier and liberator; claiming enemy territory is a homecoming. Though the occupation of Pyongyang was no less brutal than those south of the thirty-eighth parallel,[5] *The Martyred* establishes an identity between occupation and liberation to construct a narrative that moves from liberation to loss. The novel follows Lee's intelligence mission over the course of this occupation, during which he discovers a shattering truth that lays bare political alliances, including his own.

Lee's initial jubilation is tempered, however, by the sight of "the ugly, bullet-riddled buildings of Pyongyang" (3), and he faces one particularly desolate image: his office window looks out at the remains of the Central Presbyterian Church, a "gray carcass of a cross-topped bell tower where the bell was clanging" (3). Ringing with each blast of wind, the church bell tolls the destruction of the city and, fittingly, accompanies Lee's mission: he is assigned to investigate the murder of twelve Christian ministers by North Korean communist agents—and the minister of the destroyed church is among the martyred.

Lee learns that communist soldiers incarcerated the Christian ministers on June 18 and executed them on June 25, day 1 of the Korean War. This crime presents an opportunity for propaganda, not only as proof of communist viciousness but also because the martyred ministers can be packaged as anticommunist heroes. The propaganda campaign faces an obstacle, however: though twelve ministers were murdered, fourteen were rounded up. Miraculously, two survived and were released: one has gone mad as a result of the ordeal, but the other, Shin, is a mystery. The drama of *The Martyred* lies in uncovering the truth behind Reverend Shin's survival: was it "divine intervention" (16), as he claims, or is he, as many townspeople suspect, a Judas? Over the course of the novel, we learn that Shin was spared because he was the only one strong enough to resist his captors. Hence what Shin cannot reveal is that the martyred were themselves weak.

Both the military and the church are deeply invested in the purity of these martyrs, and the novel's matched military and religious plots significantly echo a modern history of intertwined political and Christian aims in Korea. Protestant missionaries famously ingratiated themselves with the Korean court in the late nineteenth century, and over the course of the twentieth century, Christianity established itself as the religion of both the political elite and the dispossessed.[6] The church "was closely allied with a progressive reform movement in late Confucian Korea (1884–1905) and with nationalist activism in the colonial era (1905–1945)" (Park 2003, 4). Indeed, despite missionaries' attempts to separate their religion from political turmoil, Christian churches became "a political training ground" for Korean nationalists during Japan's occupation (Park 2003, 4–5). Yet the church that operated as a vehicle for anticolonial movements served shifting political masters after 1945: Christians led the postwar authoritarian regime of South Korea.[7] Korean Christianity has thus proven itself to be inseparable from—and indispensable to—a broad spectrum of political ends, whether progressive or repressive.

The Northern regions of the country were particularly fertile ground for Christianity.[8] Because of a long history of missionaries in the region and a wealth of charismatic converts who grew sizable congregations, in the early twentieth century, Pyongyang was known as "the Jerusalem of Korea" (Lee 2010, 23). In fact, the Central Presbyterian Church whose skeletal remains haunt *The Martyred* has a storied past: its legendary minister was an important leader of the Great Revival of 1907, in which an outpouring of declarations of faith swept through the population.[9] These searing expressions of devotion convinced formerly skeptical missionaries that the natives were capable of true belief,[10] and revival followed revival—another great wave took place in the years immediately after the end of Japan's occupation—into the present day, in which revivals continue to be a significant part of Korean Protestant practice.

The most remarkable single session of the Great Revival took place in the Central Presbyterian Church, which reportedly seated fifteen hundred congregants. In *The Martyred,* this church has been reduced to rubble, but Reverend Shin's church is unscathed. The novel presents a striking contrast between the two structures: against the ruins of the Central Presbyterian Church, Shin's First Presbyterian Church seems almost too grand. Hence, like the miraculous survival of the reverend in the hands of the enemy, his church, too, is untouched. When Captain Lee marvels over "the towering church of red brick" (33), he learns from Colonel Chang, his superior, that the church was intentionally saved because it possessed "strategic value" (34), and despite its magnificent appearance, it was the site of a vicious battle. The church's serene facade and bloody conflict aptly characterize its minister: Reverend Shin, too, conceals his own terrible knowledge.

To preserve the sanctity of the murdered ministers, Shin sacrifices himself. He names himself a political traitor and proclaims not only that his fellow captives were valiant but that they forgave him. Shin confesses twice: once before a small group of ministers, the second time before his congregation in the First Presbyterian Church. These confessions elicit a surprising response, as in the first instance, when the ministers "hurried over to Mr. Shin, embracing him, touching him, begging him to speak no more for he had said enough; they prayed then and there; they blessed him; they confessed and repented their past complacency and meek submission to the enemies of their god; and they took him into their hearts as one of them, as their sacrifice" (112). This response astonishes Captain Lee, but these ministers are closely hewing to the tradition of revival in Korean Protestantism: the emotional displays of the Great Revival were inspired by the confession of a Canadian missionary, who tearfully admitted to his own failure to reach the locals.[11] In Shin's case, too, it is his failure that inspires these ministers, who claim him as "their sacrifice." Shin's second confession takes place in a special service he has called in order to proclaim, "It was I who betrayed our martyrs!" (120). Though he is initially met with jeers, by the end of the service the voices of the congregation echo his cries of "Hallelujah! Amen!" (124). Shin calls out to them, "You! Sinners! Down, down on your knees and repent!" and the entire congregation kneels (124). In reenacting the Great Revival, Shin sacrifices himself to serve a greater aim: he preserves the martyrs and inspires a desperate populace brutalized by war.

The army officers, however, puzzle over this sacrifice. Captain Lee responds to the skeptical Colonel Chang, who asks, "Where do they get this ability, even liking, for suffering?" "'There is one thing peculiar to Christianity, Colonel,' I said. 'Someone died for their sins, for their salvation, and this happens to be the son of their god'" (119). Chang retorts,

"A very strange notion," muttering, "Sacrifice, martyrdom," but he is delighted by Shin's effect on his congregation because their revived belief aligns with his political aims. Despite its strangeness to the colonel, the reverend's sacrifice readily folds into his military aims: from the start, the mission for the military intelligence unit had been to put on a memorial service for the martyrs, and in the wake of Shin's public confession, the event proceeds without a hitch. The memorial service brings together religious, military, and political leaders, and later, in the final section of the book, we see Shin marching in the streets as part of a demonstration "expressing the people's protest against the Chinese intervention and their entreaty to the United Nations for a speedy retaliation" (176): "In the center, somberly flanked by the twelve portraits [of the martyred], Mr. Shin walked slowly, his body erect in a black overcoat" (177). The novel first introduced Reverend Shin hidden in his study, wracked with anguish over the failings of his brethren, but over the course of the story, he is transformed into an important anticommunist leader.

In moving from the pulpit to the street, Shin is following in the foot-steps of the Protestant converts who preceded him: the leaders of the 1907 Great Revival took active part in the March First Independence Move-ment in 1919, which triggered international condemnation of Japanese brutality in Korea.[12] The 1919 movement did not succeed in overthrowing the colonial regime, and those who took part paid a heavy price—the minister of the Central Presbyterian Church, for example, was jailed for more than two years. Indeed, the movement is perhaps most famous for its martyrs, and in *The Martyred*, the brief occupation of North Korea in 1950 is presented as a failed enterprise that produces martyrs. Over the course of the novel, every character comes to revere Shin, who ultimately achieves iconic status. In the final chapter, we learn of numerous sightings of Shin, who is almost certainly dead: in the words of one of his acolytes, "If I were to believe all of their [Northern refugees'] stories, well, Mr. Shin is everywhere in North Korea" (196).

■ "SO WE ARE GOING TO ABANDON THE PEOPLE!"

Captain Lee, however, refuses to fall under Shin's spell. As Shin's beauti-ful fiction aligns with the military propaganda effort, Lee reflects, "I had been tricked into a sort of nice little game, in which both the pursuer and the pursued skillfully staged a clever play of intrigues, of plots and counterplots, all this only to reveal that they were fellow conspirators, after all" (127). Lee disapproves of both religious and military lies to cast himself as the text's lone truth-teller. Contemplating Shin's dilemma, Lee declares, "I would tell the truth" because "the truth cannot be bribed"

(50).[13] The philosophical stance taken by Lee elevates truth above ideological contexts, and Lee's resistance to such plots is particularly evident
in his single battlefield memory: he recalls digging open a cave in which
the communists sealed hundreds of political prisoners and pulling out
amid the corpses "a human hand almost skeletal" (17), a barely living
man. Once rescued, this body falls prey to photographers, who capture
its gruesome visage: "Out of the bloated toothless mouth oozed dark,
yellowish liquid, and flies" (18). Suddenly enraged, Lee begins "smashing
the cameras, chasing those cold eyes from my man" (18). Lee destroys the
cameras, which would presumably put this image to propagandistic use,
but he cannot save "my man." Yet this terrible figure would be salvageable
within a Christian context; he clearly recalls Lazarus, but Lee cannot raise
his man from the dead. We may read this instance as emblematic of Lee's
resistance in the novel: he decries ideological aims, but in the absence of
them, he can do nothing for his people.

Though Lee denounces "plots and counterplots," he is forced to harbor
a far more damaging secret: the impending military evacuation of Pyongyang. In fact, the memorial ceremony that marked the culmination of the
novel's matched Christian and propaganda campaigns coincides with the
first wave of the retreat, which launches a new narrative thread—and
in pointed contrast to the religious and military efforts to assuage the
people, this new operation simply slips away from them. Lee learns that
Chinese forces have smashed their lines and that evacuation is imminent,
but under orders from above, he can say nothing, even when UN leaflets
are later dropped, falsely promising democratic victory. Thus, even as Lee
critiques Reverend Shin for not telling the truth about the martyrs, Lee
must conceal a more terrible truth: that his military forces will not stay
and fight. When he shares this official secret with the army chaplain, the
chaplain makes clear the enormity of this information: "So we are going
to abandon the people! My people!" (153). Against this evocation of "my
people," Lee's efforts to shield "my man" appear not only futile but narrow: his antipropagandistic stance certainly could not revive his dying
man, and his ultimate inability to tell this very large and damaging truth
simply abandons the people.

Cast in the shadow of the retreat, the final portion of the book moves
toward a strange, inward denouement. The weary populace and demanding
congregants fall away in this closing movement, in which Lee and Shin
come to share a singular understanding. After his two confessions—the
first to his fellow clergymen, the second to his congregation—Shin makes
a third, private confession to Captain Lee. In a feverish exchange, Shin reveals that he himself does not believe in God and sees nothing after death.

This truth finally moves Lee: embracing Shin, he whispers, "Forgive me! I have been unjust to you!" (160). Shin's revelation opens a hidden reserve of feeling within Lee: "And for the first time since the war, I abandoned myself to uncontrollable tears, my tears, my contrition—for my parents, my countrymen, and for those many unknown souls I had destroyed" (161). The scene presents a perversion of confession and conversion—a negative image of Christian revival. Lee's contrition has no redemptive value, and in pointed contrast to the chaplain's cry against abandoning his people, Lee abandons himself in this intimate scene. Perhaps we may read this final instance as Shin's greatest sacrifice: he offers up his own belief to move the dispassionate Captain Lee.[14] Thus inspired by Shin's apostasy, Lee follows the form of revival even in the absence of belief. In this extraordinary scene, we trace religious forms into profane content.

The Martyred thus generates a structure of sacrifice and revival that its protagonist perversely follows. The culmination of this faithless sacrifice takes place when Lee finally departs from the city. He is part of the final convoy out of the city, after which the bridge out of Pyongyang is bombed by American soldiers to halt enemy forces. As Lee nears the bridge, we hear Americans for the first time in the novel: Kim writes, "English mingled with Korean. Planes flew overhead in the dark heavens" (182). Upon hearing "a series of shattering explosions," we see the Americans: "a few parka-clad American soldiers in the truck ahead of the jeep were looking out of the canvas cover. A voice cried out, 'There goes the God-damned bridge!' Another shouted, 'Oh, Jesus! Look at that!' I got out of my jeep and looked back toward Pyongyang. The doomed city was in flames" (183). In their loose, profane way, the American soldiers identify the city as the ultimate martyr, as Christ himself. The casual blasphemy of these American voices mimics and undercuts the narrative of persecution and resurrection laid out in the novel. Pyongyang will burn, but it will never rise again. The fact that American soldiers voice these sentiments reveals an aspect of the occupation of Pyongyang largely unseen in the novel. *The Martyred* considers a failed occupation within the framework of spiritual renunciation, but the presence of the United States at this critical juncture unmasks this operation as a failed attempt at rollback. Hence, though Lee can match occupation to liberation in the context of civil war, U.S. involvement can only be read as an imperial foray into enemy territory. The forsaken city, irredeemable within the novel's Christian context, lays bare the Cold War alliance between South Korea and the United States.

The large-scale movement of military retreat in the novel's final section is matched with Lee's inward retreat, in which Shin's private confession of nonbelief refocuses Lee: no longer a reluctant witness to military maneuvers couched in religious terms, Lee moves into the center of the tale to ponder his own losses—but this interior focus is no less separable from the larger political context of the war. The night of Shin's confession of faithlessness in fact began with American rations—Lee invites Shin to join him in a meal in his chambers "if he did not mind tasting American food" (158)—and later in the book, a second American meal marks the conclusion of the retreat: "On that Christmas Eve I withdrew early to my quonset hut, where I had a solitary supper of American rations. I was reading a Japanese translation of Aurelius' *Meditations*" (184). This "solitary supper" ties together multiple strands in the text. In reading the private diary of a Roman emperor who contemplated stoic virtue in daily life, Lee arrives at a discovery of non-Christian morality. That Lee reads Aurelius on Christmas Eve underscores his preference for stoic over Christian virtue—pragmatic survival over sacrifice and a distant promise of resurrection.

December 24, 1950, has a further significance: it is the date of the final retreat of U.S., UN, and South Korean forces from North Korea. Thus, in reading a Roman text at the far end of a failed occupation, Lee confirms the limits of a Christian framework in a novel shot through with Christian revival. Moreover, Lee is reading in Japanese, a reminder of the last occupation and a marker of his educational attainment. Before he joined the army, Lee was an instructor in the history of human civilization at a university in Seoul (1), and his bookishness at this moment reminds us of this past. Learning Japanese was one of many colonial policies, and privileged students went to Japan for their advanced studies. This small detail of translation is the only mention of the colonial period in the novel, and its presence on this of all days suggests that American rations are akin to Japanese translation because both are hints of imperial rule. Imagined alongside Japan's occupation, U.S. intervention is unmasked as itself an imperial venture. Lee's solitary journey is framed between two American meals; perhaps the truth of Lee's self-discovery is that his individual development is an American one.

The Cold War alliance between South Korea and the United States subtly reinforces all of the ideological maneuvers within the text. Just as Christianity in Korea is inseparable from Korea's modern history of alliance with the United States, Captain Lee is no less inscribed within the sphere of American political influence. In reading the final and solitary journey instigated by the reverend's confession of faithlessness, we discover in Captain Lee a figure of retreat: the novel begins in the Northern capital and moves ever southward, all the way to Pusan and concluding on the shores of an island off the Southern coast. If we read Lee's movement against the progression of the Korean War, which saw the line of fighting move up and down the peninsula, we see that Lee never breaks from his southward drive. And in the context of the Korean War, to travel south is to travel west: the overlay of Cold War onto civil war transformed local vectors, and Lee's journey ultimately turns him toward the United States.

■ "AWAY FROM KOREA AND TOWARD THE UNKNOWN . . ."

Reviewing *The Martyred* for the *New York Times,* Chad Walsh claimed that Kim's "purpose here is not to tell the deeds of war but to probe the involutions and ambiguities of conscience—the meaning of suffering and evil and holiness, the uncertain boundaries between illusion and truth." Similarly, in his *Los Angeles Times* review, Robert R. Kirsch (1964) applauded the novel for delving into a "second plane," in which "we see these men as allegorical figures, taking their meaningful and symbolic roles in a modern passion play, roles with which we who live in the modern world play as well." The novel's reputation was secured through this "second plane," which transported its foreign figures inward, into a modern play of symbolic meaning, to reach an American audience.

Kim carefully framed his tale within "the involutions and ambiguities of conscience" in the opening pages of the book: *The Martyred* is dedicated "to the memory of Albert Camus, whose insight into 'a strange form of love' overcame for me the nihilism of the trenches and bunkers of Korea." Kim cites from the conclusion of Camus's 1951 *The Rebel,* a lengthy meditation on political crises that enshrines a true rebellion inseparable from solidarity: "Man's solidarity is founded upon rebellion, and rebellion, in its turn, can only find its justification in this solidarity" (Camus 1957, 22). *The Rebel*'s lyrical, final section, titled "Beyond Nihilism," closes with the rebel whose "strange form of love" (304) binds him to the suffering people, and Kim's dedication presents himself freed from nihilism through Camus's insight.[15]

In thus signaling his literary and philosophical ambitions from the start—and it is worth noting, too, that Kim takes Camus's Hölderlin epigraph from *The Rebel* as his epigraph for *The Martyred*[16]—Kim aims well beyond the middlebrow accounts of Asia typical of the postwar era. And yet Kim's novel does not challenge superpower aims; *The Martyred* in fact dismantles the critique it seems to mount against colluding military and religious plots by ultimately aligning its protagonist to the imperial designs of the Cold War. Indeed, the heady conflation of occupation and liberation Captain Lee expresses upon his first arrival in Pyongyang sets the template for the novel's grander scheme, in which the skeptical protagonist finds resolution within an American imperial scene.

This Cold War accord provides a further resonance with Camus: in *The Rebel,* Camus pitted his loving rebel against the nihilism of what he termed "Historical Murder" (287), violent revolution fueled by historical materialism—a critique that fellow existential luminary Sartre took as a direct attack. In 1952, these two comrades spectacularly broke with each other in a brittle, public exchange over *The Rebel.* Ronald Aronson (2004, 118) significantly frames their split within the Cold War: "We have to see their rupture in its true colors—as the product of a distorted choice. The Cold War confused political thinking, destroyed friendships and individuals, and deformed the left." Hence, "although Camus was never a partisan of capitalism and Sartre was never a Communist" (5), they were conscripted into the Cold War's grand ideological divide. Camus, the dashing revolutionary of World War II—far more active in the Resistance than Sartre—became caricatured as a disappointing moderate after the war, as in Susan Sontag's (1963) portrait of Camus as a "noble, stoical, and the same time detached and compassionate" (5) figure marred by an "intellectual weakness" (3) that never troubled the more abrasive Sartre. Camus's disciplined rebel, who argued that "rebellion in itself is moderation" (Camus 1957, 301), came under heavy critique, and Camus's critical paralysis with regard to Algeria branded him, in the words of Albert Memmi, a "colonisateur de bonne volonté."[17]

Camus's moderation provides a critical lens for understanding the complex detachment of *The Martyred*'s Captain Lee. In *The Rebel,* Camus followed his evocation of "a strange form of love" with an explanation: "those who find no rest in God or in history are condemned to live for those who, like themselves, cannot live: in fact, for the humiliated" (Camus 1957, 304). *The Martyred*'s Reverend Shin and Colonel Chang grapple with god and history,[18] but neither finds rest—and both are condemned to die "for the humiliated." Captain Lee survives, and in the final pages of the novel, he visits a temporary church for Northern refugees erected on an island near Pusan. In the novel's final paragraph, we see him both among and apart from the people:

> I walked away from the church, past the rows of tents where silent suffering gnawed at the hearts of the people—my people—and headed toward the beach, which faced the open sea. There a group of refugees, gathered under the starry dome of the night sky, were humming in unison a song of homage to their homeland. And with a wondrous lightness of heart hitherto unknown to me, I joined them. (199)

In turning away from the broken hearts within the church, Lee experiences "a wondrous lightness of heart." This closing scene resonates with the end of *The Rebel*, the final paragraph of which opens thus:

> At this meridian of thought, the rebel thus rejects divinity in order to share in the struggles and destiny of all men. We shall choose Ithaca, the faithful land, frugal and audacious thought, lucid action, and the generosity of man who understands. In the light, the earth remains our first and our last love. Our brothers are breathing under the same sky as we; justice is a living thing. Now is born that strange joy which helps one live and die, and which we shall never again postpone to a later time. (306)

Kim has imagined Camus's loving rebel on a distant shore: Captain Lee "rejects divinity in order to share in the struggles and destiny" of his people, and in sharing the night sky with them, "that strange joy" lightens his own heart. And yet, in contrast to Camus's resounding "we," Lee preserves his first person. The placement of "my people" in dashes detaches Lee from his people, the refugees render homage to "their homeland," and most notably, when Lee joins them, he retains his "I." This final scene frees this rebel from his people—a reading that sympathetic readers of *The Rebel*, too, applied to its lyrical conclusion, interpreted as "Camus's release from political bondage" (Brée 1972, 6). Perhaps in Captain Lee's "wondrous lightness of heart," we may read a transcendence away from the people's suffering—but toward the Cold War's "political bondage," which Camus, too, keenly felt.

The prominent imprint of Albert Camus on Kim's novel lays bare a literary ambition that presents a reversal of Macdonald's exposé of Midcult, which he indicted for packaging the avant-garde for mass consumption. *The Martyred* instead elevates middlebrow allegiances into a highbrow conundrum, all the while retaining the bedrock of Cold War political mores that would permit the reception Kim enjoyed in the mid-1960s. In thus staging an existential dilemma, Kim crafted what critics applauded as a universal plight. Susan Choi's (2011, xiv–xv) response to finally reading the novel echoes its 1964 reception: "In *The Martyred* Kim forges a drama of such devastating universality that an electrifying sense of recognition binds us to the page." In thus "electrifying" all of these years later, Choi bridges the gap of the intervening years between Kim's Korean War novel and hers—the period in which Asian American literature became a category. The revelatory link that Choi expresses demonstrates the continuing salience of a global Cold War formation of an American subject far from the domestic scene. Asian Americanists have long noted and critiqued the Cold War formation of the model minority at home, and the present reappraisal of the "global cold war," to cite Odd Arne Westad's (2005) recent study, turns us to this global counterpart, whose tortured soul takes center stage in *The Martyred*.

Richard E. Kim himself joined the South Korean military as a liaison officer to UN forces, and in 1954, he sailed to the United States to pursue his education[19]—biographical facts that make him of particular interest to Susan Choi, whose first novel, *The Foreign Student,* presents a fictionalized account of her father, also a Korean foreign student who arrived in America on the heels of his service for the U.S. Information Service during the war. Foreign students in the postwar era were newly politicized as Cold War ambassadors—as plainly evidenced in the 1945 congressional establishment of the Fulbright Scholar Program—and students like Susan Choi's father and Richard E. Kim were emblems of Cold War alignment. Such figures have long fared poorly in the recovery efforts that defined the Asian American literary canon; movement activists flatly rejected the literary efforts of foreign students deemed assimilationist. Indeed, even without the close reading of superpower alliance I have attempted here, the mainstream appeal of *The Martyred* would likely have branded it a compromised work. Yet it is my contention that the Cold War conditioning of its universal appeal makes this text significant. Kim's singular novel fashioned Cold War alliance into highbrow reading; out of a deeply unpopular conflict—the Korean War was dubbed the "forgotten war" even as it was being fought[20]—it presented a moral subject fit for serious Western contemplation. As an argument for the possibility of an American soul in far-distant and benighted lands, *The Martyred* imagines a politically aligned subject we have only begun to appreciate: products of neocolonial ventures who fashion their own transcendence out of profoundly unequal political terms.

In a 1990 lecture, Kim described his own literary development as a revelation discovered on his passage to America:

On my maiden voyage to the United States, in the middle of the vast Pacific Ocean, I came, alone, face to face with the sun emerging from the waves of the morning ocean . . . and it was then I saw the sun for the first time in my life, it speaking to me and I speaking to it.

I think it all went with my own, private exploration, discovery of my Self, now utterly alone, physically and psychologically, away from Korea and toward the unknown. . . .

And, later when I began to write in English, the "I" in Korean gave way willingly and joyously to the "I" in English—and it was like discovering and assuming a wholly new identity of Being, and, with it, a wholly new way of

seeing, thinking, cogitating and understanding, having shed the Korean
"I" that is not really "I" but that is subservient, always, to the Korean "we."
(Kim 1991, 24–25, original ellipsis)

The turn toward singularity enshrined in the passage suggests an elaboration of the "wondrous lightness of heart hitherto unknown" of his protagonist Captain Lee: in this later speech, Kim detaches his first person from a Korean subservience, and the Self he discovers belongs to the West. The "I" that Kim preserves at the close of *The Martyred* thus resonates with the "I" Kim himself discovered in English, and in overlaying his fiction with his own writerly self-discovery, we discover a Western attachment at the heart of both. Though the novel's closing passage preserves the enigma of its protagonist's belonging, the American rations that sustain Captain Lee's turn away from the suffering of his people reveal the imbrication of his morality tale within the vast frame of superpower alignment. In composing *The Martyred* in the language of the Self reborn in the Pacific, Kim transposed a distant civil war into a Western key.[21]

Josephine Nock-Hee Park is associate professor of English at the University of Pennsylvania. She is the author of *Apparitions of Asia: Modernist Form and Asian American Poetics* (2008) and *Cold War Friendships: Korea, Vietnam, and Asian American Literature* (2016).

■ **NOTES**

This material, in different form, previously appeared in Josephine Nock-Hee Park, *Cold War Friendships: Korea, Vietnam, and Asian American Literature* (Oxford: Oxford University Press, 2016), and has been reproduced with permission of Oxford University Press.

1. From Walsh's (1964) *New York Times* book review.

2. See James Kyung-Jin Lee's (1998) discussion of the reception of Kim's work.

3. As in Gaddis's (2005, 21) explanation of containment policy: "the United States would, in effect, 'draw the line,' defending all future targets of Soviet expansion, but without any attempt to 'liberate' areas already under Moscow's control."

4. See Hong (2012, 146) for an analysis of the "strategic value of fiction" in *The Martyred*. Hong cogently explains that the novel "offers a fictionalized account of UN rollback that obscures the U.S. agenda" (153).

5. See Armstrong (2003) for an account of the policies of the occupation.

6. See Grayson (2006) for an overview of Christianity in Korea, from

the initial reception of Catholics in 1777 to nineteenth-century persecution of Catholicism to the arrival of Protestantism in the late nineteenth century and its subsequent flourishing.

7. Most notably Syngman Rhee, whom Timothy S. Lee (2010, 66) describes as "a Methodist elder who on August 18, 1948 became the first president of the Republic of Korea. Backed by the USAMGIK [U.S. Army Military Government in Korea] and the rightist regime, southern evangelicals became active in national politics."

8. Ryu (2008, 672) explains that the "northwest coastal region was the most neglected place during the Yi Dynasty but American Protestantism's most successful mission field in Korea. Korean Christians in the region quickly absorbed the missionaries' capitalist spirit as well as their apolitical religion."

9. Chong Bum Kim (2006, 150) portrays this influential minister: "Considered by some to be the 'father of Korean Christianity,' Kil played a central role in the growth and expansion of Protestantism in the early stages. . . . The revivalist tradition, of which he was one of the pioneers, has become a permanent feature of Korean church life."

10. Timothy S. Lee (2010, 27) writes that "before the great revival some missionaries suspected Koreans' spiritual capabilities and the authenticity of their conversions. As the revival proceeded, however, it became obvious to them that Korean were no less spiritual than they."

11. Timothy S. Lee (2010, 15) writes, "The beginning of the great revival can be traced back to a 1903 meeting of missionaries. . . . The small group of Methodist missionaries were moved by a confession made by one of their members, Robert S. Hardie. Agonizing over his failure to develop a church in that province, Hardie confessed his shortcomings to his colleagues. Afterward he confessed similarly to some Korean believers, including those who were working as his servants. . . . Soon he became a sought-after speaker, invited to lead numerous prayer meetings and Bible conferences in the country."

12. Grayson (2006, 16) discusses the significance of the movement and the role of the church: "The March First Movement of 1919, which effectively created the sense of modern Korean nationhood, was largely the work of Korean religious leaders. . . . The Japanese harshly suppressed the movement, persecuting Christians in particular. . . . In spite of a Japanese news blackout, these events became known because a few missionaries went to China and cabled their mission boards at home; these boards in turn lobbied Western governments to condemn Japanese brutality."

13. See Kang (2007) for an analysis of factual and religious truths in *The Martyred*.

14. An anonymous reader for the journal suggested that Shin may be lying. I am struck by this suggestion, which could further demonstrate Lee's peculiar blindnesses in his own political crusade for what he deems the truth.

15. Fenkl's (2011, xxvi) introduction to the Penguin edition of *The Martyred* astutely reads Camus and Kim together: "like Camus, Kim is able to move beyond nihilism by embracing and transcending many of the enigmas portrayed in *The Martyred*." My reading layers the political context of the Cold War onto this comparison.

16. Their shared epigraph is a quotation from Hölderlin's *The Death of Empedocles*: "And openly I pledged my heart to the grave and suffering land, and often in the consecrated night, I promised to love her faithfully until death, unafraid, with her heavy burden of fatality, and never to despise a single one of her enigmas. Thus did I join myself to her with a mortal cord."

17. Cited in Forsdick (2007, 127).

18. My analysis neglects another significant character, Lee's best friend, Park, an officer in the marines whose father was the murdered minister of the Central Presbyterian Church. Like Lee, Park was a university instructor in the history of human civilizations before the war, and on his deathbed, Park leaves behind a cryptic, final note for Lee: "I have been clinging onto the precipice of History, but I give up. I am prepared to take leave of it" (308). It is tempting to read this renunciation in light of Camus's oblique indictment of Sartre's historical materialism in *The Rebel*.

19. Kim's biography shares some further similarities with his novel: as James Kyung-Jin Lee (1998, 31) notes, Kim's "maternal grandfather, a fiercely devout Christian minister," was taken prisoner by Communist forces and shot.

20. Cumings (2007, 271) contemplates the phrase: "It is daunting to learn that the first usage of this term came in 1951, two years before the war ended, but after it had entered a phase of trench warfare along what is now the demilitarized zone—and therefore rarely occupied the front pages of the newspaper anymore."

21. Kim's two subsequent books were also set in Korea: *The Innocent* (1968), a convoluted fictionalization of a Korean military coup, and *Lost Names* (1970), a series of interlinked short stories based on Kim's childhood experiences in Korea under Japanese colonial rule. *The Innocent* was poorly received, and *Lost Names* was little known until it was reprinted by the University of California Press in 1998, when it was reclaimed as a useful classroom text.

■ **WORKS CITED**

Armstrong, Charles K. 2003. "The Cultural Cold War in Korea, 1945–1960." *The Journal of Asian Studies* 62, no. 1: 71–108.

Aronson, Ronald. 2004. *Camus and Sartre: The Story of a Friendship and a Quarrel That Ended It.* Chicago: University of Chicago Press.

Belletto, Steven. 2015. "The Korean War, the Cold War, and the American Novel." *American Literature* 87, no. 1: 51–77.

Brée, Germaine. 1972. *Camus and Sartre: Crisis and Commitment.* New York: Delta/Dell.

Camus, Albert. 1957. *The Rebel.* Translated by Anthony Bower. New York: Vintage Books.

Choi, Susan. 1998. *The Foreign Student.* New York: Harper Perennial.

———. 2011. Foreword to *The Martyred.* By Richard E. Kim. New York: Penguin Classics.

Cumings, Bruce. 2007. "The Korean War: What Is It That We Are Remembering to Forget?" In *Ruptured Histories: War, Memory, and the Post–Cold War in Asia,* edited by Sheila Miyoshi Jager and Rana Mitter, 266–90. Cambridge, Mass.: Harvard University Press.

Fenkl, Heinz Insu. 2011. Introduction to *The Martyred.* By Richard E. Kim. New York: Penguin Classics.

Forsdick, Charles. 2007. "Camus and Sartre: The Great Quarrel." In *The Cambridge Companion to Camus,* edited by Edward J. Hughes, 118–30. Cambridge: Cambridge University Press.

Gaddis, John Lewis. 2005. *Strategies of Containment: A Critical Appraisal of American National Security Policy during the Cold War.* New York: Oxford University Press.

Grayson, James Huntley. 2006. "A Quarter-Millennium of Christianity in Korea." In *Christianity in Korea,* edited by Robert E. Buswell Jr. and Timothy S. Lee, 7–25. Honolulu: University of Hawai'i Press.

Hong, Christine. 2012. "Pyongyang Lost: Counterintelligence and Other Fictions of the Forgotten War." In *American Literature and Culture in an Age of Cold War,* edited by Steven Belletto and Daniel Grausam, 135–62. Iowa City: University of Iowa Press.

Kang, Jung In. 2007. "Politics and Truth: An Analysis of Richard E. Kim's Novel, *The Martyred.*" *Korea Journal* 42, no. 2: 184–207.

Kim, Chong Bum. 2006. "Preaching the Apocalypse in Colonial Korea: The Protestant Millennialism of Kil Son-ju." In *Christianity in Korea,* edited by Robert E. Buswell Jr. and Timothy S. Lee, 149–66. Honolulu: University of Hawai'i Press.

Kim, Richard E. 1968. *The Innocent.* Boston: Houghton Mifflin.

———. 1991. "Plenary Lecture." In *Asian Voices in English,* edited by Mimi

Chan and Roy Harris, 23–32. Hong Kong: Hong Kong University Press.

———. (1970) 1998. *Lost Names: Scenes from a Korean Boyhood*. Berkeley: University of California Press.

———. (1964) 2011. *The Martyred*. New York: Penguin Classics.

Kirsch, Robert R. 1964. "Korean War Story Deserves to Be Classed as Great Novel." *Los Angeles Times*, February 23, C14.

Klein, Christina. 2003. *Cold War Orientalism: Asia in the Middlebrow Imagination, 1945–1961*. Berkeley: University of California Press.

Lee, James Kyung-Jin. 1998. "Best-Selling Korean American: Revisiting Richard E. Kim." *Korean Culture*, Spring, 30–39.

Lee, Timothy S. 2010. *Born Again: Evangelicalism in Korea*. Honolulu: University of Hawaiʻi Press.

Life. 1964. "Best-Selling Korean." March 20, 125–26.

Macdonald, Dwight. 1962. *Against the American Grain*. New York: Random House.

Park, Chung-shin. 2003. *Protestantism and Politics in Korea*. Seattle: University of Washington Press.

Ryu, Dae Young. 2008. "Fresh Wineskins for New Wine: A New Perspective on North Korean Christianity." *Journal of Church and State* 48, no. 3: 659–75.

Sontag, Susan. 1963. "The Ideal Husband." *New York Times Review of Books*, September 26. http://www.nybooks.com/articles/archives/1963/sept/26/the-ideal-husband.

Walsh, Chad. 1964. "Another War Rages Within." *New York Times*, February 16, BR1.

Westad, Odd Arne. 2005. *The Global Cold War: Third World Interventions and the Making of Our Times*. Cambridge: Cambridge University Press.